*For Mary Alice, always.*

# MARKET-DRIVEN MANAGEMENT

# MARKET-DRIVEN MANAGEMENT

## How to Define, Develop, and Deliver Customer Value

SECOND EDITION

Frederick E. Webster Jr.

**JOHN WILEY & SONS, INC.**

Copyright © 1994 and 2002 by John Wiley & Sons, Inc. All rights reserved.

Published by John Wiley & Sons, Inc., Hoboken, New Jersey.
Published simultaneously in Canada.

# PREFACE

The convergence of ideas from several fields has revitalized marketing management with a new marketing concept. By many different routes, management thinking has come back to a central focus on the satisfaction of customer needs and expectations as the defining purpose of all business activity. After decades of thinking that creating value for shareholders was the ultimate objective, managers, consultants, and academic theorists have circled back to a customer-value concept of business strategy more consistent with the realities of the global marketplace and its stringent requirements for competitiveness.

For me, the most satisfying view of the world of marketing management comes from standing on the bridge between business and academe. It is essential that marketing scholars devote their energies to problems that are real and relevant for management just as it is critical that professional marketing managers stay informed about and guided by new developments in theory and research. One purpose of this book is to help strengthen the bridge by bringing together important new ideas from both business practice and scholarly research. I try to do this in an historical context of the evolution of the marketing concept over the past 50 years or so.

A major reason for the decline of the original marketing concept as a guiding philosophy management was the lack of any strong argument or empirical support for the notion that profit was a reward for creating a satisfied customer. In the past several years, however, strong new evidence has developed that builds a direct connection between creating value for customers and value for shareholders. Practical management developments have likewise forged a stronger link between customer orientation and business efficiency and effectiveness, aided in no small measure by developments in information technology. In pursuit of customer satisfaction and lower costs, disciplines such as total quality management, reengineering, and strategic planning have come back to the fundamental notion that customers ultimately determine the welfare of the business. That conclusion is the common theme among many important new management ideas and concepts including relationship management, interactive marketing, managing customer loyalty, defining every business as a service business, distinctive competence, and strategic partnering.

In this book, I have tried to combine important new academic thinking and research with evidence of "best practices" in the field of management as reported by management consultants and other business leaders. In the past several years, it has become increasingly clear that the field of marketing is undergoing a fundamental transformation. Those changes first became visible in business practice and in academic disciplines other than marketing. Academic research and teaching in marketing were somewhat slow to move away from an emphasis on individual transactions and sales results and a narrow focus on short-term (i.e., monthly or quarterly) profit maximization. This constrained view of marketing was also characterized by viewing customers as mass markets, preoccupation with short-term price inducements and "brand switching," and treating marketing as a distinct and separate management function.

This dated marketing view was in stark contrast with evolving business practice, also reflected in the strategic management literature, on customer relationships and longer term profitability, direct marketing to customers as individuals via the Internet and other media, increased flexibility and product customization for individual customers and small market niches, long-term customer retention and loyalty, and marketing as customer orientation throughout the business. In the background has been the fundamental reshaping of organizations that is occurring with the transition from large, bureaucratic, hierarchical structures toward outsourcing, strategic partnering, flexible coalitions, and networks of smaller, more entrepreneurial businesses cooperating in the shared task of creating and delivering superior value to customers. A new marketing concept is needed to guide the whole undertaking in this common purpose of satisfying customer needs.

Fortunately, the academic marketing discipline has changed substantially in the past decade and there is much recent research to underscore these important business developments and to guide the development of a value-delivery concept of strategy with a much stronger link between customer orientation and financial results. Those linkages are highlighted throughout this revised edition. It is exciting to see many ideas from marketing, strategic planning, financial management, organizational design, and information technology come together into a new concept of marketing which I hope will help set the course for continued development of this vital and changeable field.

FREDERICK E. WEBSTER JR.

*Southport, Maine*
*May 2002*

# CONTENTS

## 9 IMPLEMENTING THE VALUE-DELIVERY CONCEPT OF MARKETING STRATEGY 276

# Putting the Customer
# First—Always!

*The relationship between the man and the customer, their mutual trust, the importance of reputation, the idea of putting the customer first—always. All these things, if carried out with real conviction by the company, can make a great deal of difference in its destiny.*

Thomas Watson Jr., Chairman, IBM Corporation

The 1962 McKinsey Lectures
Graduate School of Business, Columbia University

**V**alue is defined in the marketplace, not the factory. This simple proposition has redefined the scope and focus of business firms around the world.

It isn't a new idea. In the 1950s, American management gurus, especially Peter Drucker,[1] suggested quite simply that the purpose of a business is to create a satisfied customer. Profit is not the objective, it is the reward. Among the stakeholders in any company, the customer comes first because all of the others are served best when the customer is satisfied.

Nothing could be simpler to understand. A satisfied customer is willing to pay the firm well for its products and services because the customer finds value in them. Value is created for the shareholders in the form of profit when the customer pays the firm a price that is greater than all of the prices the firm itself paid for the goods and services that it has combined into its own product offering. Thus, value is created in the marketplace by customers who perceive value in the firm's product offering.

This simple truth had barely begun to take hold across American industry in the late 1950s and early 1960s when another management concept, *strategic planning*, came along. At first, the marketing concept and strategic planning were integrated into a common concept of long-range planning. Over time, however, an apparently more sophisticated analytical framework from the field of financial management increasingly dominated strategic planning, and the customer's point of view once again receded into the background.

Return on investment, the Holy Grail of strategic planning, viewed profit as the *objective* of business activity, rather than the *reward* for creating a satisfied customer. The interests of the shareholders came first. Short-term profits, usually reported on a quarterly basis, often conflicted with the long-term interests of customers.

By the mid-1980s, the decline of American business in global competitiveness was a stark reality forcing a reassessment of the conventional wisdom of strategic planning. In industry after industry, including automobiles, consumer electronics, steel, and tires, American firms lost their dominant positions to competitors from Asia and Europe who somehow seemed better able to dial into the tastes, preferences, and buying habits of American customers as well as those in the rest of the world. As the harsh realities slowly sunk into the consciousness of American management, there was a rediscovery of the marketing concept.[2]

The marketing concept of the twenty-first century comes with some new twists, however. It is now integrated with important ideas from the field of strategic planning itself and with a fundamental commitment to total quality management and customer satisfaction that has become the keystone of business survival. In one sense, it is a case of old wine in new bottles: customer orientation and total quality management are the same thing.

In another sense, however, today's marketing concept is radically different from its early form because we now understand that marketing is a total organization commitment, pervasive throughout the firm's operating systems and culture, not the province of a few specialists. Even more basically, business organizations of the twenty-first century are evolving into new forms in which the traditional functional boundaries are disappearing and the boundary between the firm and its environment is increasingly blurred.[3] Bureaucratic, divisionalized, hierarchical, functional organizations, like their cousins the dinosaurs, have evolved into more efficient organisms in a rapidly changing environment.

This book describes and analyzes the new marketing concept as the guiding force for successful businesses in the global marketplace of the 2000s and beyond. We begin by looking at the evolution of marketing out of the sales function and contrast the sales and marketing mandates. We then explore the complex relationship between the sales and marketing functions and some of the reasons for the frequent confusion of these two different perspectives.

# THE EVOLUTION OF MARKETING AND BUSINESS STRATEGY

## Marketing in the 1950s

Let's look at the origins of the marketing concept more carefully starting in the 1950s. We need this historical perspective to understand the roots of the marketing concept, the subsequent criticisms of it, and how it changed American business. This analysis will also help us to understand why the eminently sensible prescriptions of the marketing concept, which sound so reasonable in theory, have been very difficult to implement and maintain in business practice.

We can take the year 1950 as our starting point. Consider these facts:

- The population of the United States was 151 million (compared with 281 million in 2000).

- Gross National Product (GNP) was $288 billion compared with $9,861 billion in 2000. If we adjust for inflation by using constant 1982–1984 dollars, 1950 GNP would be $1,195 billion compared with $5,726 billion in 2000. On a per capita basis, this is $7,870 in 1950 versus $20,347 in 2000, an increase of 159 percent in constant dollars.

- Personal consumption expenditures went from $192 billion in 1950 to $6,728 billion in 2000. Making an adjustment for the effects of inflation, again using 1982–1984 dollars as the constant for comparison purposes, total personal consumption expenditures would be $797 billion in 1950 compared with $11,572 billion in 2000. On a per capita basis, adjusted for inflation, consumption expenditures went from $5,287 in 1950 to $15,036 in the year 2000, an increase of 184 percent and significantly more than the rate of growth in production.

- The average consumer in 1950 enjoyed a material standard of living only one-third that of today.

In 1950, the United States was still recovering from the effects of World War II, when much of the country's productive capacity was focused on the military effort and consumer products. Durable goods especially, such as household appliances and automobiles, were in very short supply. Conditions for consumers improved rapidly in the late 1940s. Before the postwar economic recovery was complete, however, the country was brought into another major military conflict when President Truman, in June of 1950, ordered American forces into South Korea after that country was invaded by troops from North Korea. The Korean War continued until a truce agreement was signed in July 1953, putting the United States economy back into a peacetime mode. While the early 1950s did not bring the same austerity conditions that consumers had faced in the mid-1940s, they certainly prolonged the period of economic recovery from wartime conditions.

As American industry turned its attention to satisfying consumer needs, companies began to experience the benefits of the postwar baby boom. The birth rate in the United States (per 1,000 population) went from 19.4 in 1940 to 20.4 in 1945, 24.1 in 1950, and 25.0 in 1955, peaking at 25.3 in 1957. It then declined steadily for the next two decades, except for a small increase in 1969–1970, reaching a low of 14.8 in 1975–1976. The 1980s saw a slow increase up to 16.7 in 1990, when the rate again began to decline. The annual rate recently has held steady around 14.5 births per thousand total population, less than 60 percent of what it was during the mid-1950s. Rapid increases in the number and size of young families was a major driver of consumer demand when the marketing concept took form.

In the post-Korean War years, American industry looked optimistically at a growing market of young families with increasing incomes. Younger families needed both the durable goods required for establishing their households as well as the packaged goods and other nondurables that provide the necessities and conveniences of everyday life. Established households still had pent-up demand for durables from the war years. (Services accounted for only 32 percent of personal consumption expenditures in 1950 compared with approximately 60 percent today.)

## The Old Marketing Concept: Stimulating Demand for What Factories Produced

Markets became increasingly competitive following the war years of the 1940s and 1950s as new and old firms alike sought to attract consumers. As conditions of economic scarcity waned, consumers were given a larger array of choices. New product development activity increased rapidly, fueled in no small measure by the major increases in research budgets, almost half of which had been government funded, that had accompanied the war effort. Companies began to diversify out of their core businesses, oil companies into petrochemicals, for example, and rubber companies into plastics, creating new competitors in many industries. With more competing brands and the virtual end of supply scarcity, consumers could demand more precise and total response to their needs and wants. The Age of the Consumer had begun.

Changing marketplace conditions were a major stimulus to the development of the customer-oriented marketing concept. Increased competition for the consumer's patronage called for more care in understanding and responding to consumer needs and wants. Up until this time, the definition of marketing was essentially that of selling what the factory could produce. The focus of management was on products and production, not on consumers. Marketing was responsible for stimulating demand; it was different from "selling" or "sales" in that it also included advertising, sales promotion, and other forms of mass communication. Marketing management was also responsible for market research and sales planning, including forecasting and budgeting, helping manufacturing decide how much to produce. Marketing departments were found only in large companies, however. In the vast majority of firms, the little marketing activity to be found resided in the sales department.

Prior to the development of the marketing concept, the goal of marketing activity was to produce a sale, to maximize sales volume. Profitability was not a major marketing concern. The basic assumption was that sales volume was the key to profitability. The more the sales and marketing people could sell, the higher the profit the firm could expect as it spread its fixed costs over larger production volume and reduced variable cost per unit as well.

Selling, product planning, pricing, and distribution were seen as separate management areas, each with a unique set of problems to be managed by specialists. Much of what we think of as marketing today was found in a sales department, managed by the Sales Manager. In addition to responsibility for the salesforce, the sales department would include advertising, sales promotion, sales correspondence and service, and perhaps marketing research, if such a function existed in the company. The role of marketing was to make the sales department as effective as possible in moving the merchandise, supporting it with advertising, sales promotion, market research, and recommended pricing actions.

In most firms, product planning was not a marketing activity. Rather, products were the responsibility of the research and development, engineering, and manufacturing people. The idea of an integrated "marketing mix," blending product, pricing, promotion, and distribution policies and conscious strategic analysis of the interactions among them, had not yet gained acceptance.

Such was the world of the early 1950s: growing markets, increasing competition, companies focused on their current products and production capacity, marketing dominated by selling functions, and consumers with increased spending power and increased discretion in how they would spend it.

## CUSTOMER ORIENTATION AS A NEW IDEA

Perhaps the wisest viewer of this scene was Peter F. Drucker, a management consultant, lecturer, writer, and college and business school faculty member. Born in Austria in 1909, Drucker was educated in Germany in economics, politics, and the law. He worked for several years in England before coming to the United States in 1937. As a frequent advisor to banks and corporations, a reporter on economic affairs for newspapers and business journals, and a professor of politics and philosophy, he brought a unique perspective to the changing business environment in America. He saw things in a different way from the typical manager and management theorist.

It is fair to say that Drucker was the academic father of the marketing concept with its central tenet of customer orientation, the basic assertion that the company should put the customer first, always. In his famous book, *The Practice of Management,* published in 1954, Drucker addressed the fundamental question: What is a business? His thoughts were revolutionary:

> If we want to know what a business is we have to start with its *purpose. . . .* There is only one valid definition of business purpose: *to create a customer.*
>
> It is the customer who determines what a business is. For it is the customer, and he alone, who through being willing to pay for a good or service, converts economic resources into wealth, things into goods. What the business thinks it produces is not of first importance—especially not to the future of the business and to its success. What the customer thinks he is buying, what he considers "value," is decisive . . .
>
> Because it is its purpose to create a customer, any business enterprise has two—and only these two—basic functions: marketing and innovation.[4]

Drucker believed that marketing, as opposed to selling, was an American invention, created by "the assumption of responsibility for creative, aggressive, pioneering marketing by American management." He noted that Cyrus McCormick, the inventor of the mechanical harvester, also invented market research and analysis, the concept of market share or "standing," modern pricing policies, the sales/service specialist, parts and service supply to the customer, and customer credit. McCormick did all of this before the middle of the nineteenth century, to create markets for his invention.

Drucker saw the traditional American manager's attitude of "The sales department will sell whatever the factory produces" being replaced by "It is our job to produce what the market needs." In contrast, he believed that "In Europe there is still almost no understanding that marketing is the specific business function—a major reason for the stagnation of the European economies of today."[5] (By the end of the 1970s, however, European and Asian competitors were teaching lessons on customer orientation to the Americans.)

Drucker went on to explain:

> [Marketing] is so basic that it is not just enough to have a strong sales department and to entrust marketing to it. Marketing is not only much broader than selling, it is not a specialized activity at all. It encompasses the entire business. It is the whole business seen from the point of view of its final result, that is from the customer's point of view.[6]

As a good example, Drucker pointed to the General Electric Company which had developed a new marketing approach, beginning in 1947 in some affiliated companies. By 1950, these methods had been more or less completely adopted throughout the company. The new General Electric approach emphasized *integration of all marketing functions and an analytical perspective, based on market research.* In its 1952 *Annual Report,* General Electric had proclaimed the importance of putting the customer first in the process of production planning, attempting to build consumer appeal into the product from the design stage on. General Electric reported:

> [General Electric] operating managers were presented with an advanced concept of marketing formulated by the Marketing Services Division. This, in simple terms, would introduce the marketing man at the beginning rather than the end of the production cycle and would integrate marketing into each phase of the business. Thus, marketing, through its studies and research, would establish for the engineer, the designer and the manufacturing man what the customer wants in a given product, what price he is willing to pay, and where and when it will be wanted. Marketing would have authority in product planning, production planning and inventory control, as well as the sales, distribution and servicing of the product. This concept, it is believed, will tighten control over business operation and will fix responsibility, while making possible greater flexibility and closer teamwork in the marketing of the Company's products.[7]

General Electric was clearly in the vanguard in implementing the marketing concept. What it called the "advanced concept of marketing" combined customer orientation, market research, and integrated marketing. It saw the need for marketing to begin with the conceptualization of the product and its planning, not with the factory's finished product. It made a clear distinction between the new customer-oriented marketing concept and the old selling approach to marketing.

In addition to General Electric, there were a number of other large companies such as IBM, Procter & Gamble, and General Foods, and their CEOs, championing the marketing concept. In the consumer packaged goods area, these included Pillsbury and its president, Robert J. Keith. In a 1960 article, Keith described Pillsbury's progression from a production orientation to a sales orientation to a marketing orientation and, ultimately, to *marketing control*. He compared this "marketing revolution" to the revolution caused by Copernicus' paradigm-shifting proposition that the earth revolved around the sun rather than the reverse. In this case, the company was seen to revolve around the customer rather than the customer around the company.

Keith believed that the experience at Pillsbury was one that would be followed by every company seeking continued improvement in profitability. The core of the marketing orientation at Pillsbury was the development of a brand manager organization which had evolved out of the advertising department as a method of achieving marketing integration, a system already in place at Procter & Gamble and other leading packaged goods companies. The move from marketing orientation to marketing control was basically a shift from short-term to long-term orientation in the business, from marketing tactics and operations to overall business policy and strategy, all focused around the consumer. Keith had a strong vision of the marketing revolution:

> Soon it will be true that every activity of the corporation—from finance to sales to production—is aimed at satisfying the needs and desires of the consumer. When that stage of development is reached, the marketing revolution will be complete.[8]

In the minds of many executives, the marketing concept was being accepted as a new management philosophy, a new concept of what it means to be a business, as Peter Drucker had proposed.

It is important to understand Drucker's early statement of what the marketing concept is, and what it is not. It is not a statement of business strategy or tactics. It does not offer a clear road map or checklist or "do-it-yourself" guide. In fact, it says little about *how* to become customer-oriented. Nor is it a guide to organization structure for improved marketing. It is especially important to remember that, according to Drucker, *marketing should not be a separate business function at all.* It certainly doesn't urge, as its critics would subsequently claim, that the firm should have a strong, separate marketing department. The notion of marketing "empire building" is not part of the marketing concept.

What the marketing concept offers is a statement of management philosophy, a basic set of values and beliefs to guide the organization. As McNamara, a management consultant, noted, the marketing concept is:

> . . . a philosophy of business management, based upon a company-wide acceptance of the need for customer orientation, profit orientation, and recognition of the important role of marketing in communicating the needs of the market to all major corporate departments.[9]

Today, we see the marketing concept as a statement of *organizational culture,* an agreed upon set of shared values among the employees of a company representing a commitment to putting the customer first in all management and operations decision making. It calls for everyone in the organization to think about their job in terms of how it delivers value to customers. Note that Drucker specifically talked about *value* for the customer as the necessary driving force and vision for any successful company.

At the forefront in the implementation of the philosophy of the marketing concept was the Manager of the Marketing Research Service at General Electric, John B. McKitterick. McKitterick was comfortable at the interface of the worlds of business and academe, stayed current on the marketing literature, and spoke frequently at professional meetings on the subject of the marketing concept. While he noted that marketing textbooks and journals had been advocating the importance of being "market-oriented" for decades, what was new in the late 1950s was the fact that business managers were beginning to implement these ideas. But it was the ideas, the subtle change in meaning hidden in words, that fascinated McKitterick. He saw the focus of management shifting away from the customer as the *means* to profit and toward serving customers as the *end purpose* of business activity. Profit, he said, was becoming less the end objective of business and more a condition that must be satisfied.[10]

While we might disagree with the implication that customer satisfaction and profit are competing objectives, the important point in McKitterick's opinion is that management was elevating the customer's interest into the primary position in the business planning process. A key concept here was that of *market segmentation*. Based on the fundamental premise that no firm could do an equally effective job of delivering value to all potential customers, the marketing concept called for the firm to analyze its potential markets carefully, identifying those customers whose unsatisfied needs it could best serve.

## Marketing and Innovation: A Company's Two Basic Functions

Drucker, it will be recalled, said that every firm has only two basic functions—*marketing* and *innovation*. Merely being "customer-oriented" in the philosophical sense was not enough, nor was marketing skill, narrowly defined; constant innovation in order to deliver better value to consumers in a competitive marketplace was also a basic requirement. McKitterick made the point forcefully:

> [A] company committed to the marketing concept focuses its major innovative effort on enlarging the size of the market in which it participates by introducing new generic products and services, by promoting new applications for existing products, and by seeking out new classes of customers who heretofore have not used the existing products. . . . [O]nly thinking of the customer and mere technical proficiency in marketing both turn out to be inferior hands when played against the company that couples its thought with action and actually comes to market with a successful innovation. . . . *So the principal task of the marketing function in a management concept is not so much to be skillful in making the customer do what suits the interests of the business as to be skillful in conceiving and then making the business do what suits the interests of the customer.*[11]

## Implementing the Marketing Concept

Implementation of the marketing concept requires five steps:

1. Developing a culture of customer orientation.
2. Emphasizing profitability rather than sales volume.
3. Deciding how to compete: Market segmentation, targeting, and positioning.
4. Developing an integrated marketing mix.
5. Defining organizational responsibility for marketing.

## Customer Orientation and Profitability

The commitment to innovation and customer-oriented business decision making is only the first step in implementing the marketing concept. This commitment establishes the culture of customer orientation that is the foundation of the marketing concept. It is absolutely essential, the basis on which all strategic activities must be built. But by itself it is incomplete as a business strategy; it says nothing about how to create and deliver customer value profitably.

The next step is to shift the focus away from sales volume and toward profitability. When managing for profitability, not sales volume, the firm is focusing on the value its products create for customers in the competitive marketplace. Profit does not come at the expense of the customer, as some would argue. On the contrary, it is the best possible measure of the value that has been created for customers.

Declining profitability is a signal that the company's product offering is becoming less effective, relative to substitutes and competitive product offerings, in delivering value and satisfying customer needs. It may often be the result of aggressive attempts to expand sales volume by serving a larger portion of the total market, requiring higher expenditures on promotional activities and low prices. This is where the concept of market segmentation becomes essential to our understanding.

Market segmentation, targeting, and positioning constitute the third set of requirements for implementing the marketing concept and deserve special emphasis as they are the heart of marketing strategy.

## Market Segmentation, Targeting, and Positioning

Market segmentation recognizes that customers have distinct needs, preferences, and buying patterns. It is the process of analyzing the market in order to define, creatively, distinct groupings of customers for whom the firm has the potential to offer superior value. These different groups will respond differently to the firm's product offering and communications.

Market targeting involves developing products and communications aimed at specific parts of the total market in order to more effectively and efficiently compete. Market targets should be those segments that offer the best return on marketing investments and the greatest profit opportunities. One of the drivers of the product lifecycle, in which profit margins begin to erode following the early growth stage of the market, is increased competition from market nichers who selectively target parts of the total market with a superior product offering.

The inevitability of the product or market lifecycle brings us back to the centrality of innovation in the marketing concept. The successful firm must continuously improve its product offering in order to remain competitive. Inefficiency and lower profit margins inevitably creep in when the company relies on heavier promotional expenditures and aggressive pricing actions to prop up sales volume for an increasingly obsolete product aimed at multiple market segments. Superior marketing skill is a myth when applied to obsolete products in an undifferentiated or incorrectly segmented market.

Positioning is the process of developing the value proposition, which differentiates the product offering from its competitors in the customer's mind. It is implemented through communications—personal selling, advertising, sales promotion, publicity, and so on. All brand elements such as company and brand name, logos, packaging, promotional materials, and labeling are part of the positioning process. Positioning is critical to the success of the product offering. For many product offerings and market targets, the product positioning is more enduring than the physical product itself. Brand image and positioning may remain constant while the product is continuously refined and improved in response to changing customer preferences and technology.

## Integrated Marketing

The fourth requirement for implementation of the marketing concept is to develop an *integrated* approach to the marketing policy variables of market segmentation, product, pricing, promotion, and distribution. The concept of integration itself is rather subtle and complex. It has three dimensions: priority, completeness, and synergy.

Prioritizing marketing decisions means putting the elements in proper sequence. First must come the market segmentation process, selecting those customers that the firm is to serve. By committing to serve a particular set of customers, the company is committing to develop a particular set of competences, resources, and skills that will define the firm in the future. *The selection of markets to be served is the single most important decision that any firm makes.* It is even more important than the product offering. The product is a variable that can be tailored to the customers' needs and wants if the firm has chosen its customers so that they match up with its unique competitive capabilities.

Second in decision priority comes the product itself. Is the product offering consistent with the best available technology and designed to provide the best solution for the customer in the customer's use situation? The product offering must be continuously refined, improved, updated, and expanded if the firm is to be successful in meeting and exceeding customer expectations, which change over time in response to the promise of competitive product offerings. The concept of the product must go beyond the core, physical product itself, and even beyond the "expected" product in the mind of the customer, which includes all of the service features, which are required to make it available to, and usable by, the consumer. It must be "augmented" with additional features and services that exceed the customer's expectations in ways that are important to the customer.[12]

The third decision priority is pricing, which is part of the product offering and determines the economic value delivered to the customer as well as the value to be captured by the firm. In fact, a given price level may be a design objective in the development of the product offering. The customer's use situation and competitive product offerings may define a rather narrow range of pricing opportunities. Pricing must also recognize the need for promotional expenditures and reseller profit margins in order to play its proper strategic role in the marketing mix.

Following market segmentation, targeting, product development and positioning, and pricing, which define the firm's product offering (and its business-level strategy which can be thought of as the answer to the question "How do we want to compete?"), policies relating to distribution and promotion, or marketing communications, must be decided on. There may be tradeoffs to be made between reliance on resellers in the form of wholesalers, retailers, and other forms of distributors, and the use of a direct salesforce of company employees. In both cases, the reseller organization and the direct salesforce must be supported by advertising, sales promotion, customer service, publicity, telemarketing, and other forms of communication to optimize response to marketing expenditures.

In the process of describing decision priorities, we have also touched on the dimensions of completeness and synergy. A complete marketing strategy must be based on careful analysis and programming of all of the marketing mix elements and it must consider specifically the interactions and interdependencies among them. For example, pricing is a key dimension of product positioning. Market segmentation has specific implications for the organization of the selling effort as well as for product line development and management. Advertising message and media strategy must be consistent with the desired image called for by market targeting and product positioning. The entire effort must be coordinated at a high level of strategic management to insure that marketing decisions are both consistent and thorough.

## Defining the Role of Marketing in the Organization

Fifth and finally, organizational responsibility for marketing must be assigned. Commitment to the marketing concept and its implementation will not happen unless there is clear, high-level managerial responsibility for it. Here we encounter a fundamental dilemma, inherent in the marketing concept. On the one hand, responsibility must be assigned. On the other hand, as Peter Drucker noted so carefully, marketing is really not a separate function at all. Rather, it is the total business seen from the point of view of its ultimate purpose—that of creating a satisfied customer.

The challenge, in a nutshell, is how to make sure that everyone in the organization is focused on the customer and committed to delivering superior customer value while at the same time achieving a distinct level of competence in marketing skills and assigning clear responsibility for marketing results. Why have Marketing Managers at all? The short answer is that there must be people within the organization who are clearly "experts on the customer" and who can provide the rest of the organization with the necessary information and insights into customers' evolving definitions of value. They must also take responsibility for guiding the various organizational processes that lead to the creation and delivery of superior customer value.

We must leave this complex issue unresolved for the moment, but it is one that we will come back to many times as our analysis of the new marketing concept develops.

# PROBLEMS IN ADOPTING THE MARKETING CONCEPT

By the mid-1960s, marketing researchers had begun to study the extent to which American firms had actually adopted the marketing concept. They did this by looking at the extent to which management was committed to customer orientation and managing for profitability rather than sales volume. In addition, they frequently looked for the presence of a strong, central marketing department as evidence of the extent to which the firm had adopted the marketing mandate. As noted, this is a very controversial measure.

It became increasingly common, however, to equate strong marketing with a large marketing department. Hise, for example, in a 1965 study, defined a firm's adoption of the marketing concept as including:

- Customer orientation.
- Profit orientation of marketing operations.
- "An organizational structure in which all marketing activities are performed by the marketing department, and where the chief marketing executive is accorded a place on the company's organization chart equal to that given the top financial and manufacturing executives."[13]

He found that the companies surveyed were doing market research and surveys and giving marketing partial responsibility for product development but in general were not managing for profitability. Large firms were more likely to use market research. In most of the firms surveyed, the top marketing executive reported to the president of the firm. Hise's overall conclusion was that most large and medium-sized manufacturing firms had adopted the marketing concept, especially in terms of customer orientation and organization structure, with large firms showing a somewhat stronger tendency.

In 1972, McNamara published the results of another survey of American manufacturing firms' practices with respect to adopting the marketing concept. He used primarily organizational criteria in making his judgments, including:

- The organizational level of the top marketing executive.
- The presence or absence of people with marketing backgrounds in top management positions.
- Whether marketing was centralized at the corporate or product/division level.
- The scope of the marketing research function.

He did not consider direct measures of customer- or profit-orientation, but for these constructs he used surrogate organizational measures such as the presence of marketing executives on nonmarketing committees and the presence of formal training and communications programs.

His primary conclusions were that large firms and consumer goods companies were more likely to have adopted the marketing concept than were smaller companies and those marketing to industrial customers. In large companies, where marketing was centralized at the corporate level, the role was that of a coordinating and consulting function rather than a direct operating role. In the smaller companies, and in industrial firms, there was a limited amount of integration of marketing functions, but with more of an operational focus.[14]

By the mid-1970s, it had become clear that the rather simple strictures of the marketing concept were not easily or readily accepted by most companies. Instead of true customer orientation, managing for profitability, and integrated marketing at the business unit level, what was often found was continued product and manufacturing orientation, continued emphasis on sales volume rather than long-term profitability based on customer satisfaction, and weak integration among marketing functions and of marketing with other functions like research and development and manufacturing. In most companies, sales still dominated. The job of marketing was to sell what the factory could produce.

The original marketing concept saw marketing as a function that pervaded all aspects of the business, putting the customer in the center of all operational and strategic decision making. The objective was to do the best possible job of satisfying customer needs. At both General Electric and Pillsbury, for example, it was stated explicitly that as the marketing function came to fruition, all operations management, from product design to production planning to manufacturing to inventory control and distribution, would ultimately be coordinated, integrated, and directed by marketing. This vision was clearly stated by Keith's fourth phase in the development of the marketing concept, that of *marketing control.*

Instead of a blurring of the boundaries between the traditional management functions (sales, finance, manufacturing, engineering, etc.) called for by the move to total customer orientation, the functional boundaries grew higher and stronger. In large consumer goods companies, marketing had typically become the dominant managerial function and now provided a large portion of the top management of the company. In smaller companies and in firms serving industrial markets, marketing, if it existed at all, was relatively weak. There was still manufacturing and engineering dominance and there was a sales volume and selling orientation. Marketing was typically a staff function, perhaps within the sales department or else as part of the administrative structure reporting to the president or chief operating officer.

Champions of the marketing concept were troubled by what they saw in the mid-1970s. It had not lived up to its promise of revolutionizing American business. It was becoming clear that many of the companies in several key industries were facing non-American competitors who were taking significant market share and apparently much more in touch with the American consumer. Automobiles, consumer electronics, office machines, and photographic equipment and film are just a few of the industries that were under siege.

Why was the marketing concept, so simple an idea to understand, so hard to implement in practice? There are three areas to consider:

1. The validity and soundness of the marketing concept *per se.*
2. Errors and shortcomings in its implementation.
3. Inherent conflicts with other management functions.

## Flaws in the Marketing Concept

This chapter has stressed, as did Drucker, that the marketing concept is a management philosophy, a way of thinking about the business and its fundamental purpose: to create a satisfied customer. From a societal point of view, customer orientation is the strongest source of legitimation for business as an institution, especially for a business grown too large to be controlled by its owners and their wishes for business purpose. In its simple form, where its intent is most clear, the marketing concept does not contain significant *strategic* content. It says virtually nothing about *how* the firm should satisfy customer needs. Indeed it says nothing about *which* customer needs a firm should focus on. Because of these unanswered questions, the marketing concept has a nebulous quality about it that makes it very difficult for marketing managers and other advocates of customer orientation to defend themselves against the other management functions.

### *Difficulty in Analyzing Customer Needs*

A key part of customer orientation and integrated marketing is the use of market research to analyze customer needs and wants and to provide feedback of the results to other parts of the business. The implication is that marketing has the ability to discover, to understand, and to communicate to others the essence of customer needs. The even more basic implication is that customers know their needs. Suppose they don't. Where does that leave the marketing concept and customer orientation?

There are a number of situations where customers do not and even cannot know their own needs and wants. Consumers could not know they wanted television or electronic fuel injection or compact discs or fluoride toothpaste before they existed. A possible retort here is "Of course, but they had clearly defined needs for information and entertainment, dependable engine performance, improved musical listening, and better dental health." From a practical standpoint, how useful is that level of analysis? What good does it do a firm in the radio manufacturing business to have its marketing research learn that people want better information and more entertainment?

The real challenge for the firm is *to create new markets*, not just to serve existing ones. The legendary success stories—Ford, Disney, IBM, Hewlett-Packard, Federal Express, Apple, AOL, and the like—did just that. These managers did not start with a clean piece of paper when they asked customers what they wanted. They had a vision of a capability to produce a unique product or service that would revolutionize the way customers solved a problem. They could lead their customers into the future, especially if they listened to customers as they developed and refined the features of their product offering. They were committed to leading and educating their customers in the use of their products. They had a vision.

Not all real business opportunities are as revolutionary. Consider those instances in which customers can come closer to expressing their unsatisfied needs, for example "I would like to have a toothpaste that will make my children want to brush their teeth three times a day and that will prevent cavities." There is still the question of whether the company has the capability to develop the called-for solution or whether the solution is even remotely technically feasible.

In his classic statement of the marketing concept, "Marketing Myopia," Ted Levitt built a convincing argument that the business should define itself not by its products but by the nature of the basic customer needs it was committed to satisfying.[15] His examples of firms in the industrial graveyard because they failed to do so included railroads and buggy whip companies. The argument was that the railroads should have defined themselves as being in the transportation business and that the buggy whip manufacturers should have been able to develop new lines of business to serve the automobile owner. Putting aside the fact that government regulation prevented it, there seems little point in telling a railroad that it should go into the trucking business to compete with the truckers or into the airline passenger business to keep the customers who used to travel by rail. The buggy whip people could probably have used their leather-crafting skills better in making belts or hats than in trying to develop new products for the automobile market. There are fundamental questions about the capability of the firm, its resources and skills, and even more basically its values and mission, that must be answered before we can match up the strategy of the business and a set of market needs.

## Understanding What the Firm Can Do Well

The market alone cannot tell the firm what to do. A creative process is required to look at the market, understand potential customer needs and wants, consider the basic capabilities of the firm, conceive potential product offerings based on the present and potential capabilities, design and develop such products, and actually make them and deliver them with the full bundle of supporting services to a clearly defined target market. It is just as important to understand the firm's capabilities as it is to understand customer needs. The marketing concept does not deny this fact, it just doesn't say anything about it.

A literal interpretation of the marketing concept would suggest that the firm should take information from the marketplace as the sole basis for deciding what to do. Somehow, this implies that the market itself provides not only information about customer needs but also the criteria that tell the firm what to do. Carried to this extreme, of course, the marketing concept begins to make less and less sense. To that extent, therefore, the marketing concept is an incomplete management philosophy.

One insightful commentator, Andrew Kaldor, a management consultant, addressed this issue in the early 1970s with his concept of *Imbricative Marketing*, a phrase that, not surprisingly, never caught on. "Imbrication" is an overlapping of edges, and the concept of imbricative marketing involved four steps:

1. Identification of the organization's skills.
2. Identification of the objectives of the organization.
3. The identification of the leading part of the system in which the firm operates, which can be thought of as its position in the value chain.
4. The identification of market needs compatible to the organization's needs.[16]

More recent authors have made much of the concept of the firm's "distinctive competence," but Kaldor was using the concept in 1971:

> By concentrating on the firm's competencies, the concept of imbrication attempts to outline the areas in which the firm may actualize its potential. It is a

framework for strategy selection because it includes the firm and its environment, recognizes the repercussive nature of policy making, and concentrates on those areas in which the firm can maximally utilize its resources. Thus, the framework defines those areas of choice confronting the firm through the conjunction of the freedom the environment allows the firm and the capabilities within the firm. The integrity of the firm is preserved by interpreting and translating information about the environment from the perspective of the firm and not from the perspective of the environment.[17]

No firm can be all things to all potential customers. If the marketing concept was to be a useful management tool, not just a statement of corporate culture and business purpose, it would need to be expanded to include a more strategic focus on matching up market needs and the firm's capabilities.

## Errors in Implementing the Marketing Concept

Beyond the conceptual problems with the marketing concept, which it is fair to assume many managers had not thought about deeply, there were a number of problems at the implementation level, including:

- Failure to make customer orientation the true priority.
- Underinvestment in marketing.
- Weak performance by the marketing organization.
- Creation of a marketing bureaucracy.

### The Difficulty of Making Customer Orientation the Priority

First, for many companies the adoption of the marketing concept was mostly at the conceptual level. It is easy for top management to *say* we are committed to the customer. That has the familiar ring of "motherhood and apple pie." It is harder to make the resource commitments to marketing information systems, strategy development, processes for identifying and developing professional marketing management talent, and organizational structures necessary to keep the total organization focused on the customer. It may be even harder to develop and maintain a true culture of customer orientation, a set of values and beliefs that puts the interests of the customer first, ahead of those of all the other constituencies and stakeholders served by the organization.

Not all chief executive officers (CEOs) are truly committed to putting the customer first, even if they say they are. Many CEOs clearly put their shareholders first; all too often, shareholders' interests dominate, in terms of the priority of return on investment and quarterly earnings per share. Especially in publicly owned corporations where large institutional investors (notably pension funds) often control huge blocks of stock, top management would seem to have little choice but to make short-term profit the number one objective.

The argument that, over the long run, all constituencies including the shareholders are served best by putting the customer first is a bit nebulous, especially for financial analysts whose job is to focus on return on investment. The marketing concept's assertion that profit is the reward for creating a satisfied customer and that the firm that does the best job for the customer will be the most profitable has lacked sound empirical support until quite recently and may appear to its critics to be little more than wishful thinking.

If top management does not truly put the customer first, they have put something else first—usually earnings per share. The rest of the organization can figure this out in a hurry and will behave accordingly, especially if they are evaluated and rewarded in terms of short-term measures of profitability and financial performance.

## Underinvestment in Marketing

The marketing concept requires specific resource commitments, most of which do not pay off in the short term. There is an obvious requirement for information from the marketplace about customer needs, wants, preferences, buying habits, and usage patterns, and about competitive product offerings. This information must be collected and professionally analyzed. Models must be developed for examining relationships among market characteristics, marketing actions, and customer response to marketing effort. Professional marketing requires the development of truly professional marketing personnel and marketing information systems.

These are long-term investments with long-term payoffs and long-term strategic consequences for the firm. Budgeting for these investments puts the marketing function in direct conflict with other management functions for scarce financial resources. Such requests may conflict directly with the short-term profit orientation of the firm.

The marketing department may be trapped in a self-fulfilling-prophecy cycle: Lack of investment in information and analysis, resulting in failure to develop the professional marketing personnel and analytical systems necessary to identify and track the strategic and financial consequences of marketing actions, makes it difficult to justify rigorously the request for funds to develop and maintain such systems.

As financial management gained ascendancy in the 1970s, the marketing function in many companies looked less professional than its other management colleagues who had often been trained more completely and more rigorously in the management and analytical disciplines. To quote one executive:

> Marketing tends to be peripatetic. They do less homework than the other business functions such as finance, manufacturing, and engineering. They tend to fly by the seat of the pants and their approach is much less documented. They are less even, more in-and-out than the other functions. I have great affinity for the marketing people. I like to talk to them. But when they go away I wonder if they were really listening.[18]

## Weak Performance by the Marketing Function

All too often, marketing promised more than it could deliver. This is true both on the academic side, where marketing scholars were struggling to develop a rigorous analytical base for the marketing discipline, and on the business side where marketing departments were often staffed with people poorly prepared for their responsibility.

From the academic perspective, it is fair to say that management science, using the tools of rigorous mathematical and statistical analysis, had not lived up to its promise in marketing.[19] Although there had been a lot of "over promising" in the 1960s and 1970s, that is not the principal point here. Rather, there is a fundamental difficulty inherent in the nature of marketing problems for the manager who wishes to justify marketing expenditures by establishing cause-and-effect relationships between marketing actions and sales and profit results. In a competitive marketplace, where consumers are exposed to thousands of selling messages from dozens of competing suppliers, where customers have limited ability to process information and a number of other constraints on their decision making, where every sale is the result of many complex interactions between marketing variables and buyer characteristics, it is virtually impossible to find strong causal relationships.

The financial manager can run a computer model to predict return on investment given assumptions about risks and interest rates. The manufacturing manager can rather precisely determine the amount of production output that will result from specified inputs of raw materials, machine time, workforce hours, energy, and other factors. The marketing manager must often answer "It all depends . . ." when asked to predict the results of a given investment. At best, the manager may be able to specify *what* it depends on. More commonly, he or she may not be able to get to even that general level of analysis.

In the best companies, marketing management talent was being recruited from leading universities and exposed to rigorous in-house training and management development programs. Such excellence was characteristic of the large consumer packaged goods companies like Procter & Gamble, General Mills, and Gillette, and some of the more prominent industrial firms like General Electric and IBM. In many other companies, however, as will be readily admitted by their managers, marketing was still seen as an adjunct to the sales department. Field sales managers were brought into headquarters to head a poorly conceived marketing operation. The long-term, strategic, research-based requirements of the marketing concept were superseded by the short-term, tactical, intuitive emphasis and skills of the sales manager who continued to be under pressure to produce maximum sales volume in the short term.

In a 1980 study of top management views of the marketing function, many of the respondents commented on the separation of sales and marketing. The president of one of the "Big 3" American automobile companies commented:

> The auto companies are in the Dark Ages. They confuse sales and marketing. The "sales and marketing guys" are all sales guys. They don't sell cars to the public, they sell them to the dealers. The auto companies do not see that they have any incentive to become customer and marketing oriented.[20]

The chief executive officer of a major paper products company, with over 30 years of experience in a variety of both consumer and industrial businesses, commented from this broad perspective:

> The marketing concept is only 25 or 30 years old and to get it understood and accepted is the biggest challenge any organization faces. Marketing tends to degenerate into a sales orientation and into an exclusive concern for marketing communications. . . . In industrial companies like this one, the experience ladder is usually built on direct sales or a related function, and this can create a very narrow viewpoint. They bring the values of a salesman into the marketing function, partly because they feel they have been successful and have been promoted into marketing. In an industrial organization, there is an almost inevitable pressure from individual customers that creates a short-term orientation, a concern for specific orders, specific customer problems, and specific requests. It is a continuing uphill battle to get marketing people to see their

job in broad strategic terms. It is difficult for anybody to think broadly, reflectively about what they do. But salespeople will never be able to develop a marketing plan. There are many, many more salespeople in the typical organization than marketing people, and this also helps to explain why the sales viewpoint tends to drive out the marketing viewpoint.[21]

## Marketing Bureaucracy

Over time, the marketing department became a distinct organizational entity in many companies, driven in part by the inherent conflict between the sales and marketing viewpoints. Assigning marketing responsibility to sales organizations in general did not work very well. Marketing was identified with marketing research and product development, while sales was associated with promotion, distribution, and pricing. Integrated marketing required something more.

Despite the urging of Drucker and others that marketing was really not a separate business function at all, it was necessary to find organizational mechanisms for implementing the marketing concept. There must be responsibility established for market information, market analysis, and integrated marketing—coordination of the parts of the marketing mix and of marketing with other functions, especially manufacturing and distribution.

In the consumer packaged goods firms, organizational responsibility typically resided in a brand management function. Here, marketing was a line management function with profit-and-loss responsibility implemented through a rigorous annual budgeting process. Some firms in industries such as paper, chemicals, office machinery, and computers also found it possible to organize around product managers or market managers who had clear profit and loss (P&L) responsibilities.

In many other cases, however, marketing remained a staff function, reporting through a sales vice president or marketing vice president to a chief executive officer such as the president. Within the marketing function, there were managers of advertising and sales promotion, market research, and sometimes product development, distribution, packaging, public relations, and publicity. Pricing responsibility was often diffused across marketing, sales, and financial management. Sales was frequently a separate function, with its own vice president, reporting separately to the CEO.

Organizational separation of marketing and sales created a number of issues of responsibility and coordination. Some firms attempted to manage the inherent conflict with a kind of matrix organization in which salespeople also had a "dotted line" responsibility to a product manager or market manager. Seldom did these arrangements work well. Again, the sales viewpoint tended to dominate. The product or market manager was a general without troops. Market development activities, for example, would receive inadequate attention from a salesforce focused on making the sales revenue numbers for the current period. Marketing planning remained an advisory or consulting function with unclear responsibility for results and was often viewed as an impediment to quick response in the increasingly competitive marketplace.

If marketing was a separate staff function, it was not a profit center but a cost center. It had a budget and a staff, clearly assigned costs, and no assigned revenue. When the cost-cutting, downsizing, and delayering mandates of the 1980s and 1990s came along, marketing departments were in a very exposed position. Marketing staffs were reduced significantly and in some cases eliminated altogether. The rationalization was sometimes that of the old marketing concept—marketing should not be a separate staff function at all; rather it is the responsibility of the businesses, the operating units, to become customer-focused and market-driven. Reducing marketing headcount at the corporate level, however, didn't mean that better marketing would result at the operating unit level. The basic problems of the marketing concept and its implementation remain, regardless of the level in the organization to which they are assigned.

Having marketing as a separate function also had another negative consequence: It let the rest of the organization "off the hook" in terms of customer satisfaction. Other functional managers could follow the mandates of their own disciplines, not the customer's requirements. (If the marketing department is going to worry about the customer, the other departments can go about their own business.)

When marketing became a function, it was no longer a focus. Someplace along the line, marketing orientation was substituted for market or customer orientation. Perhaps it was Pillsbury's Keith with his concepts of marketing orientation and marketing control who unwittingly first made the substitution. It should come as no surprise that managers of other functions were not ready to buy into the notion of a firm controlled by its marketing department.

## Conflict between Marketing and Other Management Functions

When marketing exists as a separate management function, there is an inherent conflict with the other management functions. Under the marketing concept, marketing among all the management functions is the one charged with responsibility for telling the rest of the organization what to do. It is marketing's job to research customer needs and wants and to direct the firm's product development, manufacturing, and distribution activities, and indeed all other support functions from credit to human resources to purchasing to financial management, toward the delivering of maximum value for customers. Marketing is charged with being the *expert on the customer,* for keeping the rest of the organization both informed about and focused on the customer. Marketing is an advocate for the customer's point of view.

There are two problems with this:

1. Managers in other functions have other constituencies that must be served and satisfied.
2. Marketing is not alone in thinking that they know best what is in the customers' best interests.

Any organization is a complex coalition of interests. According to the stakeholder theory of the firm, each of the company's functional specialists is responsible for securing the favor and serving the needs of a group of persons and organizations who provide resource inputs to the firm or who place constraints upon its activities:

- Financial managers are accountable to the firm's shareholders, banks, and other investors.
- Purchasing managers must manage relationships with suppliers of raw materials, components, services, and other inputs to the operations of the business.
- Engineers and scientists represent the scientific community and are caretakers for a body of professional knowledge.
- Human resource managers and line managers share responsibility for the employees who contract with the firm.
- Manufacturing management is accountable to multiple constituencies including the employees, the owners of the productive assets, vendors, and customers.

It is the job of top management to coordinate and manage the trade-offs between these potentially conflicting interests.

The marketing concept asserts that customers should be first among equals, that is, they are the constituency that must be served first because customers have veto power over all of the other decisions made within the organization. If the customer doesn't buy, the other inputs and constraints become irrelevant because the firm will be out of business. This should give legitimacy to the mission of the marketing function to make the rest of the business customer-oriented.

Managers in other functions may honestly believe that they are putting the customer's interests first when they look at things from their own internal/company perspectives. The research scientist, the engineer who specializes in product development and design, the manufacturing manager, the purchasing manager, and all the rest are not willing to concede that their own viewpoint about what serves the customer best is in error. A manufacturing manager for a chemical company once said to me, for example: "I'll tell you what is best for the customer—it is what runs best through my plant!"

R&D people are certainly entitled to the view that they know better than the customers themselves what is in their best interest because they, the scientists, have a better view of what is possible. They know the technology, the customer doesn't. Some may think they even know better than customers themselves what is best for the customer. This can be a problem especially in firms dominated by the disciplines of physical or biological sciences and engineering.

## Can the Marketing Concept Improve Organizational Performance?

A final, and perhaps most basic problem with the marketing concept is that there was virtually no convincing evidence that a commitment to the strictures of the marketing concept would actually improve profitability or other measures of organizational performance. The argument that profit was a reward for creating a satisfied customer seemed to be one based on faith rather than hard data. It would be a hard argument to prove, because the relevant profits were *long-term* profits. Furthermore, concepts like *customer orientation* and *integrated marketing* would prove very difficult to make operational, observable, and measurable. (Research has begun to provide the necessary connections as described in Chapter 7.)

In the absence of empirical support for the argument, and given the marketing concept's call for a long-term, strategic view of a firm that put the customer's needs first, it was no surprise that the emphasis on strategic planning and sophisticated financial management that evolved in the 1970s would revolve around short-term measures of profitability such as cash flow, return-on-investment, and earnings per share. The current interests of the shareholders, and sales volume as the key to short-term earnings, would continue to dominate firm management at the expense of the interests of customers and long-term profitability. Global competitors found an interesting opportunity in the United States, the largest domestic market in the world, where management attention was not sharply focused on the changing needs and preferences of an increasingly sophisticated consumer.

## SUMMARY

Thus, the marketing concept ran into rough times as it matured. While no one argued with the basic wisdom of customer orientation, managing for profitability, and integrated marketing, getting the marketing concept implemented proved to be very difficult work. First, there was the problem of the rather weak strategic links of customer orientation back to the resources, skills, and other competences of the firm. It was often not clear that the customers could say what they needed or wanted or whether it was reasonable to assume that customers should be able to direct the development of potential technological and other capabilities.

Second, there were difficulties of implementation including the tension between the demand for short-term earnings based on current sales volume and the need for a long-term, strategic focus on future earnings requirements. Short term tended to drive out attention to long term; sales dominated marketing. Firms that underinvested in marketing tended to weaken their marketing activities, undercutting the ability of the marketing function to gain credibility with the other management functions and contribute to organizational effectiveness. Marketing didn't always live up to its promises.

A separate marketing department and the development of a marketing bureaucracy added to the problem. If marketing and sales were separate functions, there was an inherent conflict that was usually won by the sales department. If the company had not made a commitment to a strong marketing department, as opposed to simple lip service to the concept of being customer-oriented, it was easy for the other management functions to refuse to be guided by the market information provided by a marketing department. Information is the key, and to be useful it must be credible. If marketing has low credibility, the other functional managers can in good faith hold onto their belief that they know best what is in the customer's best interests.

A new marketing concept would have to address these questions, but in the context of the new organizational forms that have emerged in the global marketplace—*network organizations* consisting of smaller, more entrepreneurial business units; some as traditional divisions of larger corporations; others in the form of joint ventures; strategic alliances to develop new technologies; strategic partnerships with vendors; and a variety of long-term relationships with resellers, customers, and suppliers of services of all kinds. The traditional functional, bureaucratic, hierarchical, divisionalized corporate structure defined by the pyramid of its organization chart and its shiny corporate offices is obsolete. As these new organizational forms have evolved, the marketing concept had to be reinvented for the twenty-first century.

That is the purpose of this book.

# 2 Strategic Planning and Marketing

*The strategic aim of a business [is] to earn a return on capital, and if in any particular case the return in the long run is not satisfactory, then the deficiency should be corrected or the activity abandoned for a more favorable one.*

Alfred P. Sloan Jr.

Quoted in Ansoff
*Corporate Strategy* (1965), p. 1

The marketing concept, articulated as a management philosophy in the 1950s, melded into a broader concept of strategic planning in the 1960s and the marketing concept was soon overshadowed.

A financial management orientation dominated the strategic planning process in the late 1960s and into the 1970s. Firms were seen as investment portfolios of businesses (defined as product/market combinations) with the objective of maximizing return on investment. The attention of top management was focused on the challenge of allocating financial resources among the businesses in the portfolio in a way that maximized total return to the shareholders.

It wasn't until the mid-1980s that business leaders began to revisit the fundamental notions of customer orientation and integrated marketing that had been popular 25 years before. Many managers spent years trying to repair the damage done to competitive positions by the emphasis on short-term financial objectives and to recreate their companies as customer-focused, market-driven businesses. Unfortunately, the efforts to regain customer relationships were often driven by an emphasis on sales volume, not profitability, using price cuts and sales promotion in an attempt to restore market share.

In this chapter, we examine the evolution of the marketing concept into strategic planning and back again, leading to a new value-delivery concept of marketing and business strategy.

# EMERGENCE OF LONG-RANGE STRATEGIC PLANNING

As the ideas of the marketing concept were gaining popularity in the 1950s, managers were also developing the practice of *long-range planning*. This was an attempt to get beyond annual sales forecasting, budgeting, and production planning and adopt a longer time horizon that would permit more careful development and commitment of financial and human resources. Long-range planning was distinct from product planning, which was part of the product development process.

Also in the late 1950s, an interest developed—especially on the academic side—in rigorous, quantitative approaches to management decision making. The field of management science and decision analysis was based on mathematics, statistics, economics, and psychology. The curricula of leading business schools very quickly began to teach these more rigorous approaches to decision making and to apply them in the functional fields of finance, production/operations, and marketing. The analysts these schools trained would soon find their way into corporate staff positions.

In his famous study, *Strategy and Structure,* published in 1962, the business historian Alfred Chandler concluded that the evolution of the country's largest and most successful corporations had followed a consistent pattern. He observed that successful firms were those that had been able to identify changes in the external environment that created new opportunities and required some fundamental changes in the way the firm managed its operations. These firms had been able to adopt new strategies as required by the changing environment and to implement them through new organizational forms. It was the willingness to change organization form and structure as required by the changing environment that distinguished these successful firms, enabling them to implement effective strategies. Chandler's observations led to a simply stated conclusion: *Structure follows strategy.*[1]

The result of the evolutionary process that Chandler had identified in these successful companies was the now familiar organizational concept of centralized policy making and decentralized control, through a profit-center form of organization. Large, bureaucratic, divisionalized companies must balance the need for consistency, coordination, and control on the one hand with the need to push decision-making responsibility and authority down and out into the operating units on the other.

One of the management issues that must be addressed in such arrangements is how to achieve the proper balance between attention to current operating problems and longer term strategic challenges, between short-term and long-term decisions, given the inevitable tendency of operating management to focus on short-term problems and results. Formal, long-range planning was a method for keeping the entire enterprise moving in a coordinated fashion toward the achievement of long-term objectives. The practice of long-range *strategic* planning—planning that focused on the long-run strategic objectives of the firm—emerged in the 1960s as a new discipline, a new management practice to address these needs.

## Three Types of Decisions: Operating, Strategic, and Administrative

An early voice bringing these ideas together in a coherent framework was that of H. Igor Ansoff, then a professor at Carnegie Institute of Technology, noted for its rigorous approach to the study of industrial management. Ansoff's approach to the concept of strategy, one of several, is particularly interesting for our purposes because it highlights the confusing and often conflicting relationship between strategic planning and the marketing concept. In his book *Corporate Strategy,* Ansoff spelled out the differences among three types of decisions: operating, strategic, and administrative.[2]

### Operating Decisions

Operating decisions allocate the firm's productive resources to various activities, determining the levels of the various physical, financial, and human inputs into the firm's operations. Ansoff gave the following examples of operating decisions:

- Pricing.
- Marketing strategy (his words).
- Setting production schedules and inventory levels.
- Relative expenditures for R&D, marketing, and operations.

In an early example of how confusing the use of the word *strategy* can be, Ansoff asserted that marketing *strategy* is an operating decision, *not* a *strategic* decision.[3] Operating decisions were said to have a primarily internal focus, while strategic decisions had an external focus. From the beginning of the field of corporate strategy, there has been confusion and uncertainty about the relationship with marketing as a concept, as a discipline, and as a business function.

## Strategic Decisions

Strategic decisions were defined by Ansoff as those that establish what business the firm is in. They do so by selecting from among many alternatives for the firm's product-market mix, the products to be offered and the markets to which they will be sold. Apparently, Ansoff did not consider the choice of products or markets to be marketing decisions. As noted, marketing was defined as a set of operating decisions. This becomes significant as we consider what will happen to the acceptance and implementation of the marketing concept. Ansoff was also specific as to the objective of strategic decision making: to select a product/market mix that maximizes the firm's potential return on investment.[4] The emphasis on financial criteria was inherent in a more rigorous, economics-based approach to management decision making that focused on the optimum allocation of the firm's scarce resources among investment alternatives.

## Administrative Decisions

Administrative decisions establish the shape and structure of the firm. The objective of administrative decisions is to structure the firm's resources in a way that maximizes the firm's profit performance potential. According to Ansoff, administrative decisions include those relating to:

- Development and acquisition of productive resources like raw materials and personnel.
- Organization of the firm, including authority and reporting relationships.
- Flow of work and information.
- Location of facilities.
- Design and management of channels of distribution.

There is a strong argument that the design of distribution channels and supply or "value" chains, which are both examples of strategic partnering, are strategic, not administrative decisions.

## How the Marketing Concept Fits into Strategic Planning

Thinking back to the marketing concept and relating it to Ansoff's schema, if product-market selection is a strategic decision and distribution is an administrative decision, then the balance of what Ansoff would call marketing is pricing and promotion (personal selling, advertising, sales promotion, etc.) decisions, which he saw as operating decisions. Marketing was one of the functional competences that the firm needed to maintain. In Ansoff's words:

> *Marketing* is taken as a broad activity concerned with creating product acceptance, advertising, sales promotion, selling, distributing the product (including transportation and warehousing), contract administration, sales analysis, and, very importantly, servicing the product.[5]

As a practical matter, it would seem more appropriate to consider sales-force management issues as administrative in nature, but that is a small point. Ansoff's concept of corporate strategy and three types of decisions implicitly broke marketing into administrative and operating decision components and explicitly separated marketing from strategic decision making. It was a reversion back to the days before the marketing concept, when marketing was equated with selling. Ansoff added distribution and service as part of the marketing function but specifically excluded concern for customer focus and innovation. These were now the province of "strategy," although the marketing concept had intended to provide a long-term, strategic focus for the business.

## Long-Term Challenges versus Short-Term Focus

Ansoff observed that management, under the pressures of day-to-day business life, tended to approach decisions sequentially, and that attention to short-term operating problems tended to drive out attention to long-term strategic issues. If a problem was identified (e.g., sales volume that was below forecasted levels), management tended to treat it first as an *operating* decision—that is, to adjust the level of resources (e.g., by increasing advertising or decreasing the rate of production). If the problem persisted, it would next be defined as an *administrative* decision—resulting in some change in the structure of the firm or in the nature of its resources (e.g., reassigning sales representatives or managers or perhaps reorganizing the production department).

Only if the problem still persisted would it be defined as a *strategic* problem, one that questioned the company's commitments to products and markets. In familiar words, the focus would shift from asking "Are we doing things right?" to "Are we doing the right things?" Strategic decisions were those that required a realignment of the firm's resource commitments with a changing market environment.

Looking at the problems large corporations such as General Motors (GM) and IBM experienced in the 1980s, as they have attempted to downsize, realign, and refocus their organization into smaller, more flexible business units, we can see the processes Ansoff described working. Only after a series of operating and administrative decisions failed to stop the erosion in sales and earnings did top management at GM and IBM face up to the need for fundamental strategic shifts and total reorganization. Both strategic and structural change had been too slow. Cited as an example of a successful firm in Chandler's studies, GM emerged three decades later as an example of what happens when a firm does *not* respond to a changing environment with a changed strategy and organization. It could equally well be cited as an example of a firm that had lost touch with its customers as well as its ability to innovate new solutions to customer problems. IBM, under the leadership of Louis Gerstner, successfully redefined itself as a service organization with a much stronger customer focus. Recent changes at the top of GM, including the appointment of Robert Lutz, a seasoned industry executive noted for his innovativeness, to refocus on new product design and new product introductions, show that the process of rejuvenation is far from complete despite improved profitability.

## Creating a Strategic Planning Function

A clear concept of corporate strategy and strategic planning required ongoing surveillance of the changing environment so that important developments could be seen as they occurred rather than being detected after-the-fact through their problematic impact on operations. This called for a separate, centralized strategic planning operation that could assume responsibility for this critically important function of environmental assessment, objective analysis of the strengths and weaknesses of the firm, and a carefully managed process of matching up the firm's capabilities with changing market opportunities.

Separate strategic planning departments insulated the critical strategic planning process from the exigencies of short-term operating problems. In this manner, the company could overcome the basic management tendency to focus on short-term operating and administrative decisions and to lose sight of the need for strategic response to a changing environment. Management could make an up-front judgment about whether a given problem was primarily operating, administrative, or strategic in nature rather than proceeding sequentially, using trial-and-error to identify the most important, strategic issues. Strategic planning moved the firm from a pattern of lagged responses to a changing environment to one of anticipatory or self-triggered responses.

Strategic planning also addressed an important limitation of the marketing concept identified in Chapter 1. The marketing concept called for customer orientation and directed the firm to concentrate on satisfying customer needs. It did not say how the firm should go about determining which sets of customer needs it should focus on. Product development was to be guided by market research on customer needs, wants, and preferences. However, the marketing concept offered no guidance as to how the firm should decide in which areas to concentrate its efforts at improvement and innovation in response to changing customer needs. The marketing concept said nothing about which markets to serve or which technologies to develop and exploit in creating products for those markets.

Implicit within the marketing concept, but not clearly developed, was the mandate of market segmentation—dividing the total market into a set of smaller, more homogeneous segments within which buyers had similar needs and patterns of response to product characteristics and communications. After those segments have been identified and analyzed, the strategic problem is to choose among them and to tailor the firm's offerings for each. Should the company try to serve all segments or select one or a few? This is the market targeting and product positioning problem. Ansoff incorporated these fundamental notions and made them explicit in his concept of strategy—the selection of markets to be served and products to be offered in those markets. How should a firm decide which markets to serve and which products to offer in those markets? Ansoff saw these as strategic decisions, not marketing decisions, as he attempted to keep marketing and strategic planning distinct from one another.

## The Financial Emphasis of Strategic Planning

Corporate strategy as a distinct field had a predominant financial emphasis from the very beginning. Ansoff followed traditional economic wisdom in assuming that the long-term objective of any business was profit maximization, an assumption in the microeconomic paradigm that puts the interests of the owners first, ahead of all other participants in the business system. He also recognized, however, that it was virtually impossible to predict accurately the stream of profits from a given business—defined by the commitment of resources to a product/market.

After considering issues involved in forecasting and measuring profitability, Ansoff stated clearly that, in his theory of corporate strategy ". . . the primary economic objective is to optimize the long-term rate of return on the equity employed in the firm."[6] The problem of corporate strategy was to allocate scarce financial resources across the portfolio of businesses (product-market combinations) in ways that maximized return on investment.

Ansoff rejected classical capital investment theory as the basis for his theory of corporate strategy because it provided only a mechanism for evaluating and ranking alternative investment projects. It did not address the prior problems of defining strategic challenges and opportunities and searching for investment alternatives. Instead, he based his theory, in part, on a new approach to traditional portfolio selection theory proposed by Clarkson.[7] Clarkson's enhancement of Markowitz's[8] original model allowed the incorporation of flexible decision rules and multiple objectives, depending on the situation and preference of the investor, including attitudes toward risk. The new approach appealed to Ansoff because it incorporated important qualitative considerations while retaining rigorous analysis.

The virtual impossibility of accurately predicting long-term profitability remained. How could a firm pursue a goal of maximizing long-term return on equity if long-term profit could not be forecasted? Ansoff proposed to "abandon efforts to measure long-term profitability directly and to measure, instead, characteristics of the firm that contribute to it."[9] The variables that he chose as surrogates for long-term profitability set the stage for the rapid demise of the customer-focused marketing concept. We return shortly to a specific discussion of these surrogate measures.

## Key Elements of Strategic Planning

The fundamental purpose of strategic planning was to insure the survival, growth, and profitability of the firm over the long term in a changing and potentially hostile competitive environment. Any firm faced two basic challenges: maintaining its competitive strength and continuously improving its internal efficiency. These two challenges can be thought of as simply the revenue and cost elements of the profit equation.

To maintain its competitive strength, the firm needed to grow at a rate at least equal to the rate of market growth. Failure to do so would result in loss of market share. Thus, *market share* becomes a key strategic variable in the most basic sense. Second, the firm must grow revenues and profit margins in ways that minimize seasonal and cyclical fluctuations. Such fluctuations can lead to inefficient use of assets from under- and overutilization of capacity, causing reduced return on investment and diminished competitive strength. *Stability*—of sales, growth rates, and earnings—thus becomes an important strategic objective. The twin strategic objectives of growth and stability dominate the strategic planning process.

Turning to the efficiency/cost elements of the profit model, the factors to be considered include the firm's skills in R&D, management, and the labor force, the age of physical assets including plant, equipment, and inventory, the rate of turnover of its financial assets and inventories, the ratio of sales to inventories, and the rate of return being earned on sales. These relationships are summarized in Figure 2.1.

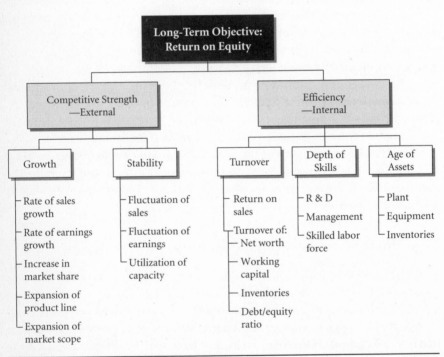

**FIGURE 2.1** The hierarchy of strategic objectives: Surrogates for long-term profit/ROI Maximization. *Source:* Adapted from H. Igor Ansoff, *Corporate Strategy* (New York: McGraw-Hill, 1965), 53. Used with permission.

## Surrogate Variables for Profitability

It has often been said that what gets measured gets emphasized. When management incorporated surrogate variables for profitability identified by Ansoff and others into formal strategic planning systems, it focused management attention on specific, short-term operating measures. In pursuit of long-run maximum returns on equity, guided by the twin objectives of competitive strength and internal efficiency, Ansoff's framework identified a number of operating measures to guide management, as described in the following sections. Subsequent authors quickly adopted and expanded these ideas.

### Sales Growth

The objective of continuous sales growth at or above the rate of market growth presages a goal of increased market share. The position of the firm relative to its competitors is a fundamentally important determinant of the firm's competitive strength. Market dominance is a source of market power, permitting more control over pricing and a larger expenditure for sales—and market—expanding activities like R&D and marketing/selling.

### Market Share

Increasing market share is essential to improve efficiency of the firm relative to competitors. Market share becomes important because of the *experience curve*, the phenomenon of a constant percentage reduction in cost per unit each time the cumulative volume produced by the firm doubles. This is a first cousin to the older concept of the learning curve. Logically, the argument is that the largest firm, in terms of total units produced over its lifetime, should be the most efficient, lowest cost producer. (Note the implicit, questionable assumption, however, that all firms share a common production technology.)

### Earnings Growth

Profits must increase to permit reinvestment in skills, resources, and assets. If the firm is to grow at, or preferably above, the rate of market growth, it needs to continually reinvest in human and physical resources, in the development of new sources of raw materials and components, and in R&D. The funds to support this investment must come from operating earnings as well as from new capital investment.

## Growth in Earnings per Share

Improved performance attracts new capital. The firm with the best earnings per share should be able to attract more new investment at lower cost than firms with weaker earnings performance.

## Innovation

Addition of new products and product lines is vital. Because of the dynamics of the competitive marketplace and product lifecycles, with declining profit margins over time, new products are the lifeblood of the business, the engine for growth.

## Customer Growth

New customers expand the customer base and reduce the dependence on a few large customers. Major dependence on one or a few large customers is a sign of strategic weaknesses and relatively low competitive strength. These large customers can demand increasingly lower prices by means of threats to take their business elsewhere. The loss of a major piece of business would also contribute to substantial instability in sales and earnings.

## Stability

Excessive seasonal or cyclical fluctuation in sales and earnings can cause the loss of competitive position through inefficient use of resources. Orderly investment decisions, the logic of the experience curve, and the need for continuous improvement in skills, resources, and the product mix call for stability in sales and earnings. Otherwise, the firm can find itself in situations of over- and under-capacity, leading to higher relative costs and weakened competitive position.

These core concepts came to dominate the strategic planning field. Many of the ideas were developed and promoted by managers and consultants, not only by academic thinkers and writers. Some of the nation's most respected and most successful businesses, such as General Electric, Norton Company, Champion International, and GTE, sometimes in collaboration with major consulting firms such as McKinsey & Company and the Boston Consulting Group, began to popularize and promote these ideas. *Market share* became the Holy Grail, followed closely by the importance of steady *revenue and earnings growth* from growing markets, a focus on becoming the *low-cost producer* by exploiting *the experience curve,* and *stability* in earnings growth enhanced by *diversification* into unrelated businesses to spread risk and balance seasonal and cyclical trends that might characterize certain industries.

## Defining the Business: Satisfy Customer Needs or Develop Technical Competence

While this book cannot offer a complete review of Ansoff's model of corporate strategy, one other important feature that is directly relevant in its connection to the marketing concept is an emphasis on the firm's productive and technological capabilities. The basic calculus of the strategic planning approach being developed by Ansoff and others was to match up the strengths and weaknesses of the firm with the evolving set of competitive threats and market opportunities. Ansoff was specifically concerned with the problem, noted earlier, that the marketing concept did not specify *how* the firm should choose among the multiple market opportunities potentially available to it. He rejected the mandates of the earliest advocates of the marketing concept, especially Drucker[10] and Levitt,[11] to define the business in terms of the customer needs that the business was committed to satisfying. He argued against customer orientation in its pure form and advocated, instead, a view that focused internally on the firm's technological capabilities, the things it could do best. On the other hand, traditional definitions of the business that focused on a particular industry were also too narrow.

Ansoff believed that definition of the business in terms of customer need satisfaction (e.g., defining a railroad as being in the business of satisfying customers' needs for transportation) was imprecise and impractical. First, such definitions were too broad. It was highly unlikely that a railroad would have the skills and resources necessary to be an effective competitor in the airline or trucking or pipeline or barge business. Second, such definitions did not provide what Ansoff called "a common thread," a relationship between the firm's present and future markets that enables managers and outsiders, especially investors, to see where the firm is headed and to give it guidance on how to get there. A useful definition of the business would focus on the range of missions, customers, and products that the firm wished to pursue.

Focusing on a particular set of customers also was rejected as the common thread. Each customer has many needs and wants and a given firm can serve only one or a few of these. The customer also "belongs" to many other businesses, including many of the firm's competitors. Thus, Ansoff argues that the customer cannot provide strategic focus for a business.

## Defining the Business with a Product and Market View

Instead, Ansoff believed that the fundamental concept of *product/market scope* was the most practical definition of a common thread for a business unit. To be useful and provide the necessary guidance for management, the concept of product/market scope should concentrate on a particular set of submarkets and technologies with similar characteristics.[12] This led to the definition of four growth strategies, which Ansoff called "growth vectors":

1. Market penetration—gaining a larger share of an existing market.
2. Product development—pursuing new product opportunities for existing markets.
3. Market development—expanding present markets and finding new markets for existing products.
4. Diversification—the more risky strategy of simultaneously pursuing new products for new markets.

By focusing on the firm's strengths and weaknesses and the need to develop specific competences as a source of competitive advantage, Ansoff had addressed a serious shortcoming in the marketing concept. At the same time, however, he had softened the commitment to a customer orientation, to putting the customer first. Was this necessary? Was it wise? Does a firm really have to choose between focusing on its customers or its core technologies?

By the late 1960s, the business community initiated the development of several concepts of strategic planning and corporate strategy. They had many common themes, including:

- Adopting a portfolio approach and incorporating many of the ideas found in Ansoff's seminal work.
- Recognizing the strategic importance of growth and internal efficiency.
- Being concerned with matching up the firm's strengths and weaknesses with market opportunities and threats.
- Stressing the strategic importance of market share.

- Incorporating the criterion of maximum return on equity and attempting to address the problem of allocating scarce financial resources across a portfolio of competing investment opportunities.

Ansoff's work was a seminal influence in many respects. The concept of product/market scope as the common thread in a business became a central element in the several different approaches to corporate strategy developed by leading business firms and management consultants. Highly visible among these was Bruce Henderson, founder of the Boston Consulting Group (BCG). Henderson had been an executive at Westinghouse and worked briefly with the Arthur D. Little consulting firm before founding his own company to exploit the new interest in corporate strategy.[13] The approach promoted by BCG was built around three central concepts:

1. Strategic business units.
2. Experience curves.
3. Growth/share matrices.

Each of these concepts is discussed in the following sections.

## Strategic Business Units

The definition of a strategic business unit (SBU) made operational the concept of product/market scope and was the central unit of analysis in the strategic planning process. The term was proposed by McKinsey & Company in a study they did at General Electric in 1969, borrowing freely from the language of an internal study concluded at General Electric in 1957.[14] The general definition of an SBU was that it could be recognized as a distinct business unit selling a product or a product line to a definable market and not competing directly with another SBU within the corporation. (If businesses were serving the same market and therefore competing, they were part of the same SBU.)

In addition, the SBU was defined by a set of activities built around a common thread such as technical competence, access to critical raw materials, a dominant position in a marketing channel, or a particular management skill such as sales promotion. In practice, the definition of SBUs became highly flexible and creative. At one point, General Electric had over 60 distinct SBUs ranging widely in size and defined in many different ways, prompting one manager to comment: "I'll tell you how an SBU is defined—however the chairman wants it defined!"

The SBU was a free-standing entity with its own chief executive and/or operating officer. In the annual strategic planning and budgeting process, the SBU management team had to prepare a strategic plan that served, most importantly, as a request for funding. Corporate management reviewed the plans of the SBUs, evaluated performance against previously stated objectives and plans, considered the attractiveness of the markets in which the SBU was competing, assessed the competitive strength of the SBU in its chosen markets, and judged the management's proposed strategy for competing in those markets. Based on these evaluations, financial assets were allocated among the SBUs. Some businesses received new funding while others were depended on to provide the cash (from earnings) required to fund other businesses with greater future potential.

Defining the *served market* was a critical part of the exercise of defining a strategic business unit because this identified the set of competitors with which the business must compare itself in assessing its strengths and weaknesses. Markets were defined as sets of competitors rather than as sets of customers.

## Experience Curves

The focus on internal efficiency as the key to competitive strength led directly to a concern for achieving the lowest possible costs among firms vying for the same customers. The concept of the experience curve was developed by BCG as part of its strategic planning practice. It was an update of the old idea of the learning curve, identified in the manufacturing of aircraft in the 1930s, where it was observed that the cost of producing an airplane tended to diminish consistently over time as production workers became more familiar with the task and improved their skills. The new experience curve concept refined the old learning curve concept by noting that there was a predictable amount by which cost per unit would decline each time the total cumulative production doubled. The BCG formulation also extended the learning notion to all costs, not just those narrowly defined by manufacturing activities.

The relationship between cost and volume was described by a logarithmic function in which cost declines in an amount described by the gradually decreasing slope of the curve, the cost elasticity. For example, with a 15 percent curve, unit cost would decline by 15 percent with each doubling of volume. BCG research found this predictable consistency in cost reduction in many distinct product/market groups including long distance telephone calls in the United States, integrated circuits, life insurance policies, bottle caps in Germany, refrigerators in Britain, polystyrene molding resins in the United States, and motorcycles in Japan.[15] Experience curve effects were attributable to learning, technological innovation, and economies of scale. Many solid econometric studies have confirmed the existence of the experience curve, often by studying the decline of *prices,* as a surrogate for costs, over time.

To have a favorable cost position, a business (SBU) needed to achieve a dominant position in its served market, thus assuring that it would be furthest down the experience curve and thus the low-cost producer. The name of the game was *dominant market share.* One strategy for exploiting the potential of the experience curve was to use price to gain a dominant market position, thus moving down the experience curve faster than competitors as well as discouraging competitive market entry.

A number of critical assumptions are operating here, each of which is subject to debate:

1. It is assumed that all competitors face the same experience curve; otherwise, the comparison is invalid. This in turn requires the assumption that all competitors are using approximately the same production technology.

2. It is also assumed that market share is highly correlated with cumulative production. There is no consideration of the possibility that a late entrant into the market could adopt a newer, more efficient product form or production technology, and achieve both a dominant market share and a low-cost position without having the largest cumulative production volume.

3. Another assumption is that all cost components decline at the same rate. Whereas the analysis is performed on total costs, the implicit assumption is that costs of manufacturing, selling, distribution, and so on are all declining in similar fashion. In fact, the relative changes in individual cost elements may vary widely and behave differently over time.

In addition, there are all the issues associated with administrative rules for allocation of costs among products and activities. The data for performing experience curve cost analysis are provided by normal company cost accounting methods with all of the arbitrary rules-of-thumb they employ. These become especially serious issues when many of the relevant costs are joint costs, shared by multiple products and activities.

## Growth/Share Matrices

In the strategic planning process, as top management appraised the plans and performance of the multiple SBUs and determined where to allocate financial resources, the major problem was how to apportion scarce resources, especially cash, among the competing investment opportunities. The strongest business opportunities, those with the greatest potential for maximizing return on investment, were those with the strongest growth prospects and those in which the firm could achieve a dominant competitive position. The central idea was that there were certain basic economic rules in the marketplace that could be analyzed and that determined the success or failure of a business. It was necessary to understand these structural characteristics of markets as barriers to competitive entry and as contributors to competitive strength. The growth/share matrix provided a mechanism for making the necessary comparisons in the context of different competitive market structures.

While the BCG product portfolio became the best known and most widely used of the growth/share models, several others were developed including the company position/industry attractiveness matrix developed by McKinsey & Company for General Electric, the Arthur D. Little product lifecycle/market position matrix, and the Shell Chemical International product portfolio.[16] In each model, the two most important dimensions in the matrix were the company's market share/competitive position and the market's rate of growth, the latter being a proxy variable for stage in the product lifecycle. We will look more closely at the BCG model.

In the BCG model, the two dimensions are industry growth rate and market share. Industry growth is said to be high if it is more than 10 percent, low if it is less. Market share is defined as market share *relative to the market share of the largest competitor,* on a logarithmic scale. Thus, a firm's position is measured by dividing its market share by the largest competitor's share. The result is a number that is more than one if the SBU is the dominant competitor, and less than one if it is not dominant. Why is *dominance* the critical concept? Because of the logic of the experience curve. If the SBU is not a dominant player, it has an inferior cost position and is an inefficient competitor with weak prospects for success in this market.

These definitions result in a two-by-two matrix as shown in Figure 2.2. Various names have been used to describe the businesses that end up in each of the four boxes. In our terminology, the *Stars* are the businesses with high growth and dominant market position. They require substantial investment for growth and are users of cash. Despite their cash requirements, they are

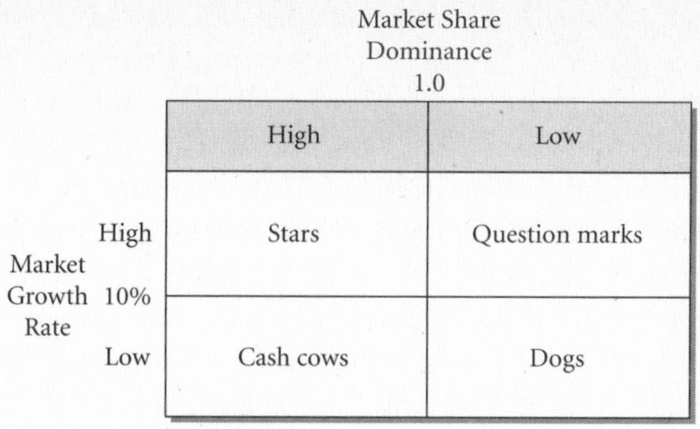

Market Share
Dominance
1.0

| | High | Low |
|---|---|---|
| High | Stars | Question marks |
| Low | Cash cows | Dogs |

Market
Growth 10%
Rate

**FIGURE 2.2**   The Boston Consulting Group growth/share matrix.

the most sought after SBUs, the most attractive. They are the subject of a *Growth* strategy.

The businesses with good growth characteristics but an inferior market share position have been called *Question Marks, Problem Children*, or *Wildcats*. They also need cash to finance their growth but their prospects are uncertain because the company has a relatively weak competitive position. They do not have a clearly defined strategic role. They must be fixed, strengthened, and repositioned, or else removed from the portfolio. They are candidates for either a *Fix* or *Divest* strategy.

The SBUs characterized by a strong competitive position in a slow-growth market are the *Cash Cows* for the corporation. Because they are operating in slow-growth markets, they do not require major new investments. Also, the firm's dominant position confers a degree of market control that may permit some price premium. Significant sales volume is also likely to mean a favorable cost position. For all of these reasons, firms with strong positions in slow-growth markets can be sources of cash for reinvestment in other SBUs. They are often selected for a *Harvest* strategy. This begs the question: Wouldn't these businesses continue to grow and be stronger if they were allowed to continue to invest?

The weakest performers in the portfolio are those businesses that have a weak position in a slow-growth market. These are the *Dogs*. Given the prospects of slow growth, a weak competitive position, and the likelihood of zero-to-negative returns on investment, these SBUs are identified for a *Divest* or *Withdrawal* strategy, freeing up funds for investment in businesses with better prospects.

As this brief review suggests, the product portfolio was concerned primarily with sources and uses of cash and the allocation of financial resources among competing investment projects, not with how to manage those businesses. Nothing in the growth/share matrix suggests the specific business strategies appropriate for a given SBU. Saying that a business is a Star or a Question Mark or a Cash Cow does not say what the firm must do to compete effectively in that business. (The Arthur D. Little and Shell Chemical International models go on to the next step and suggest broad categories of appropriate generic strategies for each box in the matrix but still do not prescribe specific business strategies.) The growth/share matrix could help decide strategic issues at the *corporate* strategy level: "What businesses do we want to be in?" It could not specify a *business* strategy: "How should we attempt to compete in the business we have chosen to be in?"

Also, the focus on cash flow led, by definition, to a relatively short-term orientation. Corporate management's fundamental question was whether to continue to invest funds in this business in the next year or whether to use it to provide funds for other businesses. Financial urgency usually called for a relatively short-term orientation in assessing business prospects. Taking cash from a healthy Cash Cow often meant that its life span was shortened considerably as the firm lost market share and brand equity. It was doomed to become another Dog.

Market share was in many respects the most important strategic indicator of competitive strength. More than one CEO, most notably Jack Welch of General Electric, announced that his company was not going to stay in any business where it could not be in the number one or number two competitive position. In the hundreds of firms that developed a strategic planning competence, usually in the form of a Manager of Strategic Planning with a supporting staff, the focus on market share was paramount.

This led to some interesting managerial behavior as SBU managers, to protect their businesses, tried to define their served market in such a way that they were indeed in the number one or number two position. Defining the boundaries of any market is never an easy task. The temptation to tautological argument is great. In his last letter to General Electric shareholders before he retired in 2001 as chairman and CEO, Jack Welch commented that his emphasis on being Number One or Number Two had been a mistake because:

> It leads management teams to define their markets narrowly to nonsensical levels, and has caused General Electric to miss opportunities and growth.

It is easy for a manager to try to dismiss a major competitor by observing that they have a different product strategy and a different market niche and therefore should not be considered as being in the same business. Thus, there was a time when the American automobile manufacturers dismissed the European and Japanese marques that were beginning to appear in the United States because these cars were smaller and supposedly less safe and poorly made, and not competing for the same customers.

Notice how long it has been since we last mentioned *customers*. Nowhere in the strategic planning approach and in product portfolio analysis was there any consideration of customers. Markets were defined as collections of competitors. Competitive strength was defined not in terms of satisfying customer needs but in terms of achieving a dominant position based on lowest total cost. Basic concepts of customer value were simply not part of the strategic planning conversation. In many respects, the strategic planning approach, with its emphasis on return on investment, cash flow, market dominance, low cost, and markets defined as sets of competitors, was in direct conflict with the marketing concept and its focus on customer orientation, innovation, and long-term profit as a reward for creating a satisfied customer.

## PIMS: PROFIT IMPACT OF MARKET STRATEGY

In the beginning of the formal strategic planning discipline, arguments about the central importance of market share were based largely on the logic of economic analysis. There was little empirical support for the notion that higher market share would lead to higher return on investment. That was to change with the advent of the PIMS project at General Electric.

The *Profit Impact of Market Strategy* (PIMS) project grew directly out of the corporate strategic planning department at General Electric. After the McKinsey & Company consulting project had been completed in 1969, the company reorganized itself around 43 SBUs, a sharp reduction from 190 separate business plans that the CEO had to review under the old organization. (The CEO at the time, Reginald Jones, told me that it took a full six to eight weeks of his time each year to review these.) These 43 new SBUs (the number expanded to more than 60 over time), each of which might contain several businesses, covered 23 of the 26 two-digit Standard Industrial Classification (SIC) codes used by the U.S. Bureau of the Census. General Electric was a highly diversified company competing in virtually every industry imaginable.[17] General Electric management recognized that this breadth of experience offered a natural laboratory for examining the fundamental determinants of competitive strength and business performance. To follow up on this possibility, the PIMS program of research was launched in 1972. Later, the PIMS project left General Electric and was set up as the independent Strategic Planning Institute, eventually attaining a database of more than 450 companies and 3,000 business units.[18]

## Importance of Market Share to Profitability

The basic methodology of the PIMS project was *regression analysis,* a form of correlation analysis in which *n* variables are arranged in an *n* by *n* matrix and the correlation of every pair of variables is determined. Equations are then built which combine variables in terms of the strength of their association with the *dependent* variable, that variable whose values the analyst is interested in explaining and predicting. In the initial PIMS analysis, the dependent variable was profitability, measured as return on investment. There were 36 other, independent or explanatory, variables in the database that could be examined for their influence on the profitability of a business. Among all of the variables examined, it was *market share* that had the strongest association with return on investment.[19] This finding was entirely consistent with the theory and conjecture of the strategic planning school and gave new life to the belief in the strategic importance of market share.

To put these results into perspective, it is helpful to understand a bit more about the nature of the PIMS database, especially because the critics of the PIMS findings often focused their attention on the quality of the data. Among the variables in the PIMS database, in addition to market share, were things such as advertising expenditures, product quality, stage in product lifecycle, type of business (service, durable goods, etc.), frequency of product changes, rate of technological change, type and number of customers, average size of purchase, and several items taken from the profit-and-loss statement or balance sheet (sales, percentage of revenue spent on purchases, R&D expenditures, fixed assets, profits, etc.). The data were provided as answers to a series of questions by the managers of the business. Product quality and price were assessed *relative to competition.*

The finding of the importance of market share was subsequently duplicated, dissected, and expanded by other PIMS researchers. The result was surprisingly robust. Many studies confirmed the strong relationship of profitability (ROI) and market share. Critics were quick to point out, however, that correlation does not imply causality. It would be a mistake to use the PIMS regression results to argue that market share *causes* profitability, although that was the argument of the early strategic planning theorists. We could just as well argue, using the PIMS findings, that *profits cause market share*—perhaps by giving the business the resources that it needs to invest more heavily in promotion and R&D. Still others could argue that *both* profits and market share might be caused by some third variable like product quality or loyal customers.

In fact, the early PIMS finding of the correlation between market share and profitability, when analyzed further, showed that the major factor explaining the relationship was the ratio of purchases to sales. The firm with the largest market share seemed better able to achieve economies of scale in its purchasing expenditures. While there was no particular theory to explain this result, it was a strong statistical finding. Several later studies found the same result—that the large-share firms have the lowest ratios of cost of purchases to sales.[20]

## Reducing Price to Improve Market Share

A possible interpretation of the findings of the strong association between market share and return on investment is to conclude that the firm that increases its market share will increase its profitability. Note that this is a problematic conclusion because the statistical finding is based on a "cross-sectional" analysis that makes comparisons among many businesses, whereas the proposed conclusion makes an assertion about changes in a single business over time. Nonetheless, the argument can be made that a firm that increases its market share is moving down the experience curve faster than its competitors and that a dominant market share will provide the low-cost position and resulting competitive strength.

How can a firm improve its share of market? One way is to lower prices. Especially if the firm is selling a relatively undifferentiated product, customers might readily shift their purchase preference to the firm with the lowest prices. One possible interpretation of the market share findings could lead to the strategic argument:

Volume Strategy

Low Price → High Share → High Volume → Low Cost → Profit

This can be called a high-volume/low-cost strategy, the combination of high volume and low cost supposedly leading to higher return on investment.

It was a strategy frequently advocated by BCG and others who were impressed by the strength of experience curve effects.[21] The problem is that the combination of low price and resulting low margins makes it difficult to earn above-average returns on the large investment necessary to support the high-volume strategy, especially if high-cost debt is used to finance the volume/growth strategy.

Such a strategy can also lead to disaster if the company gets its price cutting ahead of its cost cutting, anticipating (sometimes based more on hope than analysis) that greater volume will produce the necessary cost improvements. Many companies have been trapped by this bad assumption with the result that margins decrease and turn negative due to lower prices, even as volume increases. The result is increasingly unprofitable volume. There is nothing magical about the experience curve. Cost improvements do not come automatically with volume. Rather, they result from careful, programmatic attempts to reduce specific costs. Cost reduction must be managed.

The business landscape is littered with the remains of companies that tried to use price to gain share to achieve low cost and, finally, above average return on investment. They are found in many industries including airlines, automobiles, consumer electronics, computers, food, paper, and retailing. Even Japanese industry has not been immune from the negative consequences of low-price, high-share, high-volume strategies for which they have been well known and, in some cases, emulated. In the 1990s, the Japanese (and Korean) automobile industry faced declining world demand for its products, excess plant capacity, and increased cost of capital, putting some of the weaker players into a loss position and leading to a trend of industry consolidation through mergers and strategic alliances.

## Quality Is Related to Market Share

Further analysis of the PIMS database, which was adding many new companies and businesses into the 1980s, suggested that the relationship between market share and profitability was more complicated. Market share did not influence profitability directly.

Some studies found many examples of small-share firms enjoying superior rates of return. Others found that both market share and return on investment tended to be jointly determined by other factors including product quality, marketing expenditures, management skill, luck, and unanticipated changes in the environment, such as entry or exit of a major competitor, a change in government regulations, or the introduction of a new technology. Others found the suspected reverse causal link between profitability and market share—profits leading to higher share. In general, it was often found that the magnitude of the relationship between market share and return on investment was very small. And always there was lurking in the background the basic question of how a market was to be defined in order to calculate market share.[22]

It became obvious that low margins, which would be characteristic of low-price competitors, were typically *not* associated with above average return on investment, even for firms with dominant market share. Rather, it was a combination of *high price* and low cost that yielded superior profitability. Is high price and low cost a contradiction? Isn't higher quality associated with a higher price because of higher cost? Yes and no. High price *is* associated with high quality, because customers are usually willing to pay more for a better, more differentiated product. It is *not* necessarily true that high quality leads to high cost. In fact, the reverse may be true. In many situations, *quality costs less.*

The common way to think about the relationship between quality and profitability is what has been called a "margin strategy," as contrasted to the high-volume/low-cost strategy or market dominance strategy:

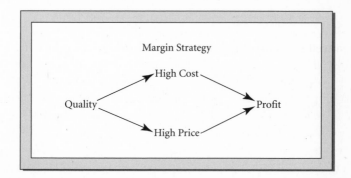

With a margin strategy, the company is typically pursuing one or more well-defined market niches, a set of customers with needs and wants that are served by the unique features and superior quality of a differentiated product. The margin strategy is usually also a market-niching strategy.

A well-known author in the strategic management area, Michael Porter, offered some evidence in support of the notion that either a volume strategy or a margin strategy could produce superior results. He proposed that firms should be clear about which of the two strategic options they were pursuing and not try to find some combination or compromise of the two. Firms that were "stuck in the middle," with neither a superior quality/market niching strategy nor a dominant, low-cost market position, were those that had the lowest return on investment.[23]

The assertion that low cost and high quality are mutually exclusive is debatable. Another way to think about the relationship between market share and profitability is to see both market share and low cost as driven by superior quality. If customers really value the superior quality supposedly being built into the product or service, the demand for it will be higher and it will command a relatively higher price. In this instance, what we can call simply the "quality strategy," superior quality leads to both high volume and high margin, and volume, in turn, produces a favorable cost position:

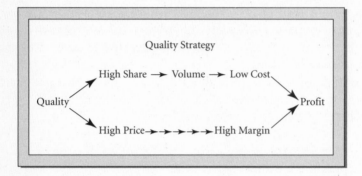

Further analysis of the PIMS data led the officers of the Strategic Planning Institute to move away from their focus on market share and toward an emphasis on product quality (actually, "perceived relative product quality," in recognition of the fact that the data were based on managers' perceptions of their product quality relative to that of competitors). One PIMS study, using a more sophisticated analytical technique called *causal modeling,* showed no evidence to support the argument that high quality was incompatible with low cost relative to competitors. It was found that the higher prices associated with higher product quality did not deter market penetration. Thus, quality had a positive effect on return on investment, not directly but indirectly, through its influence on market share, which yielded both higher volume and lower cost.[24]

The PIMS researchers then attempted to disassociate the market share arguments from those based on experience curve effects, as advocated by Bruce Henderson and BCG, and to associate market share with quality.[25] Reinterpretation of the PIMS data reinforced the conclusions of the quality strategy model discussed earlier. Today, the first of the PIMS Principles is stated as:

In the long run, the most important single factor affecting a business unit's performance is the quality of its products and services, relative to those of competitors.[26]

The firms with the most favorable performance were those that had been able to dominate a market niche, not the whole market, with superior quality that offered both the advantages of high-price/high-margin and the low costs associated with higher volume. The basic wisdom of a strategy of product differentiation, market segmentation, and positioning was confirmed, and the low-price-driven experience curve strategy was discredited.[27]

## Delivering Value to Customers to Increase Market Share

One of the most interesting examinations of the relationship between market share and profitability was conducted at the Stanford University Graduate School of Business in a study published by the Marketing Science Institute.[28] The authors revisited the question of the direction of causality between share and profit and the role of product quality, using both PIMS and Federal Trade Commission (FTC) "Line of Business" data. What makes this study especially interesting is the model used to analyze the data—"the value-delivery theory of competitive advantage." Conceptually, it puts the customer's definition of value back into the center of strategic focus.

The central proposition of the value-delivery theory is that sustainable competitive advantage has its roots in the ability of the firm to deliver superior value to customers at a profitable cost, not in the "structural barriers" to competition at the core of the experience-curve-based arguments. A business may capitalize on a particular set of skills in selecting, producing, delivering, or communicating superior value to a target market. That skill set could be unique to the firm or one in which it is merely superior to its competitors. These skills may reside in individuals, in technological capabilities, or in business systems designed and managed by the organization. Market share is the result of superior value delivery, as is profitability. Profit and market share are caused by the same forces.

This strategic formulation brings us back to a point of view consistent with the original marketing concept: *Profit is a reward for creating a satisfied customer.* Market share is also not a strategic objective; it is a result. In their analysis of the PIMS and FTC data, these authors could find no instance in which market share had a significant, positive, and temporally prior influence on return on investment. In fact, they found stronger evidence of reverse causality—higher profit can lead to higher market share.

Significant environmental discontinuities or "shocks" were factored into the value-delivery model in terms of their effect on the customer's definition of value and the resulting change in the skills and resources that the firm needed in order to deliver superior value to customers at a profit. Profitable firms were those that had the management skills necessary to redefine strategy and reconfigure the resources and skills of the organization to fit the new market requirements. The more profitable firms were more likely to have the skills and resources, and the financial strength, necessary to respond to the changing environment. For these well-managed firms, discontinuities and shocks created an opportunity to improve their market position. This finding certainly echoes Chandler's conclusions three decades earlier: *Successful firms are those that monitor and respond to a changing environment with new strategies and organization structures.*

In the strategic planning discipline, and in the related field of marketing strategy or strategic marketing, product quality and value delivery have replaced market share and low cost as the key strategic variables. The ascendance of such strong, new brands as Federal Express, Honda, Intel, Lexus, Microsoft, Charles Schwab, and Southwest Airlines helped to focus management attention on the central importance of product quality in determining market share. Market share was seen as a result of superior business strategy based on product quality, not as a strategic objective by itself. Simplistic thinking about the value of market share had been an expensive mistake for many firms.

## COMPETITOR-CENTERED VERSUS CUSTOMER-CENTERED PLANNING

The most important contribution of strategic planning may also have been its critical shortcoming. Strategic planning focused the firm on its competitors and its strengths and weaknesses relative to them. It introduced the basic notions of market structure and competitive forces from economic theory into management thinking. Market share was the summary measure of competitive strength. Product quality was assessed relative to competitors. It was important to have dominant market share in order to have a favorable cost position relative to competitors. Strategic planning, especially with the incorporation of the experience curve, focused the attention of industry on cost as a strategic variable. This was an extremely important development as American firms faced global competitors, many of whom had favorable cost positions based on lower labor costs, government support, and lower cost of capital.

But the customer fell out of the equation in this market view. A market was defined as a set of competitors, an "industry," not a set of customers with needs and wants that must be satisfied. (This definition of a market as an industry becomes a real problem as the traditional boundaries between industries break down in a world of strategic partnerships and network organizations. Competitors come in new forms.) Product quality was defined in terms of managers' perceptions of their product quality relative to that of competitors, not in terms of the ability of the product to satisfy customer needs better than the products of competitors.

The new strategy of value delivery reintroduced the customer into the concept of business strategy. The firm is assessed relative to its competitors in terms of its ability to deliver superior value, as perceived by the customer.

The other major contribution of the strategic planning era was to recognize that the firm's distinctive competence had to be taken into account, along with customer needs and wants, in defining the strategy of the firm, its selection of those product/markets where it wished to compete. The original marketing concept had left some important questions unanswered. Strategic planning put the company and its competence into the concept of business strategy whereas the marketing concept had focused only on the customer's needs and wants.

A more complete approach to planning business strategy combines both customer-centered and competitor-centered analysis and matches the company's distinctive competence with a set of market needs and wants that is less than completely served by competitors. It focuses on the customer in developing a definition of value and then assesses the skills and resources of the firm in terms of its ability to deliver superior value compared with competitors. Effective business strategy must be based on a balanced combination of competitor-centered and customer-centered analysis. The goal is a strategy that permits the firm to deliver superior value to a well-defined set of customers in the competitive marketplace, capitalizing on its unique sources of competitive advantage. Every strategy problem must be approached in terms of "The Three C's": Customers, Company, and Competitors.

## A NEW BALANCE: CUSTOMERS, COMPANY, AND COMPETITORS

The key strategic concept here is that of the *value proposition,* a statement of how the firm proposes to deliver superior value to customers and to differentiate itself from competitors. The value proposition is important both internally and externally. Internally, it focuses the attention of everyone in the business on customer requirements. Externally, it is the means by which the firm can position itself in the minds of customers. The value proposition should be the firm's single most important organizing principle.

Day and Wensley have offered a new framework for balancing the analysis of customers, the company, and its competitors in a strategic planning framework as summarized in Figure 2.3.[29] In the center of their model is *superior customer value,* seen as the major determinant of the firm's strength relative to competition. The other source of advantage is *lower relative cost.* Both of these are assessed relative to competitors, but it is the *customer's perception of value relative to competitors' product offerings* that is important.

These positional advantages are based on the firm's distinctive competence, and its superior skills and resources. But, there is nothing automatic about superior skills and resources leading to positional advantages. Whether the firm's distinctive competences can be turned to positional advantages depends on the quality of the analytical and strategy formulation skills of management. Chief among these is the ability to understand customers and their needs. In formulating strategy, management must understand how customers define value based on their needs, wants, and product use systems, and how they evaluate the firm's offering relative to those of

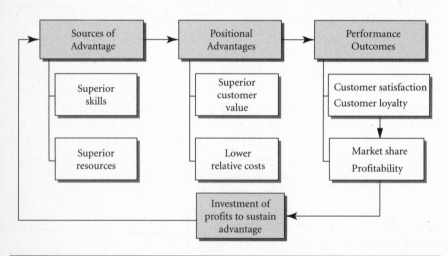

**FIGURE 2.3**   A value-based view of business strategy. *Source:* George S. Day and Robin Wensley, "Assessing Advantage: A Framework for Diagnosing Competitive Superiority," *Journal of Marketing* 52, 2 (April 1988), 1–20, at p. 3. Reproduced with permission of the American Marketing Association.

competitors. Management must also understand their competitors' business strategies, critical skills and resources, and value propositions. How do they propose to satisfy customer needs? On what basis are they trying to deliver superior value? What are their strengths and weaknesses? Thus, customer-centered and competitor-centered analysis blend in creating a concept of value delivery for a target market, based on the company's own unique skills and resources as a source of sustainable competitive advantage.

Just as turning the company's potential sources of advantage into real positional advantages in the marketplace requires superior skills in strategic analysis and planning, so does the achievement of positive performance results depend on the ability to manage the firm's positional advantages and to implement the strategy successfully. The quality of the tactics, programs, and systems developed and employed by the business to implement its strategy is just as important as the quality of the strategy itself. Strategy formulation and implementation are inseparable determinants of business performance.

The old approach to strategic planning emphasized strategy formulation and had little to do with actual implementation. This was reflected in the separation of the strategic planning department from the operations of the business. Portfolio models looked at strategy from the corporate perspective: What businesses should the firm be in? The answer to the business strategy question—How should we compete in those businesses?—was phrased simplistically in terms of low-cost/high-volume or high-quality/market-niche strategic options. How to do that, how to implement the business strategy, with functional-level strategies for marketing, operations, R&D, and so on, was not addressed.

Strategic planning was dominated by analysts and professional planners on the corporate staff acting as advisors to top management. The people who were actually charged with responsibility for operating the businesses profitably were involved to the extent that they provided the required information and business plans, frequently requiring weeks and months of preparation and presentations. In many cases, the corporate strategic planning process became so time consuming that operating management lost track of the details of running their businesses. They had to focus all of their attention on achieving bottom-line financial results as called for by their strategic plan and their role in the business portfolio. Thus, long-range strategic planning had the undesirable, even self-defeating, result of focusing corporate management on long-term "strategic" objectives (primarily financial) while focusing operating management attention on very short-term, usually quarterly, goals.

In the new value-delivery view of strategy, business performance is measured by the outcomes of customer satisfaction and loyalty, leading to market share and profitability, as well as traditional measures of sales volume and profit margins. This causal sequence—from customer satisfaction, loyalty, and repeat purchase to profitable sales volume—is essential to understanding the new viewpoint embodied in the value-delivery view of strategy. Remember that Ansoff's principal measures of business success, given the futility of predicting long-term profitability, were relatively short-term measures of sales growth, market share, earnings growth, and so on. None of those measures reflected customer preference or satisfaction. In the new view, market share and profits are the rewards for creating a satisfied customer. Back to the marketing concept!

Assuming that the most basic long-term objectives of the firm are survival and growth, as precursors to maximizing the value of the firm, management must reinvest profits in the maintenance and enhancement of the critical resources and skills that define its distinctive competence and are the source of its unique, sustainable competitive advantage. While the owners' interests are vital, they are not paramount. In the old view of strategy, the shareholders' interests were put first. The objective was to maximize return on equity. In the new view of strategy, the customer is first among equals because the customer must want the company's products and be willing to pay a reasonable price for them if any of the other constituencies of the firm—owners, employees, managers, suppliers, and so on—are to achieve their objectives over the long run. The price the customer is willing to pay is the ultimate measure of the economic value created by the firm and is in the final analysis the only source of profits for the shareholders.

It is the unique responsibility of top management to balance the claims of all constituencies and to optimize the total performance of the firm. More and more, top management is recognizing the wisdom and necessity of putting the customer first to survive and prosper in the global marketplace.[30]

# A VALUE-DELIVERY BUSINESS MODEL

An integrated approach to maximizing the long-term value of the enterprise, and thus value to shareholders, by focusing on delivering superior value to customers is captured by a model of the business that contains four crucial elements that summarize the value-delivery concept of strategy that has been developed in this chapter:

1. Customer selection—the definition of market targets.
2. Creating the value proposition.
3. Developing a model for capturing a fair share of the economic value that has been created for customers.
4. Selecting strategic partners in the value-delivery process.

In the following brief discussion of each of these steps, we review the key ideas developed in this chapter. Later chapters develop these concepts in greater detail. In this chapter, we introduce the fundamental idea of a business model that defines the zone of potential profit opportunities and brings together customer value and shareholder value.[31]

## Customer Selection

The central idea in a customer-centered view of business strategy is that customers define the business by the demands they place on it. Thus, customer selection is *the critical strategic choice.* The definition of the business starts with the customer.

No firm can be all things to all potential customers, so the firm must decide which customers it wants to serve, based on its unique capabilities, its "distinctive competence," as a source of competitive advantage. What can it do well? More importantly, it must decide what customers it does *not* want, those it cannot serve well and profitably. This is the fundamental distinction between marketing and selling: Marketing means knowing what customers you don't want; from a narrow selling perspective, every customer is a good customer and every order is a good order. The hallmark of a sound and profitable business model is *selectivity.*

## Creating the Value Proposition

To repeat a now familiar definition: The value proposition states how the firm proposes to deliver superior value to its chosen customers. If a firm elects to serve multiple (clearly defined) product/markets, it will have multiple value propositions unique to each business. The value proposition must be based on the firm's unique strengths and resources as they define its superior ability to deliver customer value and differentiate it from its competitors. The value proposition is important internally, keeping all members of the organization focused on the business strategy and value delivery, as well as externally, communicating the firm's value offering.

Developing the value proposition is in many respects similar to the concept of product positioning, but positioning is essentially a communication strategy. Embedded in the value proposition is the essence of the firm's business strategy. It is more than communication. It is a fundamental commitment of resources and a statement of company values and mission.

## Developing the Value Capture Strategy

Neither customer selection nor creating the value proposition is easy, but developing the value capture strategy, or profit model, is probably the greatest challenge. How will the firm make a profit? How will it retain its fair share of the economic value created by its product/market strategy? Part of this is a pricing problem, but the problem is more complex than pricing. How will the firm maintain strategic control over the relationship with customers and partners in the value chain so that it has the power necessary to earn a fair return?

Elements of the pricing problem in creating a profit model include how to charge for the multiple pieces of the total product offering and how to reward resellers. If the business strategy is built around a "bundled" product offering to achieve differentiation, such as an integrated process control system for a manufacturing plant, then the question is how to obtain a price premium that covers all of the costs of integrating the various pieces of the bundle as well as the individual components such as parts, software, installation, postsale service, repair, and so on. Or if the strategy is to sell "unbundled" products and services *a la carte,* how can the firm compete with other sellers of each of the pieces of the total system without cutting prices to unprofitable levels. Each part of the product offering must be able to claim superior features and performance versus competitors. How much is the customer willing to pay for the company and product brand image and distinctiveness? How strongly can the firm's product be differentiated from that of its competitors?

Reseller or "trade" margins are always a pricing challenge. How much must be offered to distributors, dealers, value-added partners, retailers, and similar channel members to reward them fairly for the functions they perform in completing and delivering the product offering to the customer? Will they retain their intended gross profits and reinvest them in developing superior customer value or simply pass them on to aggressive customers in the form of price cuts? Similar issues are involved in the relationships with the firm's suppliers and the prices that must be paid for their contribution to the company's product offering. Whether the firm is in the role of seller or buyer, it faces a number of challenges in developing and implementing its strategy of value capture and profitability. The foregoing comments barely scratch the surface of this complex problem in developing a profitable business model.

## Defining Position in the Value Chain

As already noted, no firm can be all things to all customers. Every company needs multiple partners in delivering superior value to customers. Some of these partners will be suppliers of products that become part of the company's own product offering; others will be part of the company's go-to-market system, helping to communicate the value proposition and distribute it to customers.

These choices of strategic partners determine the scope of the business—how many activities it will perform itself and how many will be performed by partners. To illustrate, many companies depend on partners to perform such essential functions as transportation, financing of transactions, after-sale product service, and disposal of products at the end of their useful life. Many also depend on partners for key parts of their marketing mix such as advertising, field sales coverage, and market research studies. Current experience suggests that the best performing firms have defined their scope quite narrowly, focusing on those areas where they can maintain worldwide superiority.

There are important connections between strategic partnering and the firm's value-capture strategy. Managing customer relationships and strategic partnerships are covered in Chapters 5 and 6. The essential definition of the firm remains its relationships with its customers. The brand name on the product, the firm that actually has the ongoing relationship with the customer is the focal point for all of the other value providers. Maintaining that customer relationship is essential to long-term profitability.

## SUMMARY

This chapter completes our historical overview of the evolution of the marketing concept from its origins in the 1950s and 1960s through its eclipse by strategic planning in the 1970s and 1980s, then into a new value-driven concept of strategy in the 1990s and 2000s. The failure of the original marketing concept to address the fundamental issue of matching customer needs with the things the firm could do best left unanswered the critical question of how the firm could find sustainable competitive advantage. Strategic planning addressed that issue but redefined markets as collections of competitors and obliterated customer-orientation.

The integration of long-range planning, capital budgeting, and the marketing concept into a new discipline of strategic planning shifted attention in many American companies away from customers and toward competitors and the interests of shareholders. Thinking of firms as portfolios of investments emphasized short-term profitability (ROI) at the expense of long-term relationships with satisfied customers. Newly emerging competitors in many global industries from automobiles to financial services were able to take advantage of the opportunities this created for providing superior value to customers.

The value driven concept of strategy has emerged out of a reconsideration of the relationship between market share and profitability. The conclusion that market share *caused profitability* proved to be overly simplistic. Rather, *quality* as perceived by the customer has been identified as the critical strategic force leading to both lower costs and higher sales (and, thus, higher market share), which combine to yield superior profitability. Strategy must be based on analysis of the company, the competition, and the customer, identifying those opportunities for the firm to deliver superior value to customers based on its distinctive competences. The firm's *value proposition* becomes the primary organizing force for the business. Before the value proposition can be turned into profitability, it must be embedded in a business model that begins with customer selection and includes a carefully crafted strategy of value capture and a positioning of the firm in the value chain with strategic partners.

# Marketing as Process: Quality, Service, and Customer Satisfaction

# 3

*A manufacturer is not through with his customer when a sale is completed.
He has only then started with his customer.*

Henry Ford

*My Life and Work*
Garden City, NY: Doubleday,
Page & Company, 1922, p. 41

The simple notion of customer orientation was matched up with the concept of distinctive competence to create a new understanding of the basics of business strategy. Marketing strategy and strategic management, once distinct disciplines, have merged into a value-delivery concept of market-driven management. Delivering superior value to customers is now understood to be the only path to sustained profitability. As noted in Chapter 2, there is growing evidence that customer-perceived quality is the primary driver of both market share and profitability.

While marketing strategy researchers and management consultants were discovering that quality was the critical strategic variable, the total quality management (TQM) movement was gaining a strong foothold in American industry. Japanese firms had for decades been learning and following the precepts of the American fathers of the quality movement, W. Edwards Deming and Joseph Juran (born in Romania but raised in the United States), with almost religious zeal. Japanese industry had created the Deming Prize to honor Mr. Deming and to encourage total quality management (TQM) that would spur Japanese firms to world-class competitiveness. Only in the 1980s did American firms begin to pay serious attention to the dictates of a commitment to total quality.

TQM and the value-delivery concept of strategy have much in common. The total quality movement has been a major force for the revitalization of the marketing concept. More and more, businesspeople and academics realized that TQM and customer orientation were really the same thing. While some companies and their management had continued to be advocates for a customer-centered view of the business throughout the 1970s and into the 1980s, many more had not. It was only when quality was defined, under the pressures of global competition, as the major issue facing American industry that the shift back to putting the customer first began to occur in earnest. Even then, the path was not a direct one.

## How Not to Define Quality

Not all views of quality put the customer first. Some are internally focused and use product-oriented, technical definitions of quality—meeting specifications for product dimensions or performance, defects or rejections per thousand pieces produced, visual standards for fit and finish, and so on. When quality is defined simply by statistics about the product or the manufacturing process, there is a good chance that the customer has still been left out of the equation. Focusing on the quality of the product itself is a necessary but not sufficient condition for achieving customer-perceived quality in the delivery of the product offering.

Other definitions of quality focus on the people in the organization, processes for managing those people, their obligations to one another, and team-building in the pursuit of organizational excellence. It is common in companies with this focus to talk about "the internal customer," the people in the organization whose work is most directly affected by what the person does and who uses the output of that person's function. One well-known company promotes 10 "Quality Principles" including "Build a spirit of working together toward common goals," "Promote a climate of open communication and feedback," "Encourage and recognize innovation and teamwork," and "Provide honest, fair and equitable treatment of all and develop an atmosphere of trust and mutual respect." Those are lofty principles for organizational functioning, but they have a bearing on quality only to the extent that they prevent mistakes and avoid rude behavior in customer interactions. The customer is mentioned specifically in only two of the 10 principles: "Encourage every person to strive continually for understanding of and mutual agreement on all requirements of customers and suppliers," and "Require that products will not be shipped nor services performed if they do not meet customer requirements." (Why does this last principle need to be stated at all?)

The most aggressive and successful quality programs recognize that definitions of quality in terms of product characteristics and organizational behavior miss the point. Quality, like the marketing concept, means putting the customer first, *always*. There is only one customer, the one who pays the bills. Talk of the "internal customer," is dangerous and misleading because it puts another organizational actor first rather than the real customer. This can create all kinds of interesting internal politics and intra-organizational conflict requiring energy that could be better used to solve real customer problems in the marketplace.

## Quality Is Defined by the Customer

The true definition of quality is *meeting and exceeding customer expectations.* This definition may leave a technical expert with an uneasy feeling because it appears to be very subjective. How can you make a definition of quality operational if it relies on something as soft and mushy as customer expectations? How can you define quality in terms of people's feelings? These are good questions, but there are also answers. It *is* possible to measure customer expectations and to measure performance against those standards.

### The Customer's Definition of Value Keeps Changing

The bigger problem is that customers keep increasing their expectations and changing their definition of value as a function of their buying situation and experience with previous purchases. "What have you done for me lately?" is the standard response when a company gives its customers what they want, especially in the industrial market. Customer needs, wants, and buying habits are extremely dynamic.

When a company succeeds in meeting customer expectations, two things are likely to happen. First, the customer says "Thank you," and, realizing that this marketer has the capability for superior performance, will now expect it as a matter of course. Second, competitors improve *their* performance (or promise the customer that they will) and try harder to gain a share of the customer's business (Figure 3.1). Thus, there are three forces driving customer expectations to ever-higher levels:

1. The customer's dynamic needs and wants.
2. The company's promise and delivery of superior performance.
3. Competitors' promises that they can do even better.

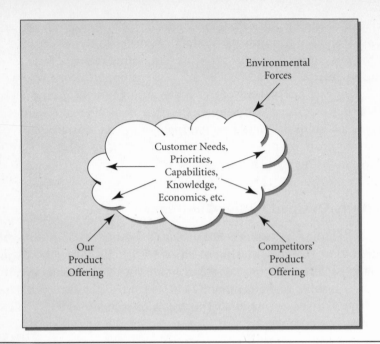

**FIGURE 3.1**   The customer's changing definition of value.

The "Three Cs" of strategy—Customers, the Company, and Competitors—become the "Three Cs" of quality. The customer's expectations change, his or her definitions of value change, and the definition of quality continues to evolve. For business-to-business marketers, there is added pressure from the fact that the *customer's* customers continue to increase *their* expectations and demands for superior performance.

Recall that customer orientation and innovation were directly linked in the initial statement of the marketing concept. Quality and continuous innovation go hand-in-hand as dual requirements of the new marketing concept. Customer expectations, technological developments, and competitive pressures intersect and combine to equate success with continual improvement. Any firm that attempts to make customers satisfied with what they currently have, that is not committed to continuous improvement in products and processes, and that is unable to offer new and better solutions to customer problems is doomed to failure in the global marketplace.

Merely promising and promoting "new, improved, better" products and services won't do the job. The firm's value proposition must be based on skills and resources that deliver value as perceived by the customer. The old definition of marketing, one limited to the functions of selling, advertising, promotion, distribution, and customer service, is worse than inadequate—it is self-defeating and certain to lead to competitive disaster and business failure. The quality revolution is real, the changes it has brought are permanent, and a customer-centered view of the business is essential. There is no other choice. Marketing has moved from a static world of "Make and Sell" to a dynamic world of "Sense and Respond."[1]

# MARKETING AS PROCESS

Viewing marketing narrowly as a separate business function is an incorrect interpretation of what it means to be customer-oriented and market-driven. Rather, marketing must be thought of as the whole business seen from the customer's point of view. Marketing is the way the customer gets to influence the company, not something the company does to the customer. A customer-centric view of marketing requires redefining marketing as a set of processes for defining, developing, and delivering superior value.

## Marketing: Defining, Developing, and Delivering Value

The new definition of marketing is built around the concept of customer value and the value chain. *Marketing* is the process of *defining, developing,* and *delivering* value to customers:

- *Defining* value consists of identifying, measuring, and analyzing customer needs and translating that information into requirements for creating satisfied customers.

- *Developing* value incorporates the activities of product development, completing the product offering with services, and pricing consistent with customer needs, competitive conditions, and the value inherent in the product bundle.

- *Delivering* value includes not only the obvious functions of distribution—transportation, storage, risk-taking, sorting and providing an assortment of goods, and so on—but also the process of communicating the product offering through personal selling, advertising, sales promotion, publicity, and display to the intended target market. Customer service functions such as applications engineering, installation, warranties, and after-sale service can be thought of as an integral part of the process of delivering value.

## The Concept of the Value Chain

The value chain describes all of the activities that must be performed from the time raw materials are taken from mines, forests, farms, oceans, lakes, rivers, and air (for many gases), combined with human labor, turned into goods and services, delivered to the marketplace, often resold several times to create additional utilities of form, time, and place, and ultimately consumed.

*Consumption* often, even usually, does not mean that the product or service disappears. Most acts of consumption result in the production of waste in the form of refuse, gases, or spent products that must be reclaimed, recycled, or destroyed. Some products, such as information services, may even become more valuable with use. The value chain doesn't end until all of these postconsumption effects have been taken into account. Value for one person may be cost for another, especially in the frequent case where there are public consequences from private consumption such as air pollution from automobile use and water pollution from construction activities.

In companies with a mature commitment to total quality management, the quality process extends back into vendors' processes and forward to those of the customer. The company operates in a fairly narrow range of the value chain and depends heavily on vendors for inputs that must meet all of the quality standards defined by customers. Integrating forward into the customer's processes may also be essential to assure delivery of the full range of benefits promised, especially if the company has capabilities that the customer does not have. For example, manufacturers of industrial coatings, such as PPG, may take responsibility for the paint spraying operations in the plants of their appliance and automobile manufacturer customers. Automobile manufacturers try to maintain control over the maintenance and parts used by customers through their dealer organizations, to insure satisfactory performance over the life of the car. Chemical companies work with their customers on training personnel, applications engineering, process improvement, and a variety of other value-enhancing services.

In addition to the flow of products from manufacturers to customers, there is also a flow of information and services that, in many instances, is more important to customer satisfaction than the product itself. There is also a continuous flow of information from the customer back to the manufacturer, providing feedback on customer satisfaction, identifying the need for additional assistance, and suggesting the need for new products and services. In the best buyer-seller relationships, both parties are totally committed to continuous improvement in their interdependent processes for creating and delivering superior value.

The concept of the value chain incorporates both the focus on the customer that is inherent in the marketing concept and the focus on the company's capabilities, resources, and skills that is inherent in the concept of strategy. Customer needs, perceptions, and use systems define value. The company's capabilities determine its ability to deliver value. The company's chosen strategic position in the value chain, and its value proposition to the customer, represent management's best judgment as to the way to achieve unique, sustainable competitive advantage within the constraints of the resources and skills it has or can reasonably expect to develop.

The new marketing concept calls for defining the business "from the outside in":

- Finding customer needs that are incompletely satisfied, customer problems that are not solved.
- Being "expert" on that class of customer problems; knowing the customers and their needs and problems better than they know themselves.
- Creating solutions to those problems through innovation.
- Communicating and delivering those solutions to a carefully defined set of prospective customers whose needs the business is committed to serving.

## Defining Marketing Processes

Thinking of marketing as process is a complicated proposition. It requires finding ways to link all of the company's value creation and delivery processes to the customer. It means getting information about customers and their dynamic definitions of value into all of the firm's activities.

George S. Day, a leading academic expert on marketing strategy, helps our understanding of marketing as an organizational process. He observes that market orientation in practice requires superior skills in understanding and satisfying customers. He identifies the two critical organizational processes as *market-sensing* and *customer-linking* capabilities that result in collective learning throughout the organization. He explains that these capabilities have four components:

1. Knowledge and skills.
2. Technical systems—linked databases.
3. Management systems for creating and controlling knowledge.

4.  Values and norms ("culture"), which are the embodiment of what it means to be customer oriented.

Consistent with the value-delivery concept of strategy, Day asserts that market-sensing and customer-linking are the core processes for creating economic value. They provide the basis for achieving competitive advantage and customer value, which leads ultimately to performance outcomes such as sales volume, market share, and profitability—in other words, shareholder value.[2]

Another useful way of thinking about the complex issue of marketing as process sees marketing as the primary generator and integrator of market or customer inputs into core business processes. This viewpoint is consistent with the assertion that the fundamental role of the marketing professionals in any organization is to be "expert" on the customer. The definition of marketing as defining, delivering, and developing customer value leads to the definition of a marketing process as any organizational process that either gathers information from and about customers, uses information about customers to design products and communications for customers, or produces outputs that are used and evaluated by customers.[3]

One model of marketing as an organizational process sees marketing as consisting of three subprocesses:

1.  Product development management.
2.  Customer relationship management.
3.  Value chain management.

In this model, the objectives of marketing are to attract and retain customers and to generate and sustain customer value.[4]

Defining marketing as these three subprocesses helps to make the direct connection between quality and customer satisfaction, between total quality management and the value-delivery concept of strategy. Each of these three subprocesses will be described briefly.

## Product Development Management

Product development management should be broadened to a concept of innovation management to incorporate the important realization that the total product offering includes all of the service dimensions of the product offering, not just the physical product or the core service. Continuous improvement in the company's response to the customer's changing definition of value requires continuous, customer-driven innovation in products and value-delivery processes.

The job of marketing is to be sure that all of these innovation activities are guided by the best possible, current, complete, and correct information from the marketplace. In some cases, this may require giving marketing specialists responsibility for managing the process, often as team leaders. In other cases, marketing experts may be assigned to work with process managers in areas such as research and development.

In many companies, key customers are directly involved in the innovation process. In business-to-business markets, these customers have been variously called *lead users, lighthouse customers,* and *compelling customers.* They are often technological leaders with an excellent sense of both market trends and technology directions. They need and value their relationships with their suppliers as part of their own value development and value-delivery strategies. The fundamental objective is to be sure that technology is market-driven and focused on finding solutions to actual customer problems and priorities.

In consumer goods companies, traditional survey research methodologies are being replaced by more qualitative, observational research methods. Getting more company people in contact with actual customers can produce very beneficial results. In both consumer and industrial markets, there is no substitute for actual observation of people using the company's products and services and understanding the problems customers are trying to solve by using them. Some companies, such as Procter & Gamble, go so far as requiring their most senior managers to spend at least one day a month in the field with customers, often in locations around the world. Other companies, such as Hewlett Packard, regularly schedule customer visits for engineering and production personnel or invite customers to visit the company's laboratories, factories, and sales offices.

## Customer Relationship Management

Customer relationships are the key strategic assets of the firm. They define the business. Even if all production is outsourced, the firm is still defined by its own relationships with its own customers. Like all assets, customer relationships have economic value. Managing customer relationships as strategic assets is an important development, replacing more traditional sales management views such as key account strategy.

The purpose of marketing is to create a customer, not just to make a sale. Profitable sales result from strong, ongoing customer relationships that are designed and managed in the context of a total business model that includes customer selection, the value proposition, the value capture strategy, and strategic alliances with partners who help deliver value to those customers. To repeat, the focus is on profitability, not sales volume. Even with strategic customers, it often makes sense to have some potential sales go to competitors.

The actual processes involved in customer relationship management are the traditional domain of salesforce and marketing channel (distribution) management. But the new concept of customer relationship management goes much further into the realm of customer databases, strategic partnering with customers, and many forms of information and risk sharing. Chapter 5 will continue a detailed consideration of customer relationship management.

## Value Chain Management

The concept of the value chain has been substituted here for the more narrow supply chain to note explicitly that resellers and other agents are often involved in the value-delivery process in addition to traditionally defined suppliers or vendors. The execution of the firm's value proposition, the maintenance of market power and control as required by the value-capture model, and securing world-class competence in developing the value offering all require carefully formulated strategic partnerships both forward (toward the market) and backward (toward physical resources and other inputs) in the value chain.

Historically, many of the activities involved in value chain management were managed with the objective of minimizing cost. Functions such as procurement, logistics, and credit were viewed as a necessary cost of doing business. Purchasing managers and transportation managers, for example, were typically evaluated in terms of how much money they saved from one year to the next. The emphasis produced results that were often inconsistent with the concept of delivering superior value to customers. Total quality management and other new management disciplines have substantially altered this traditional view while at the same time trying to achieve maximum efficiency in delivering customer value. Managing processes such as inventory management from a customer perspective is a major challenge and opportunity and puts an entirely new twist on our understanding of marketing. The traditional boundaries between marketing and manufacturing, as well as other management functions, have been blurred considerably.

The discussion of the concept of the value chain continues in relationship to the understanding of quality as customer value delivery.

## Quality Is Delivering Superior Customer Value

Quality should be defined from the customer's perspective because, as we noted at the beginning of Chapter 1, value is defined in the marketplace. In the factory, we add costs. Value is not created in the factory, it is created in the market when the customer pays us more for the product or service we have produced than the sum total of the costs we incurred to create and deliver the product/service bundle. The difference between what the customer is willing to pay and the costs we have incurred is value. Profit is a measure of the value we have created. It is the reward for creating a satisfied customer, for solving a customer problem.

Under the new marketing concept, there is more to marketing than simply understanding and serving customer needs. The new marketing concept recognizes that customers are interested in the company's total capabilities. They want to be educated about the class of problems and solutions that is the company's specialty. They expect the marketer to provide leadership in the future, especially where technical capabilities are concerned. A purchase of a personal computer, for example, is based partly on the expectation that there will be a continuous flow of product enhancements, new applications software, and other innovations.

We return to these fundamental notions concerning the value proposition in Chapter 4 where our concern will be for designing and communicating the value proposition. In the rest of this chapter, we concentrate our attention on the challenges of total quality management, its relationship to customer satisfaction, and its integral role in the new marketing concept.

## Quality and Customer Expectations: The Augmented Product

Quality is defined by the extent to which the product meets customer expectations. Here we are talking about much more than the physical product or the simple service that is being purchased. The customer has expectations for the entire product offering and defines quality to encompass the shopping, buying, after-sale, use, and disposal processes. A concept of the augmented product, developed by Theodore Levitt, helps in understanding customer expectations and their central role in defining quality (Figure 3.2).[5]

First, there is the *generic product.* In the case of physical products, it is "the thing you can drop on your foot," like a portable computer. For a service product, it is the basic service feature, like $100,000 worth of term life insurance. Generic products, even for products as sophisticated as personal

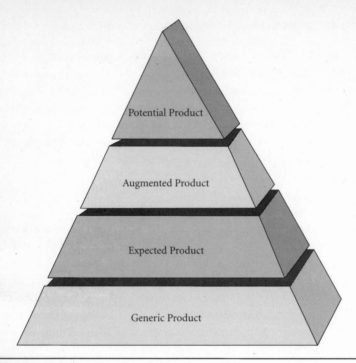

**FIGURE 3.2**  The hierarchy of products.

computers and term life insurance, and certainly for basic commodities like chemicals and air travel, tend to be undifferentiated and to be bought and sold largely in terms of price. Definitions of quality that focus on physical characteristics, specifications, and defects per thousand deal only with the generic product and fall short of the mark of thinking about quality from the customer's perspective. Every company hopes to offer more. Every customer expects more.

What the customer is buying is the *expected product* which includes the generic product plus all of the features and services, which the customer simply expects as part of the product offering. The expected product of my portable computer included a bright legible screen, easy-to-use software for word processing and spreadsheets, Internet and e-mail capabilities, rechargeable batteries, and the availability of a local dealer for product support and assistance when needed. The term life insurance customer expects efficient billing procedures, easy-to-understand explanations, a friendly helpful agent, and guaranteed prompt payment in the event of a claim. The industrial customer buying emulsifiers expects overnight delivery in bags, drums, or trailer loads, technical assistance on product applications when requested, and efficient order-entry and billing procedures.

Competitive prices are still an important part of the expected product and it is assumed that the generic product meets all technical specifications. The service bundle is also assumed to be there as part of the product offering, without the buyer's having to ask for it or to negotiate terms and conditions for its delivery. The generic product is what Levitt calls "the table stakes"; it is necessary but not sufficient to create a satisfied customer. Delivering the expected product is both necessary *and* sufficient. However, merely doing a sufficient job of meeting customer expectations may not be adequate for long-term survival in the competitive global marketplace. Simple customer satisfaction is not enough. It is better if the company can *exceed* customer expectations.

The *augmented product* includes features and services that were not expected, creating the possibility of not merely meeting but actually exceeding customer expectations. The screen on my portable computer is much larger, brighter, and easier to read, even in strong light, than I had expected. Response to commands and the scrolling feature are even faster than on my office computer. The battery recharges much faster than I had expected. I am not merely satisfied; I am delighted. The term life insurance customer was delighted to learn that the policy included a conversion option that adds a savings and capital appreciation feature. The emulsifier customer, a manufacturer of soaps and detergents, was delighted to find that the distributor who agreed to serve its requirements has excellent field sales personnel as well as technical support staff available by telephone. The customer can order for multiple plant sites from multiple distributor stocking points using the distributor's Web site to ensure overnight delivery anyplace in the United States and Canada. The distributor also offers a Total Care Program, which takes responsibility as required for reclamation and disposal of process by-products and stands ready to help with any spills, accidents, or other problems. While a large national company with an excellent reputation manufactures the chemical product itself, the critical features of the augmented product are those provided by the distributor-partner.

Can the manufacturer or distributor who offers a superior augmented product declare victory? Hardly. It doesn't take long for the augmented product to become the expected product. The customer's definition of value keeps changing. The customer may go to other potential suppliers and see if they can meet or exceed the service bundle now being purchased but at a better price. The first, successful seller has educated and informed the customer allowing the customer to exercise more discretion and power in the future. I wish I had waited for the new computer model, a dramatic new design with many new performance features and much greater power, announced one month after I bought this one. The term life insurance customer, once he thought about adding a savings and capital appreciation feature, decided to contact an investment broker, not his insurance agent. The customer has increased his or her expectations and become more demanding. The competitive battle rages. So, even the augmented product may not be enough to ensure competitive survival over the long run.

The successful firm is always thinking about the *potential product,* opportunities to innovate and serve customers better. Success requires staying ahead of customers' perceived needs and competitors' product offerings. The company cannot merely meet clearly defined customer needs. It must look at its own capabilities and work with customers to apply them in new areas, not just doing what the customer says, but also forming a partnership that looks to the future. This brings us back to the central importance of innovation in the value-delivery concept of strategy. The augmented product stresses the importance of product differentiation and the value proposition in the search for competitive advantage. The idea of the potential product keeps management's eyes focused on the future and opportunities for leading and responding to the changing customer.

## QUALITY AS A WAY OF DOING BUSINESS

Early definitions of quality, which focused on the product itself, defined it negatively, in terms of things that could go wrong. The emphasis was on measures like defects or parts rejected per 1,000 produced. Quality was defined as protecting customers from annoyances rather than delighting them with superior performance. The traditional quality measures were "defensive" measures to eliminate defects and preempt product failure.[6]

The most successful quality programs define quality not in terms of products but as a complete way of doing business, a total commitment to the customer. These marketers think of themselves as partners for their customers. In industrial markets, this incorporates the order-entry, purchasing, credit, and billing procedures; help with applications; careful introduction of new technology and new products and services as they become available; educational programs for customer personnel; and more. The partnership is based on a clear understanding of the customer's processes and how they interact with the seller's processes and careful management of their integration. They are focused on making the business partners more competitive in their markets. They go well beyond simply offering "good products."

These concepts of partnership and relationship management are also being implemented more and more by consumer marketers. It may be something as simple as the manufacturer listing on each package a telephone number or Internet Web site that customers can call for product information. Or it may be the automobile manufacturer who regularly calls customers after they have visited a dealership for service or who offers an extended warranty program at modest additional charge. It is seen in the frequent traveler programs offered by airlines and hotel chains. Hotels and campground chains offer special rates, discounts, and services to customers who join their travel clubs. Credit card companies offer not only the convenience of the card but also quarterly summaries of expenses, services such as airline reservations, special entertainment and dining packages, and travelers' checks and check-cashing privileges. They go beyond the expected product and the individual transactions and look at multiple aspects of their relationships with customers over an extended period of time.

For these sophisticated companies, quality becomes a competitive business strategy, the central theme of their business strategies in the competitive marketplace. Xerox, for example, is cited as a company that has defined quality simply as "a way of doing business, one that is focused wholly on the customer."[7] Other large companies whose quality programs have been emulated by others include L.L. Bean, Federal Express, Fidelity Investments, Motorola, IBM, Corning, Disney, and Ford.

## How NOT to Manage Quality

The quality movement produced many positive results but it also had some negative consequences. These negative aspects of the quality movement resulted from the tendency of companies, paradoxically most likely to be those with the strongest departments or managers of quality, to focus their processes of quality management internally, rather than on the customer. Unfortunately, for some companies, going after the brass ring of one of the quality prizes caused the rider to fall off of the quality carousel. By focusing their efforts myopically on their internal processes, they lost sight of the customer.

Competing for quality prizes such as the Baldrige Award (created by the U.S. Congress in 1987 and administered by the National Institute of

Standards and Technology) or the Deming Prize is a challenging and complicated endeavor. An example of what can go wrong is provided by Florida Power and Light, which for several years was touted as a paragon of TQM. They made an all-out effort to become the first non-Japanese winner of the Deming Prize and succeeded in doing so in 1989. At the height, their quality department employed 85 people and there were 1,900 quality teams involving three-fourths of their employees. Efforts were focused on the measurements called for under a very sophisticated statistical quality-review system. Unfortunately, improvements in service delivery seen by customers were insignificant. A new head of quality was appointed who described his job as trying to "clear up the mess." The quality department was reduced to six employees.[8]

## Every Business Is a Service Business

Bringing together the definition of quality as meeting or exceeding customer expectations, the concept of the augmented product, and the value-delivery concept of business strategy, produces an interesting result: It is possible and desirable to define any business as primarily a service business. Customers don't buy products, they buy a set of benefits and solutions to problems. Furthermore, the majority, now close to two-thirds, of economic activity in developed nations is in the production and marketing of services rather than physical products. Even more interesting is the fact that most of the companies we tend to think of as industrial giants with a predominance of their revenues from manufacturing activities, such as General Electric and IBM, actually derive most of their revenues and profits from the sale of services. General Electric announced in its 1996 annual report that it was redefining itself as a service business, albeit one that sells products as part of its service offering. Smart businesses sell solutions, not products.

For most businesses, the reconceptualization of themselves as a service business is an enormous challenge. Traditional ways of thinking about the business usually center on the products produced, for example, General Electric in power generation equipment, motors, and lamps, and IBM in large mainframe computers followed by smaller machines, personal computers, and a total line of peripheral equipment such as computers. The fact is that General Electric's largest and most dynamic businesses are in the services sector—General Electric Capital Corporation, NBC in television and radio, nuclear plant servicing and operations, and so on. IBM derives over 40 percent of its revenues from sales of consulting services, networking, and other service businesses, as well as 15 percent from software sales and 5 percent from financing and investment activities; only 39 percent comes from the sales of hardware.

Thinking about the business in terms of the expected product and the services provided to the customer is a way of developing a customer orientation, a way of looking at the business from the customer's perspective. It is important to think in terms of what the customer is buying as opposed to what the company is making and selling. If there is evidence that different customers expect and derive different benefits from the same product, this identifies distinct market segments that have different strategic requirements and require different value propositions. Such insights are not possible if the business is defined in terms of its products.

Defining the business as a service business helps to create a value proposition that is rich enough to capture all of the important dimensions of the expected and augmented product as perceived by customers and to define the key success factors for the business. It also points to the potential product. It leads to a definition of quality as a total way of doing business rather than focusing narrowly on product dimensions and features. It can help to ensure that the company won't go to market with an incomplete product.

## THE SERVQUAL MODEL

While the conversation about TQM began in traditional manufacturing settings, innovative adaptation of ideas about quality management to the field of services has produced some interesting new insights into the concept of quality itself. This expanded understanding of the fundamental concept of quality becomes increasingly valuable as more and more firms define themselves as being in the service business. One of the hallmarks of the concept of service quality is the importance of defining quality in terms of meeting and exceeding customer expectations, which is essential in services marketing. It is much harder to develop clear specifications for product characteristics when there is no physical, resource-based product involved.

The SERVQUAL model, a pioneering attempt to measure service quality shown in Figure 3.3, has been developed, tested, and refined in a program of research supported in part by the Marketing Science Institute and with the cooperation of many service businesses in a wide range of industries.[9] Two central features of the SERVQUAL model are the definition of quality in terms of the comparison of expected and perceived benefits and the identification of gaps in the service delivery process. These gaps identify

CONSUMER

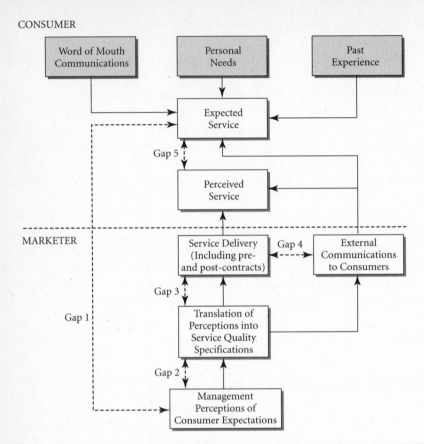

**FIGURE 3.3** The SERVQUAL Model. *Source:* A. Parasuraman, Valerie A. Zeithaml, and Leonard L. Berry, "A Conceptual Model of Service Quality and Its Implications for Future Research," *Journal of Marketing* (fall 1985), 41–50. Copyright 1985 by the American Marketing Association; reproduced with permission.

the most important ways in which the business can fail to perform in the mind of the customer:

- Misunderstanding customer expectations.
- Developing inadequate specifications for product/service performance.
- Developing products/services that do not meet performance specifications.
- Not communicating product/service benefits accurately and realistically to potential customers.

- Creating expectations that cannot be met, by overpromising in marketing communications.

# ANALYZING CUSTOMER NEEDS AND WANTS

Very often the most important gap in the delivery of service or product quality results from a failure to understand the customer's needs and wants and the product-use system in which the company's product offering will be used. The company must have procedures for gathering and analyzing the necessary information about customer needs, wants, buying habits, and usage patterns, and communicating that information to those in the organization who can use it to design, develop, produce, and deliver superior customer value. Being customer-oriented is more than a mind-set; it is, more specifically, having current, correct, and complete information, carefully analyzed about customers, their value perceptions, and their assessments of competitors' product offerings.

Providing such information is the major reason why a company needs a separate marketing function, a group of people who are responsible for being experts on the customer and communicating that information throughout the organization. The value of the marketing function is determined by the extent to which these other organizational actors place a value on and use the information provided by marketing.

These other organizational actors, including the R&D people, the product designers, the applications engineers, the salesforce, the customer service personnel, and the rest, may sincerely believe that they know better than the marketing people what it is the customer needs and wants. And, in fact, they might. Each of them, however, is likely to have a view of the customer that reflects his or her own functional bias and an incomplete understanding of the customer's total requirements.

## Establishing Cross-Functional Teams to Focus Attention on the Customer

Cross-functional teams are an important tool for implementing a TQM program. The overarching objective is to achieve the necessary degree of coordination across the traditional management functions including engineering, production, credit, transportation, customer service, and so on, and to break down the functional walls that have often prevented the delivery of the intended level of performance in the marketplace. Cross-functional teams are another mechanism for focusing everyone's attention on the customer. They must be guided by information about customer needs, wants, expectations, and purchasing and consumption behavior.

*Quality circles* are another organizational device for focusing organization actors and their actions on the customer. These small groups are typically organized within a given department or function and meet regularly to identify and discuss problems requiring action. Such groups must be given the tools and training necessary to be effective, including guidelines for identifying what is important to the customer and what is not, problem-solving techniques for identifying solutions, and organizational resources and support necessary to implement their recommendations. An important part of the quality circle concept is teaching the participants how to measure those things that are important in their operations. Such measurements should be based on a clear understanding of customer expectations and how customers define value. Quality circles without specific, on-going measurements are not likely to be effective.

The challenge is to get all of the players in the system of defining, developing, and delivering value to customers pulling together in a coordinated fashion, guided by the same vision of the customer. The first part of the challenge is to develop a common perception, a common base of information and understanding about the customer. The second part of the challenge is to develop organizational mechanisms for team-building that can cross, if not eliminate, traditional functional boundaries.

Customer analysis addresses the first part of the challenge: gathering and analyzing information about customers. Traditional survey research methods, studying a large representative sample of customers to find central tendencies in their attitudes, preferences, and behavior, are generally inadequate for developing the broader understanding of customer definitions of quality and value. The "average customer" is of little use in a concept of value delivery that looks at all aspects of the business and its relationships with customers over an extended period of time.

## Developing Customer Visit Programs

Some industrial companies, such as Hewlett-Packard, have developed customer visit programs as a way of learning more about the problems facing customers, the way in which the company's products get used, their influence on the customer's operations, and opportunities and requirements for future product development and improvements. Customer visit programs are also an important device for achieving cross-functional coordination and creating an organizational culture of customer orientation. Feedback from customer visits can also become part of the system for measuring customer satisfaction although this is not the primary purpose.[10]

Dr. Katherine Tobin, the leader of the customer visit program at Hewlett-Packard, cites the following benefits for the company:

- HP gets updated knowledge of customer environments and needs.
- HP gets updated knowledge of competitors' products.
- HP gets information to improve product strategy.
- HP engineers are educated about market conditions.
- Customer perceptions are reinforced that HP is concerned about their needs.
- Cooperation is enhanced between the R&D labs and the marketing organization.
- Better mutual understanding forms between the factory and the field sales and service organization.[11]

## Using Quality Function Deployment to Help Meet Customer Needs

Quality function deployment (QFD) is a sophisticated tool for addressing the gap between understanding customer needs and turning this understanding into clear specifications for the design of the product or service. It involves people from multiple business functions in the product development and planning effort and has the specific purpose of facilitating interfunctional cooperation. It is a planning method for translating customer needs and expectations into requirements not just for products but also for total company performance. QFD offers a specific tool for making the marketing concept operational and for matching customer requirements with company capabilities.

The concept of "the House of Quality" is a central feature of QFD. It was developed in 1972 at the Kobe shipyard of Mitsubishi and further refined by Toyota and its suppliers.[12] The central purpose of QFD is to design, manufacture, and market products that customers will want to purchase, products based on an understanding of customers' needs and wants. The House of Quality provides the conceptual map for this task, recognizing that customer wants are complex, multidimensional, and at times fundamentally in conflict with one another.

The House of Quality approach begins with a listing of the attributes that customers want. These can be identified in a number of ways; for example, by watching customers examine or use the product. These attributes are broken down into several sublevels of detail and grouped to capture overall customer concerns, using actual customer language wherever possible, to guide design decisions. Consumer research is also used to assign importance weights to various bundles of attributes, in order to assess the necessary tradeoffs given technical constraints. These result in the assignment of percentages (totaling 100 percent) to attribute groupings.

Customer ratings are also used to evaluate competitive product offerings on each attribute grouping, creating a map of consumer preferences. Designers then define opportunities for improving products, given the company's skills and capabilities, in ways that will be important to customers' perceptions of value and provide a source of competitive advantage. The House of Quality provides a visual tool in the form of a matrix with customer perceptions of product attributes on one dimension and engineering characteristics on the other. Specific target objectives for design work emerge from matching what is possible, given engineering capabilities, and what is desired by the customer. The technique can potentially be applied to any process within the company that is part of defining, developing, and delivering superior value to customers.

Quality function deployment and the House of Quality are useful tools for visualizing the relationship between customer requirements and engineering capabilities. They can be modified and creatively expanded to meet the needs of any design team. They do not offer a panacea for developing successful products but they offer a flexible approach for making a commitment to customer orientation operational.

## ANALYZING COMPETITORS THROUGH BENCHMARKING

The new marketing concept balances customer and competitor analysis. It recognizes that customer perceptions of value result from the interaction of their evaluations of the alternative product offerings available from competing firms. *Benchmarking* is a widely used technique for analyzing competitors' product offerings, identifying the best products and processes, and adapting them to the company's own products and activities.

Benchmarking has been defined as "stealing somebody else's best ideas and improving them." The practice is believed to have started at Xerox Corporation in 1979 when the company began to address its loss of market share and its unfavorable cost/price position relative to competitors, especially Japanese brands. Initially focused on product problems, benchmarking was extended throughout the company into all functions, including marketing. Now, when other American firms want to do benchmarking, they look to Xerox, which now offers training and consulting on benchmarking.

Benchmarking can be done on different divisions and functions within the company, on competitors, or on any company from which something of value can be learned that will help the business improve its products and processes. For example, the following companies have been widely recognized as world-class leaders in the designated areas:

- *Marketing:* Procter & Gamble.
- *Customer Satisfaction:* L.L. Bean, Federal Express, General Electric Plastics, Xerox.
- *Distribution and Logistics:* L.L. Bean, Wal-Mart.
- *Billing and Collection:* American Express, MCI, Fidelity Investments.
- *Product Development:* Beckman Instruments, Calcomp, Cincinnati Milacron, 3M, Xerox, Hewlett-Packard.
- *Benchmarking:* Xerox, AT&T, Ford, Texas Instruments, IBM.
- *Supplier Management:* Ford, Bose, Motorola, Xerox, 3M, Levi Strauss.[13]

The highly successful Ford Taurus/Mercury Sable automobiles were developed using benchmarking. Fifty competitive mid-size automobiles from Germany, Sweden, Japan, and the United States were analyzed in detail to discover best-in-the-world designs for everything from brake pads to transmissions to door handles. The dismantling of competitors' products, sometimes called "reverse engineering," is only one aspect of benchmarking and competitor analysis. Other forms of analysis include visiting factory sites, interviewing customers, and reviewing publicly available information, such as contained in product brochures, news releases, corporate annual reports, and trade show exhibits.

Knowing competitors' product offerings and distinctive competence can create a better understanding of how customers define value, where the company can improve its own performance in products and processes, and where it is best to avoid head-to-head competition. Benchmarking is simultaneously focused on improving performance and lowering costs in products and in all of the processes and activities involved in delivering value to customers.

While benchmarking can be performed on all of the company's products and processes, not all of them are equally important in the competitive marketplace. Especially when the focus is on internal processes like order-processing, production planning and scheduling, inventory control, and billing, while these influence the level of customer satisfaction and are thus essential, benchmarking may not be dealing with the most important issues strategically. They may define the requirements and necessary costs of being in the business, "the table stakes," to use Levitt's phrase again, but they are not likely to identify the sources of unique, sustainable competitive advantage. World-class dining facilities don't count, even if management loves them!

# ANALYZING YOUR COMPANY'S INTERNAL RESOURCES

The key to successful competition is to select market niches where the company's skills and resources will deliver the highest value to customers compared with its competitors. The company must have a clear understanding of its distinctive competences, the things that it does best. When weaknesses are identified relative to competitors, management must decide which areas must be strengthened and where the competitive weakness is likely to be an ongoing one that suggests avoiding direct battles with competitors. Analysis of internal capabilities is also the first step in developing a strategy for outsourcing and partnering.

## Defining Your Company's Distinctive Competences

When management appraises the strengths and weaknesses of the business to assess its competitive position, it needs to concentrate on those areas of capability that really matter. Among the strengths that the typical company might identify are "loyal employees, stable management, full product line, and community support." Similarly, a list of weaknesses might include "limited access to capital at reasonable rates, unresolved liability for site contamination, aging production facility, and lack of management depth and provision for managerial succession." While these are important areas and issues, with weaknesses that should be addressed by the commitment of additional resources, they do not define key success factors in the competitive marketplace.

The central calculus of strategy is to match the firm's capabilities with customer needs in the competitive marketplace. In Chapter 1, we observed that the old marketing concept only addressed one side of the equation—customer needs, and was silent on the question of identifying the firm's capabilities. We mentioned the concept of "imbricative marketing" as an early attempt to blend the consideration of company capabilities and market needs. In Chapter 2, we saw how long-range strategic planning attempted to address this issue specifically with the concepts of product/market mission and strategic business units and lost sight of the customer in the process, when markets were defined as collections of competitors. Capability was narrowly defined in the portfolio approach to strategic planning as the ability to achieve the position of lowest-cost producer and the ability to dominate a market, to achieve the largest market share.

A distinctive competence is something that the firm does well, better than any of its competitors *and* that is valued by its customers. There is a tremendously important definitional point here—the firm cannot define its distinctive competence except in the context of its chosen market. Customer selection is the critical strategic choice that any firm makes. At the same time, the selection of market targets must be based on the assessment of distinctive competences. The firm must choose those market niches where its skills and resources can deliver superior value to customers.

## The Criteria for Distinctive Competence

To be meaningful and "real" as a strategic variable, the distinctive competence must meet three criteria:

1. It must be important to potential customers in terms of their perception of value.
2. It must be knowledge-based, which often means that it is technology-based.
3. It should apply across multiple products and offer potential access to multiple market segments.

A truly distinctive competence defines an area where the company is uniquely capable among all companies in the world. Because the competence is knowledge-based, it is not easily copied. It resides in key individuals and in tightly designed and controlled proprietary systems. Patents or copyrights may protect it. Some key distinctive competences are based on information technology, including airline reservations systems (American and Delta), small package delivery systems (United Parcel Service and Federal Express), and elevator maintenance and repair service (Otis).

A real distinctive competence is at the core of a whole spectrum of products or potential products. It may become a global industry standard as a component of the products of many firms. The distinctive competence is the knowledge, not the products themselves.[14] Among some of the best-known examples of distinctive competences are Hewlett-Packard's laser-printing technology, Intel's computer-chip-making technology, Corning's capabilities in ceramics, and Silicon Graphics in computer animation. These companies' products have achieved dominant positions in the world market, often through strategic alliances with partners whose own distinctive competences create the possibility for new products through bringing together convergent technologies.

Although most distinctive competences are knowledge-based in a general sense, not all are technology-based. Marketing skills in such areas as sales promotion and media advertising are knowledge-based, often supported by sophisticated information systems. Marketing skills are core competences for Procter & Gamble, PepsiCo, and General Mills. Access to, and dominant position in, a channel of distribution may be a distinctive competence for the company, as in the case of Norton Company (now a part of Saint Gobain) in abrasives/industrial distribution and Intel in integrated circuits. A dominant channel position may preclude weaker competitors from gaining a viable place in the market.

Physical assets may occasionally be a source of distinctive competence, especially if they are based on a unique locational advantage, such as access to a scarce raw material. In most cases, however, physical resources do not offer a unique, sustainable competitive advantage because they are susceptible to duplication, often with improvements, by competitors. Unique production skills, however, meet the tests of distinctive competence because they are likely to be embedded in skilled production workers or in technology-based systems and proprietary knowledge.

The definition, development, and nurturing of distinctive competences is a key step in a program of total quality management and the implementation of the new marketing concept. It defines the competitive arena in which the company is going to strive to deliver superior value to customers, the things it promises to do better than any other business in the world.

Distinctive competences define areas where the firm must invest heavily if it is to maintain its competitive advantage. Given the inevitable progression of customer expectations, competitive imitation, and technology, the company must continue to develop the relevant knowledge, skills, and capabilities by reinvesting profits or obtaining new capital as necessary. Distinctive competence is intertwined with the need for continuous innovation, identified as a key element of the new marketing concept. The most advanced marketers focus on developing capabilities, not products.

# MEASURING COMPANY PERFORMANCE BY OBTAINING CUSTOMER FEEDBACK

The final and perhaps most important step in total quality management is developing a program for measuring customer satisfaction and providing feedback of the results to all members of the organization. Customer feedback measures the last and most important gap in the service delivery process—the difference between what customers expected and what they perceive was actually delivered by the company. Customer satisfaction measures must find their way into systems for evaluating and rewarding individual performance. In this way, quality becomes the most important strategic driver for the entire company. Customer satisfaction must be linked to the methods by which people are evaluated and rewarded if the company is to succeed in putting the interests of the customer first, always.

## Defining What to Measure

A maxim for public speakers advises, "Tell them what you're going to tell them; tell them; tell them what you told them." That is also not bad advice for measuring the successes and failures of a total quality management program. The process must begin with the customer and we might paraphrase the steps as "Ask them what they expect; give it to them; ask them if they got what they expected."

The first step in the process is to determine customer expectations. How do customers define value? What do they expect? The essential point is that quality is defined by the customer so standards for evaluating company performance must also be defined by the customer. Internal measures, for example number of units per thousand produced requiring rework, percentage of orders shipped complete, or percentage of orders shipped within 24 hours of receipt, may be important in managing operations, delivering value, and meeting expectations, but may not reflect true customer satisfaction or lack thereof. Internal measures should be based on those parts of the process that result in true differences in customer satisfaction, such as differences between promised and actual delivery times.

Listening to customers and watching how they use products may reveal some surprises that should be the basis for measuring performance. For example, having prompt repair service for home appliances may not do much to improve customer satisfaction if the customer's primary expectation is that the product will work satisfactorily from the very beginning. Time spent waiting for a reservations clerk to answer a telephone may be more important in defining quality than the courtesy with which the phone is finally answered. Mediocre airline food may meet customer expectations while a dirty seat cushion may not.

One consultant breaks the process of customer feedback into five principles or phases:

1. *Know why* you are measuring and how the results will be used to improve performance.

2. *Let customers* define what to measure.

3. *Monitor continuously* performance versus competitors.

4. *Track the internal processes* that are tied to the results customers value as well as the end results themselves.

5. *Communicate the results* throughout the organization to everyone involved in the value-delivery process.[15]

The company must learn to evaluate itself, and its management, based on specific measures of customer satisfaction. The feedback from customers must be meaningful to people within the organization in terms of how they evaluate their own performance.

To repeat, the process must start with the customer. Focus groups, customer visits, surveys, laboratory simulations, and field observation can all be used to determine what is important to customers. The first step is to define the criteria that customers use in their evaluations. The second step is to arrange these criteria in proper priority and to put weights on the multiple criteria, basing those weights on customer research. The third step is to design measurements that capture the performance of the company on each of these important dimensions. The final step is to develop summary measures and to compile the results of the analysis in reports that convey the results of measurement to management and employees on an on-going basis.

For industrial products and services, or for complex consumer products like automobiles and major appliances, the measurement challenge may be complicated by the fact that many people are involved in the purchase and use of the product. Each may use somewhat different criteria. For example, purchasing managers may focus on price and order-processing, manufacturing managers on on-time delivery and reject rates, engineers on product performance characteristics, and customer service personnel on spare parts availability. Measurement systems must be developed that incorporate the criteria emphasized by each of the important people in the system. There are several excellent commercial research firms available to help companies with the measurement challenge. No company, regardless of size, can afford to do business today without current, complete, and correct information about customer satisfaction, integrated into a TQM program, as part of its commitment to putting the customer first, always.

## Influencing Customers' Word-of-Mouth Messages

One of the most powerful forces in marketing is *word-of-mouth,* one customer speaking to another. Word-of-mouth is a very important source of customer expectations for the performance of products and services, as noted in the model of service quality that was shown in Figure 3.3. It can be used for the company or against it. It is powerful because of its believability. When customers talk about products or companies, they are doing so based on personal experience with the product or what they have learned from another consumer/user, or perhaps what they have read or seen in the media. Because the customer appears to have no commercial interest, no intent to sell the listener anything, word-of-mouth appears to be much more objective or credible.

Word-of-mouth is motivated behavior, for both the listener and the source. The listener is motivated to learn more about the product or service, as a potential buyer and user. Listeners may actually seek out the opinions of others as part of their buying decision. It is very common, for example, for people to try to find someone who has already seen a movie, and to solicit their opinion, before actually going to see the movie (or renting the video) themselves. Industrial buyers routinely contact buyers in other companies to get information about the performance of vendors and their products.

The motivation of the source of word-of-mouth messages is more complex. People may talk about advertising and other forms of marketing communication but they are much more likely to talk about their actual experience with a product. Whether they have had a positive or negative experience, users of products and services may be motivated to talk about them in order to test and confirm their own experience. It is a way of reducing postpurchase doubt, or "cognitive dissonance," as well as gaining positive affirmation for one's decisions. It is well known that new car buyers like to show off their purchases, by talking about them and showing them to friends. This activity generates positive feedback in the form of compliments and questions that permit buyers to demonstrate their knowledge, expertise, and buying skill as well as to review the positive aspects of their decision, thus reinforcing, in their own minds, the wisdom of the decision.

For marketers, perhaps the most interesting fact is that unhappy customers are more likely to talk about their purchase experience than are those who are satisfied. The motivation of the communicator in this instance may be to seek advice, to seek affirmation for his or her negative opinions, to help a friend or colleague avoid a similar problem, or to inflict damage on the reputation and the sales of the seller. Or the negative information may simply come out of a conversation initiated by the receiver who is looking for advice, as is often the case, for example, with potential purchasers of automobiles, major appliances, or home entertainment products. You are likely to look for owners of the make of automobile you are considering and ask their opinion. When they report a negative experience, this helps you know what questions to ask the dealer or why you may wish to eliminate that brand from your consideration set. If the buyer is really unhappy with some feature or angry about some unresolved problem, this is their chance to "get it off their chest" and to seek affirmation for their decision to buy in the first place by demonstrating that they were misled, misinformed, or deceived rather than simply having made a bad decision. Their opinions will be highly believable because they are based on actual experience and are communicated within the bonds of acquaintance or friendship with no need to misrepresent the true situation.

Companies can take specific steps to increase the amount of positive word-of-mouth generated by their customers, and to intercept and manage the negative word-of-mouth or, more importantly, root out the causes of dissatisfaction. An important step in generating positive word-of-mouth is to follow up with the customer, to be sure they know how to use and enjoy the product to the maximum extent, and to help them through any difficulties in the early stages of usage and ownership. Providing customers with information that they can share with others can be very helpful, especially when their opinions are sought out by other potential customers.

## The Value of Customer Complaints

Contrary to the widely held opinion of most business people, customer complaints are a valuable business asset. Whereas the conventional wisdom is to minimize complaints and to avoid them at all costs, a moment's reflection suggests that they can have great value for any business. Four facts support this observation:

1.  Unhappy customers are very likely to complain to someone and it might as well be the company. This minimizes the negative impact

on other potential customers and its gives the company the opportunity to correct the problem.

2. Customers keep changing (increasing) their expectations and the complaint is an opportunity to understand how customers' expectations may be evolving.

3. It is the best opportunity to learn when there really is something wrong that might not come to management's attention in normal channels for weeks or months. (A burned-out light bulb in a hotel room is a good example.)

4. The cost of satisfying an unhappy customer is usually much less than the cost of acquiring a new customer.[16]

Customers who are less than completely satisfied are a fact of business life that cannot and should not be avoided. It does no good to pretend that they are not there. It is not part of the psychological makeup of every customer to be completely satisfied. Customer expectations keep changing in the competitive marketplace, making historical levels of satisfaction obsolete. A customer complaint can be a window on the changing world even when the product has performed properly. Of course, if there is a problem with the product itself, then it is doubly important that it be identified and corrected. Companies must learn to listen to the customer, not only through the traditional means of market research, but also through the vitality of a customer complaint tracking system.

Customer complaint tracking is more than the usual survey of customer satisfaction. It requires following up with at least a sample if not the total population of recent customers. It requires asking them to identify specific problems they may perceive that may not come out in the routine questioning about levels of satisfaction. The standard "How satisfied were you?" or "How would you rank our service?" kinds of questions will not necessarily reveal useful customer complaints. Customers must be asked "Why?" they assign those rankings and be given specific opportunities to tell the company about real and perceived problems. Such questions are open-ended, without preassigned response categories, so they must be analyzed one at a time using seasoned judgment. Focus-group interviews with actual customers, while they can be quite expensive, are one method for studying customer complaints. Many companies put a toll-free telephone number on their packages or product information brochures, so that customers know where to call with questions and complaints.

Feedback in the form of customer complaints provides an opportunity to hear the voice of the changing customer, to gain information to be shared with all employees who are involved in delivering value to customers, and to identify those opportunities to innovate, solve problems, and continue to develop the firm's distinctive competence in directions important to the customer.

## SUMMARY

Total quality management is completely synonymous with a commitment to customer satisfaction. Quality is defined by customer expectations. Defining, developing, and delivering value to customers is a process of understanding, influencing, and responding to customer expectations. This is a dynamic process because customer expectations keep changing as the result of the interaction of competitive product offerings and increased customer sophistication.

A commitment to customer satisfaction and total quality is also a commitment to continuous innovation on behalf of the customer. In Chapter 4, we consider the process of developing the firm's value proposition, which begins by defining the target market that the firm has decided to serve, given its unique combination of skills and resources that define its distinctive competences. In Chapter 5, we examine the management of customer relationships as an extension of total quality management in the implementation of the new marketing concept, and examine in more depth the complex connections among customer satisfaction, customer loyalty, and profitability. Not all satisfied customers are loyal, and not all loyal customers are profitable.

# Market Targeting and the Value Proposition

4

*The essence of positioning is sacrifice. You must be willing to give up something in order to establish that unique position.*

Al Ries and Jack Trout

*Positioning: The Battle for Your Mind* (1986)

Every successful marketing strategy is focused and selective. The most important strategic choice any company makes is choosing the customers it wishes to do business with. It is a choice that defines the business. It must be a *conscious* choice, based on the desires and values of the owners and managers of the business as well as an assessment of the company's strengths and weaknesses, resources and capabilities, compared with those of competitors. It should be based on a management vision of the potential of the company for creating and serving markets, for exploiting its unique strengths, and for achieving substantial profitability.

Customers define the business by the demands they place on it, by asking the firm to do certain things effectively and efficiently. The decision to provide solutions to customer problems, to work with specific customers, to accept their demands, is a commitment of resources. The choice of markets and customers shapes the business even more than the choice of products to be offered. Over time, the product offering is adjusted to changing customer needs. In a stable business, the product is a variable; the served market and the customer are the constants.

Changing the definition of the served market changes the definition of the business. Customers shape the business, which is why customer choice is the critical strategic decision. If management has not defined a strategic vision of what it wants to be, and who the desired customer is, it has no control over the forces shaping its business. A business that tries to be all things to all customers is not a business at all, because it has failed to define its product/market scope. It *should* be obvious that no business can satisfy the demands of all potential customers. But it is not.

## THE SIREN SONG OF SALES VOLUME

In contrast to the marketing concept stands the sales concept. Under the marketing concept, profit is the reward earned for creating a satisfied customer. Under the sales concept, profit is tied to sales volume. The apparent logic of a sales-volume orientation by management is rooted in marginal profit contribution. Given high fixed costs, the logic goes, every additional sales dollar helps to make a contribution to fixed costs and brings the company closer to a position of profitability. Once fixed costs have been covered, the total contribution above variable costs per unit sold "falls to the bottom line" as operating profit.

The lure of the next sales dollar is great. Think of an industry with high fixed costs, usually associated with large investments in plant and equipment or software development, and you have probably identified an industry where the sales concept is more prevalent than the marketing concept: pulp and paper, lumber, agricultural chemicals, and textile fibers are good examples.

In the late 1990s, the collapse of many Internet start-ups following the much touted "get-big-fast" strategy offered further evidence of the futility of seeking sales volume without a strong business model incorporating sound customer targeting, a clear value proposition, and a value capture strategy. One notable survivor of the get-big-fast strategy, Amazon.com, reported its first profit ($5 million) for the quarter ended December 31, 2001, and annual sales of $3.1 billion for the year, after accumulating more than $2.8 billion in losses since its founding in 1995. This profit result was aided in part by international exchange rate conversions for debt involving the new Euro currency and the deferral of some severance and restructuring costs, as well as significant improvements in operational efficiency. Even with the reported profit, the company still burned cash at the rate of $120 million for the year 2001.[1] Only time will tell whether this small profit was really a validation of Amazon's get-big-fast strategy and whether their business model was sound. If Amazon survives, it will be because it was able to shift its focus from sales volume to profitability.

## Bigger Is Often Not Better: The Republic Airlines Case

Republic Airlines, which resulted from the merger of North Central Airlines with Southern Airways in 1979 and incorporated Hughes Airwest in 1980, provides a classic example of a company almost destroyed by a sales-volume orientation.[2] In 1983, Republic was the nation's sixth largest passenger carrier, serving most of America's metropolitan areas and many intermediate-sized cities. Republic's routes reached from Seattle/Tacoma to Miami, from San Diego to Boston and Montreal (but not to Hawaii or Alaska). It carried 17.8 million passengers a total of 9.7 billion passenger miles in 1983, an average of 545 miles per passenger. And it lost about $111 million in the process.

The airline business, like most transportation businesses, is characterized by high fixed costs. Most airlines have never been able to consistently earn a return on investment that exceeds their cost of capital. There are the high fixed costs of airplanes, baggage handling and other ground equipment, airport leases, signage, local sales and operating staffs, and administration. For an individual flight, even most of the operating expenses such as fuel (25 percent of revenues for Republic) and labor (37 percent of revenues) are fixed costs that will be incurred for each scheduled flight regardless of the number of passengers. True variable costs for food (2 percent), inflight service, ground service, and so on are virtually negligible.

A major element of fixed costs for Republic Airlines was the debt burden incurred as a result of the mergers (with current debt service equal to about 6 percent of total revenues). Their fixed costs per flight were also significantly above industry norms because their aircraft, including the world's largest fleet of DC-9s, were old and inefficient, their experienced labor force earned above average wages, and their route structure was dominated by relatively short flight segments.

These conditions created a perfect setting for the trap of a volume orientation. Management focused on filling the seats and increasing the number of cities served. More cities served meant more passengers being funneled through Republic's four hubs in Minneapolis-St. Paul, Detroit, Memphis, and Phoenix onto out-going flights. In none of these hubs did Republic enjoy a dominant market position in either number of flights or passenger preference. Frequent fliers who used Republic often did so because they had to, given their originating cities and destinations, not because they wanted to. Republic's in-flight personnel were regarded as friendly and helpful but the airplanes were described as old, dirty, and poorly decorated.

Informed passengers knew that Republic was struggling for survival in the unfriendly skies created by deregulation of the industry and were worried.

An estimated 130 airlines were certified to carry passengers in the United States in 1984, many of them in weak financial condition. In addition to the familiar transcontinental carriers (American, United, and TWA) and the large regional airlines that had tended to fly north-south routes extending into the Caribbean and Latin America (Braniff, Eastern, and Delta) or east-west routes extending to international destinations in Europe and Asia (Northwest Orient and Continental), there were the start-up, low-cost, low-service airlines (People Express, Southwest, Midway, and others), as well as the commuters. Large regional carriers like U.S. Airways, Piedmont, and Western were also a major competitive factor. Republic's extensive route structure of more than 150 cities meant that it competed with all of them! (Note how few of the airlines mentioned have survived; only one of the survivors, Southwest, has successfully followed a low-price strategy and they have done so by selecting markets to serve *very* carefully!)

How to compete? Republic had no jumbo jets, few international destinations (Montreal in Canada, Mazatlan and Puerto Vallarta in Mexico, and Grand Cayman in the West Indies), and a reputation for unreliable schedules. The answer, given the lack of differentiation in its product offering, seemed obvious to Republic: price and promotion. Initially, Republic had tried to hold out against the low-fare competitors and saw its load factor (percentage of seats filled on the average flight) fall to just above 50 percent, which was below the breakeven level. Republic then decided to respond with aggressive pricing. It was committed to a "Big Airline" strategy, competing in the national market against the transcontinental carriers, the large regionals, and the new low-cost airlines as well. So Republic lowered its fares to attract passengers and continued to expand the route structure.

Advertising carried the headline "What's Bigger Than 140 Cities and Flies" and featured the tag line "Nobody Serves Our Republic Like Republic." Promotions aimed at infrequent pleasure travelers included a "Kids Fly Free" promotion with Chex cereals and a two-for-one "Pair Fare." Such promotions produced no incremental revenue on the nonfare paying passengers but were assumed to attract fliers who otherwise would not have flown. These revenues, it was assumed, were purely incremental revenue that would not have been earned without the promotion. In the meantime, it was obvious that some business travelers were taking advantage of the new low fares. Republic succeeded in increasing its load factor to well over 55 percent. It also increased its losses. Republic had a fundamentally flawed business model: nonexistent market segmentation and targeting, weak value proposition, no value capture strategy, and no strategic partnering with other airlines to serve markets beyond its own routes.

For Republic's average flight distance of 545 miles, the average passenger paid only $77.99. While Republic's costs were an estimated 15.9 cents per revenue passenger mile, its revenues were about 14.3 cents. Thus, they were losing 1.6 cents for every revenue passenger mile flown. That is bad enough for a small airline. For a Big Airline, which is what Republic aspired to be, flying 9.7 billion passenger miles per year, that is a disaster. (Republic's cargo revenues of about $125 million per year during this period, all of which are truly "incremental" in an aircraft committed to passenger travel, helped to mitigate the financial disaster, reducing the loss on operations to about $31 million, as did the sale of tax benefits and a small amount of interest and nonoperating income. Interest expense of $98 million brought the total loss to $111 million in 1983.) It was a classic case of the old saw, "We lose money on every unit we sell but we hope to make it up on volume." It would be funnier if it wasn't so true. The engine of sales volume multiplies the consequences of inefficiency very rapidly.

## New Focus at Republic

Fortunately, new management was able to get on top of the situation and reverse Republic's fortunes, with the help of a new advertising agency, Dancer Fitzgerald Sample. After negotiating a new labor agreement that reduced labor costs by about 15 percent, the new Chief Executive Officer, Stephen Wolf (who would subsequently work a similar turnaround at Flying Tiger, the freight airline, and then move on to United Airlines and from there to U.S. Airways), retrenched by cutting back the number of cities served to less than 100 and concentrating aircraft on stronger schedules out of the major hubs. The solution was found in market segmentation, targeting, and positioning.

Republic offered a number of new services aimed at the business traveler, especially the younger traveler who did not currently have a strong preference for another airline, in those markets where Republic had the advantage of service frequency and an established market position. Often, these were markets that had not attracted competition from the major national carriers—cities like Omaha, Nebraska; Rochester, New York; and Madison, Wisconsin. Instead of presenting itself as a big airline, Republic was repositioned as a regional carrier, national in scope, with service through efficient, less congested hubs. This positioning turned these less glamorous hub cities into a competitive advantage for Republic. Services for business travelers included a more attractive frequent flyer program, airport lounges, a $15 upgrade to first-class cabin, and a tie-in with Pan American Airlines that offered generous international travel awards for frequent-flier mileage.

The value proposition for the business traveler was captured in the new marketing communications program that featured "Perks" for the frequent flier. Republic's advertising carried the tag line "We Make You Feel Like Flying," which emphasized the airline's commitment to providing services for the business traveler, replacing the old "Nobody Serves Our Republic Like Republic." Republic was focused on the frequent business traveler and on those cities where it could achieve some competitive superiority in terms of schedules and service. Instead of chasing after the pleasure traveler who was interested primarily in price and who could choose when, where, and how to travel based on finding the lowest fares, Republic tailored its product offering and communications for the business traveler who had to travel to a certain place at a certain time and often had little or no discretion except, perhaps, in the choice of airline.

Republic returned to profitability it 1984. In 1985, it merged with Northwest Airlines that was headquartered, like Republic, in Minneapolis-St. Paul. The purchase price was about $884 million and the buyer acquired debt of over $600 million. From a balance sheet where shareholder's equity had declined to something around $1 million or less in 1983, the merger placed a value on Republic of almost $1.5 billion, which may have been excessive but which shows the value of a successful repositioning based on market segmentation and targeting. By focusing on the young business traveler in underserved secondary and regional markets, Republic was able to define a profitable market niche where its smaller aircraft, frequent flight schedules, and friendly cabin personnel, along with the many new services for business travelers, were able to deliver superior value.

## SEGMENTING THE MARKET AND TARGETING CUSTOMERS

The process of choosing customers begins with market segmentation. Market segmentation is both an analytical and a creative process, requiring the collection and analysis of data about the potential market and the imaginative interpretation of those data by the marketing manager. The essence of market segmentation is to break a large market into smaller pieces, each segment consisting of customers who are similar to one another in ways important to the marketer such as their needs, preferences, buying habits, usage patterns, or media exposure. Customers within a given market segment should be similar in their response to the company's product offerings and/or communications. This similarity in response is the key to market segmentation and response should be related to one or more customer characteristics that can be observed and measured.

Customers *within* a given market segment should be as *similar* to one another as possible on these important characteristics; customers in different market segments should be as *different* from one another as possible. (Statistically, this means minimizing within-group variance and maximizing among-group variance.) The customer characteristics chosen as the basis for market segmentation can be demographic (age, income, occupation, family status, type or place of residence) or psychographic (self-concept, lifestyle, risk-aversion, buying decision process). Psychographic segments are often hard to develop, however, because it is difficult to observe and measure such characteristics unless they can be related to more observable attributes such as age or place of residence.

Benefit segmentation is based on the fact that different customers are looking for different sets of benefits from the same product, although this also requires matching up some characteristics of the customer with these benefit sets. For example, benefit segments for toothpaste might be based on the relative importance the consumer places on cavity prevention, taste, or whitening. These preferences are likely to be related to the presence of children in the household and the age and marital status of the consumer. Income, education, and occupation may also be usefully correlated with these benefit preferences, making benefit segmentation feasible and operational. Often, however, benefit segments are hard to define in operational terms.

Once the company has identified distinct segments, it has the choice of trying to serve one, some, or all of those segments. In *concentrated marketing,* the company sells to one or a few segments, leaving the other segments to competition. In *differentiated marketing,* the company develops distinct product offerings and communications for each chosen segment and tries to serve two or more of them, perhaps even the total market, but in a differentiated fashion. *Undifferentiated* marketing, selling the same thing the same way everywhere, brings us back to a sales volume orientation. On the other hand, concentrated marketing can be a deathtrap if the segment is shrinking and customers are migrating into other segments as their needs change and their definition of value evolves.

Republic Airlines moved from undifferentiated marketing back to concentrated marketing. By focusing in their regional markets on frequent business travelers ages 25 to 44 who did not have a strong preference for another airline, Republic was matching up its limited resources with a relatively underserved portion of the total market.

The essence of market segmentation and targeting is in the willingness to *not* serve certain customers. It requires the ability to "just say no," to walk away from business that might be available. The ability to turn down business is not part of the genetic makeup of many businesspeople, especially salespeople. The new management at Republic was willing to let competitors have those potential customers who wanted very low fares, who were traveling strictly for pleasure and on a flexible schedule, who wanted to fly on wide-body aircraft to attractive foreign destinations. Republic made a conscious choice not to compete aggressively in the major markets such as New York, Atlanta, Dallas, Los Angeles, Miami, and Chicago, and not to try to switch the preferences of those business travelers who participated in the frequent flyer programs of American, United, Delta, Northwest, and the rest. Some of those markets were dominated by a single, large competitor whereas others were fiercely competitive with many carriers, including the low-cost operators. Republic management realized it did not have the skills and resources to compete successfully in those markets.

## Market Segmentation and Product Differentiation

Market segmentation and product differentiation are related but distinct concepts. Sometimes they are used interchangeably, which is incorrect and has led to some confusion.

Over the years, the term *product differentiation* has been used to mean three very different things. In the first instance, it means offering products with features different from those of more standardized competitive offerings. The augmented product, defined in Chapter 3, is the expected product plus additional features and services that differentiate it from competition. For example, manufacturers of commodity chemicals differentiate their products with unique services that are offered as part of the purchase price, including special packaging, transportation options, specialized applications assistance, and more. Banks differentiate their services on the basis of their more convenient locations and more helpful personnel.

The second meaning of product differentiation is related more closely to market segmentation. In this usage, product differentiation refers to the practice of offering somewhat different products for different market segments. Thus, Coca-Cola offers Coke Classic, Coke II, Diet Coke, Caffeine-Free Coke, Tab, Mr. Pibb, and many noncola soft drinks including the Sprite and Fanta brands. Globally, Coca-Cola Company owns hundreds of brands in the beverage category. Likewise, Mercedes-Benz offers a large range of models from the lowest priced C-Class up through the somewhat larger and more expensive E-Class, to the very expensive luxury sedans in the S-Class, along with the SL roadsters and M-Class sport utility vehicles, continuously adding new models in each price range. Each of these products has unique features and is aimed at a distinct market segment.

The third meaning of product differentiation is the use of communication tools, especially advertising, to make claims intended to infuse a product or service with value that is not obviously part of the service or physical product itself. For example, Budweiser beer is promoted as "Beechwood Aged," Ford promises that "Quality Is Job 1," Connecticut is "The State That Thinks Like a Business," Avis "Try Harder" and Fidelity Investments offers "Common Sense. Uncommon Results." We often talk about using advertising to create a "brand image" that differentiates the product from competitors in the mind of the customer.

Some authors have confused market segmentation with product differentiation or have mistakenly presented them as competing marketing strategies.[3] It is not a question of either market segmentation or product differentiation; market segmentation is the basis for product differentiation. Market segmentation is the strategy of conceptually and statistically identifying different market segments with different characteristics—needs, wants, preferences, buying habits, usage patterns, communication exposure, or whatever. Product differentiation is the strategy and tactics of offering products with distinctive characteristics—based either on product design and engineering, service features, or communications—to these distinct market segments.

Some authors have used the term product differentiation strictly in the third sense, as a communication strategy, and have presented it as a distinct alternative to market segmentation. This distinction is inherently confusing and it implies, incorrectly, that the firm has the choice of either doing "real" market segmentation and physically differentiating products for each defined segment, or using communication to do the job. Seldom, if ever, is that a clear strategic choice for a given product. Some of these authors also imply that there is something bogus and misleading about using communication to create a distinct brand image when there are minimal product differences. There is great value in a strong brand image for both the customer and the marketer, whether that brand is IBM, Budweiser, AOL, Mercedes Benz, or Sony. The discussion of branding continues in the context of positioning and developing the value proposition.

# MARKET TARGETING: SELECTING MARKET SEGMENTS

Market targeting, illustrated by the Republic Airlines' focus on young business travelers, is the process of selecting those market segments that the company wishes to serve. It is the most important element in developing a business strategy, the heavy half of the statement of product/market scope. It is the first part of the business model and the initial step in developing the value proposition.

The selection of target markets is a commitment of resources to delivering superior value to a specific set of customers. Who are those customers? How do we decide which set of customers to commit to? It is helpful to recall that the failure of the original marketing concept to address this specific issue—How does the firm decide which customers to try to satisfy?—was one of the major criticisms that diminished its acceptance and was a weakness addressed by the early forms of strategic planning. No firm has the capability to satisfy all the needs of all potential customers. Recognition of this basic truth is at the heart of market targeting.

For a new business, the entrepreneur's commitment could begin with the perceived needs of a set of potential clients or customers. Thus, a developer of educational software may begin, before there is a product, with a commitment to enhancing the learning of elementary school children in grades 1–4. More than one visionary has started a business or a not-for-profit undertaking because of a basic commitment to solve a particular problem.

More frequently, the vision of a business opportunity has its origins in technology—new or old, high or low—that creates the possibility for solving a problem better, for delivering superior value. Quite often the business begins with a new product idea before there is a good sense of the scope and characteristics of the potential market. The entrepreneur or company believes that the new product concept has some inherent superiority based on the firm's superior knowledge, skills, and other resources.

Underlying the new product idea is, implicitly, the concept of distinctive competence, an idea developed in Chapter 3. The commitment to develop and maintain one or more distinctive competences must be made as specific as possible. The first and perhaps the most difficult step is to define the distinctive competence. What is it that the company is really good at? What does it do, or what can it potentially do, better than anyone else in the world? The answer must go deeper than the current product form and identify the knowledge-based competences that will sustain the business.

Assuming that an answer to that question is forthcoming, then the even more important question might be phrased simply as "Who cares?" or "Who needs it?" In Chapter 3, the essential point was made that a distinctive competence cannot be defined except in the context of a market target. A distinctive competence is defined by the customer's perception of value. Thus, potential customers must value the knowledge and skill that is the basis for a distinctive competence before it becomes meaningful. How does it deliver perceived superior value to customers, in their terms? What markets does it provide access to? Having defined those potential markets and applications, the analyst must go back and look at the assumed or hypothetical distinctive competence and its related new product idea more carefully. For these specific customers, what are the purported benefits, and limitations, in the customer's product use system compared with alternative products and substitutes?

## POSITIONING: COMMUNICATING VALUE TO THE CUSTOMER

Positioning is the development of the value proposition, the statement of how the firm proposes to deliver superior value to customers. Positioning is the communication about the product, not the product itself. This is made clear by the classic definition of positioning by the authors who popularized the term, Al Ries and Jack Trout:

> Positioning starts with a product. A piece of merchandise, a service, a company, an institution, or even a person. Perhaps yourself.
>
> But positioning is not what you do to a product. Positioning is what you do to the mind of the prospect. That is, you position the product in the mind of the prospect.
>
> So it's incorrect to call the concept "product positioning." You're not really doing something to the product itself.[4]

### Developing a Positioning Statement— The Value Proposition

Positioning is strategic decision making—the analytical, conceptual, and creative processes that lead to the positioning statement. The positioning statement, or what I prefer to call the value proposition, puts the concept into words and performs two critically important functions:

1. It becomes the selling proposition to potential customers, the reason why they should do business with the company rather than its competitors.
2. It communicates to the whole organization a sense of specific purpose and direction, coordinating their efforts toward the common purpose of creating a satisfied customer.

I prefer to call this verbal statement the value proposition for three reasons: (1) It focuses on customer value and relates positioning to the value-delivery concept of strategy. (2) It goes beyond the somewhat limited notion that positioning is based solely on communication, which is a narrow definition of product differentiation as discussed earlier. I don't disagree with Ries and Trout when they say that positioning is based on communication; the point of using the phrase "the value proposition" is that the benefits and attributes featured in the communication must have their roots in the company's resources, knowledge, and skills if they are to be a source of long-term, sustainable competitive advantage. (3) The positioning statement, as the phrase is commonly used, is aimed solely at customers. The value proposition is equally important for the organization that delivers the product. It keeps everyone in the value-delivery sequence focused on the customer. An important objective of the new Republic Airlines advertising campaign, for example, was to build organization morale and to refocus service personnel on the needs of the business traveler.

Positioning and the development of the value proposition must be based on an assessment of the product offering and of the firm's distinctive competences *relative to competitors*. This is inherent in the notion that the customer defines value. The customer defines value by comparing the company's product offering with those of competitors in the context of his or her own needs, preferences, buying patterns, and use system. Thus, positioning is always done "relative to competitors." Ries and Trout pointed out that the phrase "product positioning" was incorrect; they might also have pointed out that positioning "relative to competitors" is redundant.

At the same time, it is helpful to look at competitors' positioning as part of the exercise of developing the firm's own positioning and its value proposition. For example, Republic Airlines specifically considered a positioning based on their consumer research finding that Republic's flight personnel were friendly and helpful. That positioning was rejected, however, because United's "Friendly Skies" campaign had already preempted the concept of friendliness as part of its positioning. Market pioneers often have the opportunity to protect their market positions based on preemptive communication.

## Positioning: Who? What? Why?

The value proposition, or the positioning statement, has three parts:

1. *Who* is the target customer? We have already discussed the importance of defining the target customer as the first order of business.
2. *What* are we selling? The "What?" part of the value proposition is the most basic, most challenging, and most interesting part of the problem—specifying the product concept, exactly what it is that we are selling. This may be the most difficult part of the development of the positioning statement or value proposition. It must be defined from the point of view of the customer. It also defines the competition. We cannot get a clear definition of the relevant competitors until we know what we are selling.
3. *Why* should the customer buy it? The "Why?" part of the positioning statement is the familiar problem of defining clearly the benefits for the customer, the reasons our product is better than competitors' offerings.

Going back to the "What are we selling?" question, the opportunity for creative definition of a product concept is a great opportunity to redefine the competitive ground rules, even to create entirely new markets. Federal Express did not present itself as another air freight forwarder. Rather, it was an overnight delivery system for small packages and information. Tylenol wasn't just another pain reliever; it was a strong pain reliever for people who were worried about the negative side effects of taking aspirin.

The Ford Mustang has been one of the most durable models in the history of the automobile industry and it provides an excellent example of getting the *What* right. The original concept for the car featured its Italian styling and American origins. It wasn't even called Mustang but "Torino by Ford—the brand-new import from Detroit." It was aimed at a younger customer who wanted an economical, yet high-performance "sports car" vehicle. However, consumer research on the product concept demonstrated that the potential market was much larger. It was renamed the Mustang and positioned as an inexpensive sporty personal vehicle offering economy and versatility (through availability of a wide range of options for engines, transmissions, hard and soft tops, seats, wheels, upholstery, etc.).[5] The appeal of the initial Italian sports car positioning would have been much more limited.

## Sound Positioning Creates Brand Equity

The concept of brand equity has become popular in recent years, replacing the older concepts of brand image and brand loyalty. A strong brand is a major business asset. It typically represents the investment of millions of dollars in product development, advertising, sales promotion, after-sale service, and reseller support. The returns on those investments are earned over a period of many years. It is interesting to note, for example, dominant market shares in ready-to-eat cereals are still held by three of the oldest brands—Kellogg's Corn Flakes, Wheaties, and Cheerios. Other century-old brands that have retained market leadership positions include Campbells, Ford, Gillette, Green Giant, John Deere, and Steinway.

While the term *brand equity* often refers to the brand as a business asset, viewed from the perspective of the firm and its owners, the real meaning of brand equity resides in the mind of the customer. It is the difference in the value of the product perceived by the customer with the brand and without it. One authority prefers the term "customer-based brand equity" to make this important point.[6] Brand equity is based on the customer's knowledge of, and feelings for, the brand—her ability to recognize it, to recall having seen it before, to associate it with various messages, attributes, benefits, and experiences, and to use this knowledge as the basis for decision making. In theoretical terms, there is a strong cognitive component to the concept of brand equity as well as a strong behavioral predisposition. These positive associations and predispositions in the mind of the consumer result in a more favorable response to the firm's marketing efforts for the brand, giving it a better return on its marketing investments.[7]

Thus, the concept of brand equity goes beyond the old concepts of brand image and brand loyalty. Brand image referred strictly to the consumer's perceptions, without recognizing the brand's inherent strategic value. Brand equity incorporates the fundamental notion of the brand as a business asset. Brand loyalty referred to a not-so-easily defined notion of repeat purchasing—variously measured as proportion of product category purchases, probability of purchasing the brand on the next purchase, total brand units purchased by a consumer during a given period, and so on. Brand loyalty is a rather static concept when defined this way and doesn't help to consider the possibility of brand extensions—applying the brand to new products of the same or related type.

A strong brand is very close to a distinctive competence, but these are not the same thing. The distinctive competences are the underlying knowledge and skills on which the firm develops its brand equity. These competences might include the underlying technical knowledge, for example, expertise in electronics engineering and production, as well as advertising and promotion skills that led to the successful development of the Sony brand of consumer electronics.

The brand name becomes part of the definition of quality by the customer as it creates a set of expectations for product performance. A strong brand creates high expectations. Consumers develop amazingly strong imagery around a brand name. You will never see a real human model presented as Betty Crocker, the General Mills brand symbol. General Mills learned that no woman, not even a woman's voice or hands, could be convincingly presented as the "real" Betty Crocker. None could fit the consumer's strong image of Betty Crocker.

Procter & Gamble (P&G) was reminded of the strength of customer-defined brand equity when it changed Prell shampoo from a clear green gel to a reformulated blue variety that included a hair conditioner. As Jack Trout, the authority on positioning, commented: "Consumers thought Prell was the green stuff. The guys at P&G said, 'No, it's blue.' Challenging customer perceptions is very tricky, and is generally a mistake." Loyal consumers rebelled at the change and made their voice heard. Soon, new advertising appeared with the headline "Green is back! The original formula you've always loved." Loyal customers had a strong definition of value in their minds that did not include conditioners and the changed color. The new blue product was continued but appealed to a new market segment.[8]

## The Power of Branding

It can be argued that branding is the most powerful form of product differentiation from a competitive standpoint because of the virtual impossibility of a competitor's duplicating it. Once they put major advertising dollars behind it, United Airlines had a preemptive claim on "The Friendly Skies." Nike owns "the swoosh" symbol and the phrase "Just Do It." Only Avis can "Try Harder." An established brand positioning cannot be copied except to the benefit of the original owner. Product formulations and designs can be much more easily copied than branding strategies. Pepsi-Cola and BMW can compete with Coca-Cola and Mercedes-Benz by offering a parallel range of products based on physical product characteristics but they cannot hope to compete based on the same brand images. Rather, they must make the huge promotional investments necessary to create distinct brand images for their own products and pursue their own distinct market segmentation strategies. Thus, Pepsi advertising creates a more youthful brand image and BMW is presented as a sporty performance sedan.

As noted in the discussion of differentiation, the values inherent in a strong brand image are often based on the communication strategy surrounding the brand as much as on the physical characteristics that have been built into the product. IBM may be the best example of a brand image based heavily on communication, in this instance not only advertising but also the professionalism of its salesforce and all supporting communications about the company and its products and services. IBM managers would be the first to tell you that their excellent products were often no better technically than those of their best competitors, but what really made the difference in the mind of the customer was the image of IBM as the world leader in computing and its supportive relationship with every customer. After stumbling somewhat in the fiercely competitive markets of the 1980s and early 1990s, IBM has regained its distinction as a customer-oriented solutions provider, positioning itself as "People who get it. People who get IT done."

## Turning the Brand into a Strategic Asset

Not all brands are winners. Developing brand equity is a difficult, and often expensive, strategic process. According to Kevin Lane Keller,[9] there are four steps in building customer-based brand equity:

1. Creating *brand identity*—How do we want to be known to our target customers?
2. Developing *brand meaning*—What value proposition do we want customers to associate with our product?
3. Defining desired *brand responses*—What do we want target customers to think, feel, and do about our product offering?
4. Defining desired *brand relationships*—What type of association is desired with target customers?

He goes on to explain that *brand identity* has two components: *brand awareness* and *brand salience*. Brand awareness is the customer's ability to recall and recognize. Brand salience relates to how easily the customer will recall the brand under various circumstances. Awareness is obviously the first requirement for brand equity. A highly salient brand will have both depth and breadth of brand awareness so it can be recalled easily and in many different purchase and use situations. Soft drink brands are a good example of highly salient brands.

*Brand meaning* is the embodiment of the value proposition—the meaning associated with the brand in the customer's mind, the brand image. Brand meaning also has two dimensions: *brand performance* and *brand image.* Brand performance concerns how well the product works and provides problem solution and satisfaction. Brand image relates to the less tangible and more abstract psychological and social meanings associated with the brand. Keller details five aspects of brand performance:

1. Primary characteristics and supplementary features.
2. Product reliability, durability, and serviceability.
3. Service quality—effectiveness, efficiency, and empathy.
4. Style and design.
5. Price.

And four dimensions of brand imagery:

1. The profile of the typical user.
2. Purchase and usage situations.
3. Personality and values associated with the brand, such as sincerity, excitement, competence, and ruggedness.
4. History, heritage, and experience.

Specifying the *brand responses* desired is a key part of implementing the business model by tying the brand's value proposition and positioning back to the firm's strategic objectives. Desired responses include both knowledge and feelings. The marketer needs to convey meanings associated with quality, credibility and trust, actual evaluation of brand performance, and superior performance on dimensions important to the target customer's usage situation. It is also important to be explicit about how the brand is to be regarded psychologically and socially. For example, the customer may be favorably impressed by the performance characteristics of the BMW 7 Series but even more concerned about how various people will react to his owning and driving this car.

*Brand relationships* have become increasingly important as more product and service categories have redefined competition around relationship versus transactional marketing. *Brand development* requires being explicit about the desired relationship. The dimensions of a brand relationship include purchasing loyalty, attitudinal attachment, a sense of community, and active engagement with the brand. Product categories such as beverages and cosmetics engender intense loyalty and repeat purchases. The strength of attitudinal attachments may vary significantly across segments within a given product category. Many people have strong attitudinal attachments to their car stereo equipment, for example, while others do not. A sense of community may be a key benefit for purchasers of such brands as Harley-Davidson and Saturn. Active engagement with the brand is expressed in the customer's commitment of time, money, and effort in developing the brand relationship even after the brand has been purchased, such as by visiting the brand Web site and chat rooms. For industrial customers, the relationship may be strictly transactional, or one of ongoing buying commitment, or a strong strategic partnership integrating the product into the customer's business. The choice of the type of relationship desired with the customer will be examined in greater depth in the following chapter.

Successful brand development will ensure that, over time, the firm derives increased returns from its investments in innovation, business development, and marketing communications. The brand provides leverage on all of the firm's marketing expenditures. Investors are willing to pay premium prices for the shares of companies with strong brands because the brands enhance the future earnings stream of the business. While brand equity exists fundamentally in the mind of the customer, it also can pay off in enhanced value for the firm. Customer value translates finally into shareholder value.

## DEVELOPING THE PRODUCT OFFERING

Ultimately, the value proposition must be delivered by the product offering itself. Under the new marketing concept, the product offering flows from the value proposition, not *vice versa*. The value proposition establishes the strategic direction of the firm. It is based on the selection of markets and customers to be served and a commitment to develop and maintain the distinctive competences necessary to deliver superior value to those customers. The product offering is a variable, to be tailored to the needs and desires, preferences and buying habits of the chosen market target. Over time, the product offering must change as customer needs and preferences change. It is the value proposition that becomes the guiding star for continuous innovation in the pursuit of improved solutions to customer problems.

Getting from the value proposition to the actual product offering is a far from simple task. While the core or generic product may be the starting point for developing the business, it is only the beginning. The next step is to understand the expected product, what it is the customer expects to be offered in terms of product performance, features, and service. This is the basis on which the customer will judge the quality of the product offering and be satisfied or dissatisfied. We can make a distinction between product features, those physical and service aspects that are part of the basic product offering, and additional services that add to the value of the product offering by enhancing the ease and utility of ordering, taking delivery, storing, using, and disposing of the product. This dichotomy is not a clear distinction because of the ambiguous nature of the concept of a service, but we will try to make it understandable.

Before returning to the consideration of product features and services as part of the product offering, two strategic issues in developing the product offering need consideration. First, there is the problem of defining what is required for a complete product offering. Second, there is need to define the real customer for the product, the person or organization who will benefit most from the new product's capabilities, among all of the interacting parties in the product delivery and use system.

## Marketing an Incomplete Product: Why the Gould 4800 Failed

Failure to look at the product from the customer's viewpoint can result in going to market with an incomplete product. It is amazing how frequently this occurs. A classic illustration is provided by the Gould 4800, introduced in 1969 by the Graphics Division of Gould Incorporated as a key part of its drive to become an electronics company.[10]

The Gould 4800 was the first electrostatic, nonimpact printer developed for the computer. It had the remarkable ability to print up to 4800 86-character lines per minute, the equivalent of 60 sheets of 8½ by 11 inch paper, and it was very quiet. It also had excellent graphic output and plotting capability. When shown at an industry trade show, it solicited extremely positive feedback from those who saw it as a major technical breakthrough. Here was a printing device with the potential to bridge the huge gap between the incredibly fast calculation speeds of a computer and the archaically slow printing speeds of the old inked-ribbon impact printers, the fastest of which operated at only one-fourth the speed of the Gould 4800.

Several months later, not a single order had been received. Slowly, management at the Graphics Division of Gould Incorporated began to realize that they had gone to market with an incomplete product.

The Gould 4800 required a special coated paper, and Gould had built a pilot paper-coating machine to provide the necessary paper supply. Parts for building a larger machine were on order. Unfortunately, the paper was $8\frac{1}{2}$ inches wide whereas standard computer printer paper was $14\frac{7}{8}$ inches wide and 11 inches high. The coated paper came in rolls, not sheets, and there was no provision for a device to cut the paper into page-size sheets of standard $8\frac{1}{2}$ by 11 inch office size. Neither could the machine take preprinted forms or make multiple copies. To make matters worse, each sheet of paper cut to this size would cost \$.042 compared with the price for a standard 11 by $14\frac{7}{8}$ inch computer sheet of only \$.0014, 30 times more expensive. Finally, and perhaps most basically, Gould had developed none of the communications software necessary for connecting the printer to the computer. The apparent assumption was that the customers would be so excited about the performance and potential of this new technology that they would be willing to incur the expense of writing the software themselves or would put pressure on their computer vendors to do the necessary development. The latter outcome was highly unlikely because the major computer manufacturers also had their own printers for sale.

Although it isn't directly related to the central point about the dangers of going to market with an incomplete product, one other aspect of the Gould 4800 must be noted: Very few potential customers needed a machine that could print that fast. A machine with that printing speed needs constant attention just to take away the output. A roll of paper would be used up and need to be replaced every few minutes. It turned out that the really salable features of the device, which found a very limited market, were its noiseless operation, making it attractive for applications like brokerage houses, and its graphic plotting capability, which found use in process control applications.

The Gould 4800 is perhaps an extreme illustration, but not uncommon, and offers a useful lesson. The president of Gould observed to me some years later that the principal contribution of the Gould 4800 had been as a training ground for several young MBAs who had been given the assignment, as part of their career development, of trying to turn it into a profitable business. It is a good example of technology-driven marketing as opposed to market-driven technology.

There are many other examples of incomplete products that went to market, such as raw materials without any provision for new product formulations or production processes, medical diagnostic technology without the necessary instrumentation, gardening equipment sold direct to consumers without any provision for repair service or replacement parts, and the Christmas nightmare of the unassembled toy with no assembly instructions!

## The Importance of Finding the Real Customer: Why Amicon's New Technology Went Nowhere

A customer is someone or some organization who is willing and able to pay for the benefits delivered by the product. The identity of the customer is often far from obvious, especially when the value chain and marketing channel include many actors, some of whom are threatened by the new product and others of whom potentially can profit from it, depending on the arrangements that are negotiated for bringing the product to market. The actors in the marketing channel interact with and depend upon one another in ways that determine the value of the new product for each of them, especially if it disrupts those established relationships and ways of doing business.

Incomplete products result from a failure to understand how the customer will obtain and use them and the demands that the product will make on the customer's present capabilities and relationships. At one level, the problem is simply the need to understand the limitations inherent in the customer's knowledge level and use system. Few customers will be as technically sophisticated as the product inventor and developer. At another level, the challenge is to understand all of the transactions, technologies, and economic actors in the value chain as the product moves from raw material through fabrication and assembly to incorporation into product systems that ultimately get used in some other system of production and consumption by the ultimate users. The relationships among all of the actors in the value-delivery system must be carefully considered in developing the product offering and its positioning.

Another case study illustrates this problem well. Amicon Corporation[11] owned the patent for a device incorporating a new membrane-based microfiltration technology with a specific application in human blood collection. In 1978, it was in the sixth year of the 17-year life of its patent and still did not have a product ready for the marketplace. The benefits of the new technology included the ability to return blood directly to the donor, in a continuous filtration operation, after the blood plasma had been removed for further processing. The procedure required less time than the old batch-collection process. It also allowed paid donors to contribute more frequently and it had the potential to increase the total supply of blood plasma. Costs compared favorably with the old batch-collection and batch-processing technologies.

The new process was also much safer because it assured that the donor would receive his or her own blood. Under the old batch process, blood was taken from the donor, centrifuged to remove the plasma, and then returned to the donor. There was a small but real chance of a mix-up. If the donor received another person's blood in return, the result could be fatal. The ultimate beneficiaries of the new technology, at least potentially, were blood recipients who would have an assured supply because of greater availability, the American Red Cross and hospitals who needed the blood supply, and donors who would have less time commitment and greater safety.

The stumbling block was the complexity of the blood collection system in the United States. There are both commercial collection centers and non-commercial, nonprofit agencies, especially hospitals and the American Red Cross. National companies own and operate the commercial blood-collection centers, supply the disposable products (catheters, tubing, storage vessels, and anticlotting chemicals assembled into kits) used in the batch-collection process, and process the blood plasma into blood-plasma fractions. While there may be temporary shortages of blood of a given type in a specific geographic area, the amazing fact is that the blood supply is virtually always adequate to meet the requirements of those who need it. This brings us back to a basic question in market targeting, positioning, and the value proposition: Who needs it? In this case, the problem is to determine who in the total product delivery and use system will benefit most from the new technology and, equally important, who is most threatened by it.

Another way of stating the problem is the need to understand how each of the interacting firms and organizations makes money. What is their business model, their strategy for profitability? The commercial blood-collection centers proved to have little interest in the new technology because it increased their costs and could potentially lower their revenues by increasing the supply of blood and thus reducing its market price. Also, the new technology would increase their costs. This was especially a problem for the commercial centers owned by those firms who also sold the disposable supplies. The parties with the most to gain included the donors and blood recipients, neither of whom would be a significant factor because they would not directly purchase the product/service. In the strict sense, they were not potential customers because they did not have the ability to specify or purchase the product—the blood-collection technology.

The American Red Cross was a potential beneficiary of the increased availability and lower cost of blood plasma. (Even nonprofits have to make money and worry about both their costs and their revenues.) The Red Cross had recently built a new plasma-fractionating plant in collaboration with one of the major manufacturers of disposables who was also in the blood-fractionating business. The new Amicon technology could substantially lower costs to the Red Cross of blood collection but it also faced a major investment in new product development to bring the new technology into being, as there was still no physical product incorporating the Amicon microfiltration process. Somebody still needed to develop the devices that would collect the blood and the instruments that would monitor the process. This provided a potential profit opportunity for the disposables suppliers, especially the one who had formed a strategic alliance with the Red Cross on the fractionating plant.

Once again, the Amicon example shows the need to develop a complete product offering before a new technology has economic value. It also illustrates the complexity of the product use and delivery systems that must be understood to develop a product offering that truly provides superior value to customers. Defining customers is not a simple proposition. In this instance, the actual customers for the technology, those who were willing and able to pay for it, were not those who were the ultimate benefactors, the donors and blood recipients. Rather, the customers had to be economic actors in the value chain—processors, fabricators, and resellers who themselves had to add value before there was a complete product offering for the end user and who could see an opportunity to make money by helping to develop and promote the technology.

This set of costs and benefits, specific to each of the actors in the product delivery and use system, was critical to understanding the potential economic value of the new technology. The analysis of costs and benefits for each actor could have provided a basis for Amicon to select its potential partners and to negotiate licensing agreements and other terms and conditions. These contracts could have been the basis for a profitable business model that resulted in the development of instrumentation and collection devices that incorporated Amicon's membrane technology.

Developing the complete product offering requires knowing customers and their needs. Designing the product offering requires decisions about specific product features that address specific needs and wants and offer superior value in terms of how the customer will use the product and requires knowing the total use and delivery system. Service is usually a critical part of the product offering.

## Developing Product Features

Product features are part of the basic product/service offering. They are tangible and intangible aspects of the product that differentiate it from competitive offerings and add value for customers in the target market. They represent important "selling points" in the value proposition. For example, the Toshiba cardiovascular angiographic system is said to be superior to competition because it permits viewing multiple images simultaneously, its images can be enlarged, and it has computer-enhanced color to add increased information and diagnostic capability. Today, the standard product offering for many automobiles and light trucks includes a roadside assistance program as part of the purchase price, along with all of the accessories and amenities from air conditioning and power windows to heated seats and rear-window defrosters. Many product features that used to be additional cost options today come as part of the standard product offering, an example of how the augmented product of today becomes the expected product of tomorrow.

While continuous innovation and new product features can help sustain the lifecycle of many products, service as part of the product offering is increasingly likely to be even more important in determining customer preferences and satisfaction.

# SERVICE AS PART OF THE PRODUCT OFFERING

The objective of every marketing program should be not simply to satisfy the customer by meeting their expectations but to "delight" the customer by exceeding those expectations. As noted in the discussion of total quality management in Chapter 3, the best companies have defined quality not in terms of specific product features but as a way of doing business. The expected product includes essential service elements like instructions for use and a guarantee of quality. Likewise, the key to the augmented product, the complete differentiated product, is often additional service, perhaps in the form of product upgrades as they become available, troubleshooting assistance by way of telephone or the Internet, membership in a user's group, and follow-up mailings with special promotional offers. The potential product is more likely defined by the opportunity to add additional services rather than physical product features.

## Is Delighting the Customer Profitable?

It is essential that delighted customers be willing and able to pay for the costs of the extra value added by services. Such value enhancements are often intangible and hard to value until they are actually needed and used. Steps must be taken to be sure that the customer understands the extra value that is built into the service offering. Furthermore, it has been noted that delighting the customer can have the troublesome result of increasing the customer's expectations and leading to future dissatisfaction. Thus, customer delight has additional costs—the costs of providing the extra services, the costs of communicating those benefits, and the costs associated with meeting higher customer expectations in the future. How can a firm make money in this environment? Is there a profitable value capture strategy?

One analysis suggests that there can be a positive payoff because competitive firms may suffer even more from increasing customer expectations than those who create those heightened expectations, provided that the latter can win over those customers at a reasonable cost. It is also important that customers remember their earlier delightful experience on the next purchase occasion. Under these conditions, there may be a payoff from innovation in the form of enhanced market share as well as somewhat higher margins if the marketer has a sensible pricing strategy.[12] This finding is entirely consistent with the analysis of the relationship among quality, market share, and profitability presented in Chapter 2.

## Controlling Other Elements of the Value-Delivery Process

Beyond the product itself, its features and its bundled services, the product offering includes all aspects of the customer's interaction with the company and its representatives. The purchaser of a kitchen dishwasher makes an investment that she hopes will last for many years. Her "consideration set" of possible brands to purchase will be the result of acquiring information about those brands from advertising, word-of-mouth from family members and friends, displays in stores, catalogues, promotional mailings, and other sources. When she actually begins her shopping, however, the retail clerk becomes the critical source of information. The salesperson is part of the product offering. The clerk's approach to the prospective customer, including the quality of his or her product knowledge and attitude toward work, all become part of the customer's perception of the value of the brand. In a general sense, all products can be thought of as potential solutions to a problem. The salesperson determines the ability of the product/brand to solve the problem that she brings to the buying situation, both the purchase itself and the stream of benefits perceived to derive from the product over its lifetime.

The dishwasher customer may encounter several representatives of the company over time. At least two people will arrive to deliver and install the new appliance. What kind of an impression will they make? Even though they are the retailer's employees or independent contractors, they represent the dishwasher manufacturer and they are part of the total product offering. The consumer who has questions may call an 800 number, found in the owner's manual. How annoying is the company's call management system? How courteous and helpful is the person who finally comes on the line? She too is a representative of the company and part of the product offering. Then there is the service technician, always expected to be there when needed. All of these people define the augmented product, and their ability to meet or exceed customer expectations is the key to quality.

In the total scheme of things, customer satisfaction is usually influenced as much by these human interactions as by the technical specifications and fancy features of the product itself. If your new car develops a problem on your first long trip, that is bad enough. What really makes you angry, however, is the bad attitude of the service manager and mechanic you encounter when you pull off the interstate highway into the local dealer listed in your owner's manual. That is the defining moment as far as you are concerned. Your impression of the airlines you fly with is almost completely determined by your interactions with the airlines' employees—reservations clerks, baggage handlers, gate agents, cabin attendants, and the flight captain whose voice may be the only impression you have of him or her.

The quality of the service component of the product offering is a function of the care with which the company selects, trains, supervises, motivates, monitors, and rewards the service personnel. World-class service providers like Disney, Singapore Airlines, McDonald's, and United Parcel Service are distinguished by the tight, efficient systems they have for directing the efforts of their service personnel. They provide a model for all companies to emulate. The typical industrial parts manufacturer, for example, would do well to select, train, and manage telephone receptionists, order-entry clerks, credit personnel, customer service representatives, and anyone else who interacts with customers, with the same care as Disney. Only then will it have a complete product offering with a high probability of exceeding customer expectations.

Many companies have defined quality service in simple terms such as the number of times the telephone rings before it is answered. This has the advantage of being measurable and can be monitored and reported on a regular basis to those concerned. It is the kind of thing you do to win quality awards. Most customers, however, are much more likely to care about what they hear when the phone is answered. How many times have you heard:

"Your call is important to us. All of our representatives are currently serving other customers. Your call will be answered by the next available agent."

"Your call is being answered by an automated answering system. If you are calling to report a problem press 1; if you wish to place an order, press 2 . . ."

"Good morning. Please hold."

"The guy you need ta talk wid ain't here right now."?

So much for service. What you would really like to hear is:

"Thank you for calling Centricut. This is Linda. How can I help you?"

Some of the best direct marketers, like L.L. Bean and Land's End, have excellent, well-trained, carefully supervised people supported by state-of-the-art customer information systems. After a prompt, courteous answering of the call, the representative will state his or her name and ask for either the identification number on the label of the catalogue you received or, if that isn't available, your last name and zip code. Instantly, the customer service representative can bring up your purchase record on a computer screen, including recent orders, clothing sizes, and so on, and proceed with "Thank you, Mr. Webster. How can I help you today?" If you want to return merchandise, the representative can identify it in the purchase record and tell you how to return it. If you want to place a new order, that can be done quickly and your purchase record will be updated simultaneously. Your usual payment method is clearly indicated and you will be asked if you wish to use the same credit card. Once the call is completed, the updated customer information file becomes the basis for future mailings to you according to your indicated interests and purchase patterns and is available for immediate reference the next time you call.

Such sophisticated systems indicate what is possible in the realm of service as part of the product offering. Not just direct mail merchants but industrial manufacturers and distributors like Arrow Electronics, General Electric, W.W. Grainger, and many others have learned how to use the Internet, intranets, telemarketing, and customer databases not just to lower their selling costs but more importantly to improve their customer service. By means of computer hookup via satellite or land line, or by telephone, customers can place orders, obtain product and technical information, ask for technical assistance, check on an invoice, or request a call from a field sales or service person. Often, each customer is the responsibility of a single person who is the known contact for that customer, making the system almost as personal as a direct sales call. Many of these companies call their customers on a regular basis, say once every two weeks or every quarter, to see if they need anything. Information technology doesn't have to destroy the personal relationship. It can enhance it even while lowering the costs of buying and selling.

In the world of global markets, technological product parity and the inevitable regression toward price-sensitive commodity status for most products, customers are looking for reasons to prefer one company's products over those of another. The company that is easiest to do business with is likely to get the nod. Service as part of the product offering is where the competitive battles of the future will be won and lost. Service may be the key to successful positioning and a complete value proposition.

## To Bundle or Not to Bundle?

Service as part of the product offering raises a number of important strategic issues, however, not the least of which is how to price it. Bundling is the process of incorporating product features and services as part of the product offering. As noted in Chapter 2, and in the discussion above of delighting the customer, defining product scope is part of the problem of developing the value capture aspect of the business model. While bundling may enhance the customer's perception of quality, it is also likely to increase costs. It is obviously essential that the customer place a value on the bundled product enhancements greater than the cost to the manufacturer of providing them, and the customer must be willing to pay for them. The marketer must likewise have a clear strategy for capturing some of that created value.

Bundling decisions may be based on segmentation. A good illustration is provided by automobiles. A particular model may come in several treatments ranging from a plain basic unit to a fancy luxury style. Each treatment represents a distinct price point and has its own name designation:

- The basic model for the price-conscious shopper might feature vinyl upholstery, a four-cylinder engine, standard three-speed transmission and an AM/FM radio. This customer might be a younger, lower income consumer or a senior citizen.
- The next model might have cloth upholstery, an optional six-cylinder engine, four-speed transmission, AM/FM cassette player stereo system, rear window defroster, and special trim and wheels. This model might be aimed at a younger consumer, perhaps a family with multiple drivers, who uses the car primarily for local errands and trips.
- The top-of-the-line model might include as standard features a six-cylinder with a V-8 option, leather upholstery, AM/FM cassette and CD changer, cellular telephone, five-speed automatic transmission, electric windows and seat adjustments, automatic door locks, heated and cooled seats, and other features. The target market for this model would be a high-income older customer who uses the vehicle for longer trips.

Thus, there are distinct product offerings for distinct market segments that have different price elasticities and different needs and wants.

For many products, the customer has the option of buying only the base product and then shopping for a better deal on the accessories, additional features, and services that are being offered as part of the bundled product. For example, the purchaser of a 35-millimeter camera has the choice of buying a complete kit or just the camera body. The kit might include a basic 50-millimeter lens, a flash attachment, and a carrying case. The kit will be priced at less than the prices of the individual items if purchased separately. However, the informed buyer may know that he or she can buy the same camera body separately and add lenses, a flash attachment, a carrying case and other accessories of equal or better quality made by specialist manufacturers and sold at even lower prices than the bundled price of the brand-name camera manufacturer. These so-called "after-market" manufacturers are found in many industries from automobiles, photo equipment, and computers, to diesel engines, elevators, machine tools, tractors, and plasma torches.

Any manufacturer who sells a product system is likely to face aggressive, intelligent price competition from "unbundlers," niche marketers who offer excellent substitutes for some part of the total product system at lower prices. It is likely that the marketing efforts of the systems marketers have educated customers over time to become sophisticated and confident enough in their product knowledge to make sound judgments of value. This creates the opportunity for the unbundler. Very often, the manufacturer of the bundled product system is a large corporation with layers of bureaucracy and lots of administrative overhead costs that have to be covered by its pricing. How can IBM hope to compete with a specialty printer manufacturer?

The marketer who sells a bundled product offering usually must make a significant expenditure for marketing communications to convey the value proposition that has been designed into the product bundle. Bundled product offerings are typically branded and have the associated costs of brand development and product support. The luxury car model, the camera kit, the integrated computer system, the custom-built fire truck, must be promoted based on the value that the additional cost features represent. Brand image becomes a key part of the value proposition and the total product concept must be developed in the customer's mind because, even though it is inherent in the bundle of specific product features and services, it may not be completely obvious from mere visual inspection.

Bundling makes sense economically and strategically when there are distinct market segments that need and value the performance provided by the bundled features. Bundling can be the key to product differentiation and augmentation. If customers come to expect the bundled product, this may make it more difficult for competitors to enter the market with a lower-price, unbundled product. Or, if the real value is not there or has not been promoted adequately, it may *create* the opportunity for low-cost niche players to enter the market with one or more components of the total system.

One sophisticated economic model of the bundling decision concluded that bundling could be more profitable than selling unbundled components under the following conditions:

1. When profit margins can be maintained on the bundled components at levels greater than on the individual components.

2. When the firm's components in the bundled system are clearly superior to those of competitors.

3. When there are not clear market segments that prefer to purchase components and construct their own systems, currently using competitors' components.

4. When the market is not growing significantly (which means that un-bundling would merely substitute lower margin component sales for bundled systems sales instead of attracting new customers).[13]

It is probably the case, however, that as products mature, unbundling becomes increasingly common. Product knowledge becomes more generally shared and less proprietary, customers become more familiar with the technology, the industry converges on a common technical standard, and specialized components manufacturers with lower costs pursue increasingly small market niches.

In some industries, the bundling function is typically performed by a distributor. In process control instrumentation, for example, it is common for a distributor to design a system for a customer using components from several manufacturers. A similar situation is found in data-processing systems, with the well-known value-added resellers (VARs) who cater to particular end-user markets and assemble specialized hardware and software from multiple sources to fit the needs of these niche markets. Medical systems also are frequently sold through VARs. If distributors usually perform the bundling function, it might be unwise for the manufacturer to offer a bundled product offering unless the manufacturer is also willing to market direct to end-users rather than through distributors.

## Information as Part of the Product Offering

In a general sense, every product is a bundle of information in that it contains the potential to solve a problem. You buy toothpaste, for example, based on your knowledge that toothpaste has the ability to clean your teeth, improve the health of oral tissues, prevent cavities, reduce halitosis, and so on. You cannot directly observe any of these benefits as an immediate result of using the toothpaste, but you are quite content with the promise and potential of the product to produce these benefits. It is that information that you are purchasing, not the benefits directly.

More specifically, many products are themselves pure information. The airline travel guide, the computer network, the cable television news service, and all financial services are pure information. As a product, information is very different from other products. Most products become less valuable as you use them. Many information products, like the telephone system or the computer network, become more valuable the more users they have. The seller gives up nothing when it sells an information product, as it still has the information (e.g., the airline schedules) even though it has now sold them to the travel advisor.[14]

Aided by the tremendous advances in information technology, more and more tangible, physical products contain an information component. The instrument panel of your new automobile may allow you to display such digital information as outside air temperature, speed, miles per gallon, miles since last stop, radio frequency tuned to, and whether any doors are not shut properly. Included with the owner's information is an 800-telephone number to call for roadside emergency service, a list of all dealers in the United States and Canada (and perhaps Europe, if you purchased the car for European delivery). On the car are several microprocessors continuously monitoring the performance of all systems including ignition, fuel, lights, brakes, cooling, and ventilation. Some luxury models now carry automatic dialing systems that use an installed cellular telephone to call emergency aid in the event of an accident, using a global positioning system (GPS) to locate the car precisely. The same system can be used to call for mechanical assistance or travel directions. Information is clearly a critically important part of the automotive product offering today.

In industrial markets, information as part of the product offering is even more dramatically important. Customers of a major national chemical distributor chain have instant access via satellite hookup and computer terminals at their places of business to place orders, seek technical advice, check on the status of an order, schedule delivery, check on inventory levels and availabilities, or obtain information about hazardous materials and their handling. Internet auction sites for new and used equipment and supplies, electronic data interchange (EDI), and computer-based order-entry systems are common, linking customers to their vendors as part of a just-in-time inventory system. Especially for industrial raw materials, components, and subassemblies where technical product features offer minimal opportunity for differentiation, the only effective competitive weapon is skillful use of a superior information ability to enhance the relationship with the customer. Even the most low-tech company today must consider specifically the quality of the information component of its product offering in order to develop a complete concept of value for the customer. In many industries (examples include hospital supplies, airlines, railroads, banking, drug wholesaling, snack foods, and credit cards), the fundamental key success factors in the business have been redefined around information technology and its capabilities. The value proposition is dominated by the information component of the product offering.[15] While the Internet has become a key part of many company's marketing strategies, it is only one aspect of information-based product differentiation.

# COMMUNICATING VALUE TO THE TARGET MARKET

The value proposition must be communicated to the target market. Just as the product offering is tailored to the needs and requirements of the target market, so must the communication mix be designed to be responsive to the information requirements of the target customers and their characteristic reliance on various means and media of communication. Market targeting defines the audiences that must be reached by communications. Positioning defines the product concept and the benefits to be presented, explained, and developed by the marketing communication program. Positioning also implicitly defines "the enemy," that set of competitive product offerings and substitutes over which our product offering must achieve superiority in the perceptions and preferences of the target customer.

## Managing Customer Expectations: Why Volvo's 1970s Advertising Backfired

Customer expectations are the standard against which the customer evaluates the product offering. Consumers' expectations are developed in response to their exposure to communications from many sources and from their own experience. A major objective of the marketer's communication program is to develop an expectation that its product offering will deliver superior value. This can be a two-edged sword.

Overpromising can obviously cause problems by creating expectations that cannot be met. Carefully defining the target market is the first step to avoiding overpromising. It must be clear that the target market in fact has needs and wants that are consistent with our ability to deliver superior value. Superior performance for one market segment may not be satisfactory for another. It is critically important that selling messages actually get delivered to the intended audience.

The second step in avoiding overpromising is to shun creative concepts that have the potential to produce messages that result in unreasonable expectations. For many product categories, especially consumer packaged goods, it is quite common to rely on good old-fashioned boasting to help sell the product. Words like "super," "best," "world-class," "fantastic," and "beautiful" are used routinely to describe otherwise mundane products. Consumers are accustomed to hearing this language and can put it into proper context. Such words do not imply specific claims about product performance and there is no need to provide scientific evidence to support such boastful claims.

The problem of creative concepts that produce unreasonable expectations can be illustrated by the experience of Volvo automobiles in the 1970s in the U.S. market. Volvos were designed with an emphasis on safety and durability, supported by one of the best safety engineering programs in the world. Inspection of automobile registration data showed that 9 out of 10 Volvos registered in the United States in the past 11 years were still on the road. While this sounds remarkably good, it is in fact a claim that could be made for any brand. Volvo preempted the claim. This fact became the central theme of a major advertising campaign, directed at well-educated consumers with above average incomes. The results were excellent as U.S. sales of Volvos more than doubled in a few years.

Like any car, however, most Volvos developed minor problems of wear and tear after years of heavy use and indeed there was some evidence that Volvos were treated as workhorses by their owners. Volvo owners had very high expectations for the durability and trouble-free operation of their cars, due in no small part to the advertising for the brand. Over time, some Volvo owners became dissatisfied and often complained loudly, through negative word-of-mouth comments to friends and acquaintances and even to consumer protection advocates and agencies. Volvo buyers had expected their cars to last forever. When they didn't, they were angry. The advertising program for Volvos was changed to an emphasis on the sensible nature of the person who bought a Volvo and the safety features built into the car.

Customer expectations are based on many sources of information other than direct communications from the marketer. Most important, of course, is the customer's prior experience with this and competitive product offerings. Repeat purchases of the same brand are based on strong expectations for continued superior performance. Every brand name is a promise. It stands for something in the prospective customer's mind.

Most products deliver performance that will be evaluated on multiple dimensions. Automobile and truck tires, for example, are expected to produce a comfortable ride, good gas mileage, safe stopping, sure gripping when cornering, easy steering, traction on wet highways, low road noise, and long life in terms of miles driven. Unfortunately, these features represent technical tradeoffs and no tire design can maximize more than a few of these parameters. If you want high mileage you probably have to settle for a rougher ride and reduced traction in rain and snow. Seldom does the average consumer understand these tradeoffs. If he buys a tire based on its claim of high mileage, he is likely to also expect superior performance on virtually all of the other dimensions as well. He is likely to be disappointed with the handling performance of the car when driven aggressively.

For most industrial products, especially complex product systems, the challenge of creating reasonable expectations is great. It is not likely that mass communications, such as media advertising, can do more than a small amount of the job. Knowledgeable, skilled sales representatives must be assigned to target customers and supported with carefully developed sales presentations and literature. Technical product information must be complete and easy to understand and make clear the use conditions for which the product is, and is not, designed. This is a key step in managing customer expectations and a critical part of the equation of customer satisfaction.

## Developing Value through Communication

While the value of the product offering must be inherent in the product itself, communication can nonetheless convey and enhance that value. For consumer goods and services, the principal communication methodology may be media advertising. For industrial products and services, customers may rely on the sales representatives, dealer personnel, and semi-technical printed materials of all kinds. As noted earlier, for many products and services, people who are part of the selling, delivery, installation, and repair process exert a major influence on the definition of value. They are part of the product offering, defining the brand as an experience for the customer.

Marketing communications that build brand equity increase the value of the brand for the consumer. When you receive a Cross pen and pencil set as a business gift, it has special value because of the Cross brand name. The brand has acquired that value over the years not just from its excellent design and materials but also by means of the advertising investments of the A.T. Cross Company promoting its durability, permanence, lifetime guarantee, and overall quality. The Kwik-Klik pen you received from another business acquaintance doesn't carry the same panache even though it writes just as well.

Brand equity is the return on investment in communications designed to enhance the value of the brand. Within marketing science, there is an ongoing debate about the relative profitability of advertising versus sales promotion expenditures. The latter are usually temporary price inducements of one form or another (coupons, trade discounts, offers of "free" merchandise, etc.) designed to produce incremental sales in the short term. It has been argued that these tend to diminish the value of the brand over time by creating customer expectations for lower prices. There is also the related issue of the extent to which consumers equate high quality with high price, using price as a key index of quality in the absence of clear visual and other product cues.

Because advertising is intended to produce positive effects on brand sales over the long term, usually a period of several years, it is much more difficult to measure the effects of advertising on sales and profitability. In a business climate that emphasizes short-term measures of business performance, advertising and other long-term marketing expenditures have been under pressure. There remains a basic research question whether advertising (and other forms of marketing communication designed to produce long-term results) really can enhance brand value as perceived by the customer and can build brand equity as measured by sales and profitability over multiple business periods.

While we cannot even begin to review this large and complex body of research here, we can cite a recent study that provides some evidence in support of the ability of marketing communications to build brand value for both customers and marketers. Boulding, Lee, and Staelin built a model of product differentiation and brand equity and estimated the effects of marketing communication using the PIMS database for consumer products. Their analysis looked at the combined effects of expenditures for advertising, salesforce, and promotional activities on both durable and nondurable consumer products. They conceived of product differentiation as an alternative to price competition (i.e., price-cutting) and measured the effects of communication in terms of changes in consumer sensitivity to price differences. They found that, as one would expect, expenditures for advertising and salesforce activity *reduced* the consumer's sensitivity to price while the use of sales promotion *increased* it. From the perspective of the firm, this means that advertising and personal selling expenditures reduce its vulnerability to price competition while sales promotion increases it.[16]

It is assumed that the company's advertising and personal selling use messages that do not stress price competition! The low-price competitor who spends millions promoting his low-prices will undoubtedly increase the customer's sensitivity to price, not just for his products but for the whole product category.

The research does support the conclusion that marketers who stress product benefits for the consumer through advertising and personal selling can build brand equity through product differentiation that reduces its sensitivity to price competition. This is one more piece of evidence in favor of the value-delivery concept of strategy.

## SUMMARY

Market segmentation, targeting, and positioning are the essential activities in developing a focused business strategy built around the firm's distinctive competence and its ability to deliver superior value to a well-defined set of prospective customers. Customers define the business by demanding that it commit its resources to doing certain things extremely well. Thus, selection of customers (not products) is *the* critical strategic choice for the firm. A critical function of the market targeting and positioning decision is to define those market segments where the firm elects *not* to compete.

Focused marketing, the hallmark of the marketing concept, means turning away certain potential customers and orders. For most managers, that is an extremely difficult decision and in many firms, even whole industries, the sales concept still dominates. Under the sales concept, sales volume is the key to profitability and every customer is a good customer, every order a good order. A sales orientation can result in an operation loaded with barely profitable business.

Intelligent market segmentation, targeting, and positioning lead to the development of a value proposition, a product offering, and a communication strategy designed to deliver superior value to customers. Careful positioning helps to assure that the product offering, including product features, service enhancements, and supporting communications, is complete. A major challenge of the market targeting process is to understand the complex systems of market transactions, marketing channels, and product delivery and product use systems within which the product offering will be developed and used. The problem is to find a real "customer," a person or organization who will value the product offering and who will be willing and able to pay for it. We illustrated the problem with an example (blood collection and processing) where the beneficiaries of the technology were not the potential customers and the challenge was to create a customer who could derive economic benefit from the technology.

The markets of the 2000s are increasingly characterized by long-term relationships and temporary alliances among actors in the market system. Customers, suppliers, competitors, resellers, and manufacturers exist in evolving, interdependent relationships where their distinct roles get blurred and where no firm performs more than a few specialized activities in the complex value chain. Developing a product offering that delivers superior value to end-user customers becomes an extremely complicated set of interdependent, interorganizational activities and relationships. In the next two chapters we look at the nature of this revolutionary development and examine the role of marketing within these new organizational arrangements and structures. In the old marketing concept, marketing was a management function within the firm. In the new marketing concept, marketing becomes a set of processes and activities spanning the boundaries of many organizations.

# Customer Relationship Management

*Buying and selling is essentially anti-social.*

Edward Bellamy

*Looking Backward, 2000–1887* (1888)

Customer relationship management is now understood to be one of the core marketing processes. This represents a significant shift in focus. Traditionally, the field of marketing was centered on the concept of a market-based transaction. Reflecting its origins in economics, the study of marketing was concerned with the functions necessary to execute a transaction—sellers seeking buyers and buyers seeking sellers through processes of market information, providing assortments of merchandise, holding inventory, buying, selling, risk-taking, transporting, providing credit, and so on. The marketing process was seen as ending when the sale occurred, when title to the goods transferred from producer (or reseller) to consumer. The sale was the objective and the end result of marketing effort.

Under the new marketing concept, the focus has shifted from one-time transactions to ongoing relationships. The purpose of marketing is not to make the single sale; the purpose is to create a customer. The sale is not the end of the marketing process but the beginning of a relationship in which buyer and seller become interdependent.

Under customer relationship management, customers are viewed as assets and evaluated according to their long-term profitability—revenues minus cost-to-serve—not just sales volume. The product or service enters the customer's use system and the customer becomes a source of both financial support and ongoing requirements for the business. In some cases, the customer also becomes a source of knowledge useful in innovation and process improvement (innovation management being another of the core marketing processes).

Viewing the marketing process as one of building relationships is an extension of the basic idea of customer orientation and a logical outcome of the notion that every business is a service business. When products are seen as bundles of benefits, when service becomes the critical component of the product offering, it is inevitable that we must focus on the ongoing relationship between the company and its customers. It is also logically consistent with the proposition that quality is defined by the extent to which the product/service meets or exceeds customer expectations as it is being used over time.

This chapter analyzes the evolution of marketing from a focus on transactions to an emphasis on long-term customer relationships. Differences between consumer products, including services, packaged goods, and durables, and industrial products and services must be noted. In consumer marketing, the relationship is with individuals; in industrial marketing, it is with organizations, a fundamental difference. In this chapter, we consider primarily consumer relationship marketing, including the role of information technology as a facilitator of relationship marketing. We also consider how the nature of the marketing and selling process changes with relationship marketing. In Chapter 6, the discussion continues with a focus on business-to-business customer relationships, from simple transactions to complex buyer-seller strategic partnerships, alliances, and network organizations.

## CONTINUUM OF CUSTOMER RELATIONSHIPS

This discussion of customer relationship management is organized around the idea that buyers and sellers can do business along a continuum from pure transactions to totally integrated alliances and networks. At one end, the buyer-seller interaction is controlled exclusively by market forces; at the other end, the control is strictly internal and bureaucratic, within the organization of the buyer-seller relationship itself. In the middle, there is a complex interplay of market and bureaucratic controls governing the relationship. Six stages can be defined along this continuum:

1. Pure transactions.
2. Repeated transactions/simple relationships.
3. Long-term buyer-seller relationships.
4. Strategic partnerships.

5.  Strategic alliances and joint ventures.
6.  Network organizations.

The definition of these stages is somewhat arbitrary, but they capture the basic idea that buyer-seller relationships can take many forms, from simple to complex. This chapter examines the first three stages, with an emphasis on marketing to consumers, where market forces tend to dominate. The next chapter considers marketing to business customers, continuing the discussion of long-term buyer-seller relationships and then concentrating on the final three stages where there is strategic and operational integration of buyer and seller activities. In the business-to-business marketing realm, the total spectrum from transactions to networks is found, but there has been an evolution to more complex, bureaucratic buyer-seller relationships.

## Pure Transactions

A pure transaction, the core concept with which we begin our analysis, is a very rare bird. It is possible to describe one without ever seeing one. It is found frequently in the artificial world of the microeconomic paradigm, the basis of the economist's theory of the firm.

A pure transaction occurs in a perfect market, defined as one with a very large number of competing sellers, each selling an undifferentiated product, and a set of buyers with perfect information about all product offerings, including prices. Consumer preferences are given, exogenous to the process. In this perfect market, no seller can influence the desires of any buyer. The only variable is price and the buyer is a profit- or utility-maximizer, seeking the lowest price. Each transaction is a completely independent event, not influenced by consideration of past or future transactions. All that matters is price. Market forces of supply and demand set the price.

Every marketing manager (more generally, every businessperson) is dedicated to destroying every one of the economist's assumptions. The manager wants to create consumer preference, through product differentiation and marketing communications, for a product offering for which the consumer is willing to pay a higher price. Each competitor has attempted to position itself carefully in a segmented market where it has a virtual monopoly in its chosen market niche. Most markets consist of only a few sellers, each of which is watched carefully and responded to by the others. Consumers know these competitors, interact with them over a long period of time, and continually modify their buying preferences. Each firm's pricing actions and total product offerings are monitored by the others, and competitors' actions directly influence the others' pricing, product, and promotion decisions.

In the pure version of the microeconomic paradigm, there is no product differentiation, no customer loyalty, no brand equity, no repeat purchase, no recourse to the seller, no service, no credit, and no commitment to future transactions. There is also no trust. Each party assumes that the other is motivated by greed and self-interest and is seeking to maximize only its own welfare in the transaction. The relationship is adversarial, mediated only by the price mechanism of the marketplace. *Caveat emptor! Caveat venditor!*

Perhaps the best example of a pure transaction in the real world is the purchase of agricultural commodity futures. Here the buyer buys only a contract, not the product itself. (Very few investors would want to actually own pork bellies, let alone take physical possession of them!) But even here, the buyer is likely to know personally the broker he or she does business with, and they are likely to have an on-going business relationship.

The closest the average consumer comes to a pure transaction might be the purchase of unbranded gasoline at a self-service pump in a town the person has never visited before and to which he or she never expects to return, paid for by cash inserted through a slot in a bulletproof glass window in a kiosk located between the pumps. (You may have seen this place on one of your trips.) Here there is no brand recognition, no product differentiation, no familiar face, no credit card, and no chance that the buyer will be back in the store. There is no possibility of a relationship.

Even here, however, the real-world consumer might have preferred a familiar brand name, a friendly clerk, some personal service at the gas pump, a rest room, a free cup of coffee in the store, and the opportunity to use his credit card. (Mobil Oil addressed this opportunity with its Friendly Service program at its gas station/convenience stores.) After all, the essence of a brand is that of a relationship between buyer and seller. There is usually comfort and trust, albeit of a modest type, in a brand name, and the promise of a bit more customer satisfaction in a differentiated product, tailored to the needs of the individual.

## The Sale as a Conquest

Pure transactions are rare and yet much of marketing thought and practice has been based on a transaction kind of mentality where the sale is a conquest and the relationship is adversarial. In the traditional view of marketing, the focus is on winning the next sale, not the last one. This is consistent with the old sales concept, not the new marketing concept.

Under the sales concept, it is the sale that is important, not the customer. Marketers have characteristically devoted more energy and more promotional dollars to creating the next sale than to satisfying the customer they already have.

It is also fair to say that much industrial purchasing has been based on a similar set of assumptions. Purchasing managers have usually sought the lowest price by finding a large number of vendors who will offer a similar product, as undifferentiated as possible by means of concise purchase specifications. Industrial buying was typically adversarial and in many cases impersonal. In rigorously controlled purchasing procedures, as found for example in government procurement, all transactions were conducted based on a sealed-bidding process and any attempt at personal influence was considered potentially unethical. Buying and selling were antisocial behavior, guided by the rules of the impersonal marketplace.

While the assumptions of the microeconomic profit-maximization model have served the field of economic theory well and produced an amazingly robust, rigorous analysis, they are less helpful as guidelines for the conduct of business. The narrow focus on transactions, on the sale as a conquest rather than on the customer as a long-term business asset, is potentially fatal.[1]

## Repeated Transactions Based on Differentiation and Customer Preference

Most individual transactions occur as part of a stream of transactions. Because they have antecedents in prior transactions and consequences for future transactions, these repeated transactions are not "pure" and do not meet the assumptions of the economist's model. For any consumer or industrial purchase, there is almost always some prior knowledge of the characteristics that differentiate products and vendors, some previous contact, some information about competing products including their prices, and some possibility of future transactions between the buyer and the seller. Products are usually identified by their brand names or the names of their companies. Personal services are differentiated, by definition, by the personal characteristics of the service providers themselves—doctors, accountants, lawyers, insurance agents—even when they are closely controlled by regulatory requirements. Differentiation creates preferences and preference leads to repeated transactions.

Simple convenience is another cause of repeat purchasing. Once customers have processed available information and found an acceptable product offering, they may have little incentive to spend the time and energy required to evaluate alternatives. Perceived search costs exceed expected incremental gains in utility. Increasingly, consumers find that time is their scarcest resource and saving time is a major motivator in the purchase decision process. It is easier, as well as reassuring, to buy a familiar brand and to shop in a convenient store. Familiarity is the first step away from the pure, stand-alone transaction toward a buyer-seller relationship.

Repeated transactions are common in the marketing of services and packaged goods. Marketing effort is devoted toward differentiating products, building brand awareness, and creating brand preference and loyal customers. While for most consumer goods, there is no direct personal contact between the buyer and the seller, no meaningful ongoing relationship, the presence of brand preference, customer loyalty, and repeat purchases shows that we have progressed beyond the assumptions of the economist's model and the pure transaction. Repeated transactions represent the beginning of a relationship. Products are differentiated and consumers have preferences.

With repeated transactions, a critical element has entered the equation—*trust*. The familiarity of a brand name or a salesperson contains an implicit promise of consistent product and service performance, of quality, of a purchase experience that will meet expectations. Consumers are creatures of habit because of this; we have our favorite soft drink, restaurant, convenience store, financial advisor, hotel chain, cash machine, and newspaper because we trust them. Trust is the fundamental building block of relationships.

## The Value of Repeat Business

Repeat purchases and loyal customers are the main drivers of profitability for most businesses. It costs much less to service an existing customer than to create a new one. Studies suggest that to acquire a new customer requires spending about five times more than is needed to keep an old customer's loyalty.[2] It may cost between $50 and $100, for example, for a credit card company to attract a new cardholder. For banks, automobile manufacturers, insurance companies, personal computer makers, and other high-priced goods and services, the cost will be considerably higher. Brand equity and loyal customers are valuable business assets representing the investment of large amounts of marketing dollars and effort. When former customers are lost, that investment goes with them. It isn't just the next sale that is lost; it is the profit on the stream of transactions that could have been expected if that customer had been satisfied.

An ongoing relationship with a loyal customer who is a repeat buyer is valuable in several ways:

- There are the revenue and profit margin from the future sales of the product to this customer.

- There may be lower costs associated with serving a repeat customer compared with a new customer.

- The loyal customer may be willing to pay a modest price premium and may need less price inducement such as special promotions, a point touched upon in Chapter 4.

- There is the potential for additional revenue and profit margin from selling other products to the same customer, either products already in the product line or new products to be offered in the future. This is captured in the concept of brand equity.

- Positive word-of-mouth generated by the satisfied customer can lead to sales revenue from other customers.

For the large proportion of repeated transactions, however, there is no real *personal* relationship between the buyer and the manufacturer, although there may be some minimal amount of personal contact at the retail point of sale. Thus, we do not characterize a series of transactions as a true relationship. It is a basic fact of most consumer goods marketing that the specific identity of the customer is not known to the marketer, which disqualifies the stream of transactions with that buyer as a true relationship. While the brand may represent a relationship of the customer with the product or service, the impersonal nature of the interaction does not qualify as a relationship for the marketer with the customer. Communication is one way, from marketer to customer. The customer cannot influence the company. You can't have a relationship with someone you don't know.

Furthermore, buyers of frequently purchased packaged goods and services seldom worry about the welfare of the marketer to any great extent; they place virtually no value on the relationship with the manufacturer of the brand. If one seller goes out of business, there are several others who can take its place. Familiarity and repeated transactions stop short of creating a real relationship.

## Long-Term Buyer-Seller Relationships

A relationship is characterized by a stronger connection, usually personal in nature, one that is ongoing and has multiple dimensions. In marketing, it means among other things that the buyer is known to the seller by name, that the buyer's geographic location and other identifying characteristics are known, and that the seller can communicate directly with the buyer. These are the essential characteristics of *addressability* at the core of marketing relationships. They are of sufficient duration that we can refer to them as *long-term* relationships, to differentiate them further from transactions. Providers of telephone service and banking services, for example, have always been involved in relationship marketing. They know the names and addresses of their customers, and maintain a record of their transactions over a long time period. There is the possibility of two-way communication; buyers can initiate communication with the marketer as well as receive messages from the company and expect a response tailored to the message.

A relationship also implies a degree of interdependence as well as trust. The interdependence consists in part of the expectation of a string of future transactions as well as a degree of dependence on the other for providing resources (income for the seller, products and services for the customer) that are necessary for the ongoing operations of both. Each party to the relationship is specifically interested in ensuring the survival and welfare of the other. Consumers have a real interest in the welfare of their banks, airlines (and frequent flyer programs), energy suppliers, auto manufacturers and dealers, and so on.

## Linked Operations and Interdependence

The two operations—those of the customer and those of the seller—become linked. This is true even at the household level. In fact, some interesting marketing insights come from thinking about the household as a production system. Marketers of foods, food preparation, and household cleaning items, for example, have been able to generate many new product ideas from such analysis. In some sense, each household has the option for virtually every purchased product or service of electing to produce it themselves. While this is a little far-fetched in the age of supermarkets, cash machines, shopping malls, the Internet, cellular telephones, open-heart surgery, and two-income families, it is sometimes helpful to think of how the product or service we are selling could be produced by the consumer. She can bake bread instead of buy it. She can write a letter or walk to visit her neighbor rather than use the telephone or Internet. She can pay cash rather than use her credit card. She can assume the risk of lost income rather than pay for disability insurance.

It is also important to remember that every product or service must fit into the customer's production system. If the consumer buys a coffeemaker, it will have to fit into a system of equipment, kitchen space, and supplies for preparing food. As a time-saving device, the quality of the coffee brewed may be less important than the ease with which it can be filled, operated, cleaned, and stored as part of the morning routine in preparation for going to work. The alternative for the consumer may not be to purchase another type or brand of coffeemaker but rather to move the entire production system outside of the home and purchase breakfast at McDonald's on the way to the office.

## Relationships Create Expectations

In the world of relationship marketing, buyer and seller become interdependent. Relationships entail mutual expectations and obligations. You expect to be able to go to the local grocery store and find the fresh milk that your children need, just as the store stocks it on the expectation that you will come in to buy it. That same storekeeper may set aside a copy of the Sunday *New York Times* for you, which you then have an obligation to pick up.

You may have a contract for the delivery of fuel oil to your home or your business. In both locations, you depend on the oil distributor for the flow of a material that is essential to your welfare. You may have paid in advance for the heating season's supply of heating oil at a more favorable price. The distributor offered this to you in return for the certainty that his advanced commitments to his suppliers, necessary for him to have an assured supply during the winter months, would find a market.

Your operations and those of your grocer and your fuel distributor are linked and interdependent. They represent a relationship rather than a series of transactions because you are known by name, address, purchasing habits, and usage patterns. Each party has clear expectations for the other, and there are mutual obligations to buy and to sell.

Consumer durables represent a fertile ground for relationship marketing. If the product carries a warranty and the buyer registers the purchase with the manufacturer, the basis for a marketing relationship has been established. It is still remarkable, however, how few companies who request this information from customers use it wisely to build an ongoing relationship with the new purchaser. Why should a buyer pay the postage required to send a "product registration card" back to the manufacturer, when the card asks only for information about the buyer's demographics and buying habits and provides nothing in return? While appliance manufacturers routinely try to gather information about their customers, few of them use the information to build relationships that could be the basis for future sales, even though a customer represents the potential for sales of an estimated $3,000 over a 20-year period according to one study done in the 1980s. (That number is undoubtedly much higher today.)

Automobile manufacturers do a somewhat better job, perhaps because the value of a loyal customer can be as much as $250,000 over the customer's lifetime. The auto manufacturers maintain a database with the names of every person who has purchased a new car, their address, the complete description and specifications of the vehicle that was purchased, and a variety of other information about the nature of the transaction and the buyer. The customer subsequently receives verification of the terms of the warranty, information about other product and service offerings, surveys of customer satisfaction with the dealer and the vehicle, follow-up on subsequent service visits and warranty claims, and notifications of product recalls if there are problems. Mailings to customers to follow up on service encounters and to promote additional sales of service and products frequently go to the customer over the dealer's signature. Customers expect to be supported with information and service by the manufacturer and the dealer as long as they own the car.

In industrial marketing and in the marketing of most personal services, especially financial services, relationship marketing has traditionally been more common than in consumer marketing, although consumer marketing has been changing rapidly. Personal service relationships are built on the expectation of integrity, professional competence, and, usually, confidentiality in the relationship. Often, government and professional organizations set standards for their service providers and monitor performance in ways that ensure maintenance of those standards of integrity, competence, and trust. The expectations are an essential feature of the relationship.

Expectations can be a double-edged sword, however. Meeting customer expectations may lead to satisfaction but not necessarily customer loyalty. As pointed out in Chapter 3, when customers' expectations are met, they tend to increase and the customer's definition of value keeps changing. Those increased expectations may create a problem for the marketer who does not have the capability to increase performance to meet them. In contrast, the satisfied customer may be approached by another marketer with a different value proposition. The customer can easily add that to their expectations for the company they are currently buying from. It may be difficult or impossible for the company to meet those revised expectations, especially if they are inherently contradictory—as when, for example, the customer asks company 1 to continue to provide superior service and product quality at the substantially lower price of company 2. As we discuss at the end of the chapter, the customer's increased expectations may lead the company to consider marketing alliances as a way to meet increased customer expectations that go beyond its own capabilities.

## Negotiation as Part of the Relationship

In industrial marketing and in a good portion of consumer durables marketing, even when the marketer has a list price, terms and conditions are agreed to by both parties as a result of negotiation. Prices for professional services, such as management consulting, accounting, and advertising creative services, are usually based on negotiations.

The further we move from pure transactions, the more price becomes negotiable, set by interaction between buyer and seller, not by pure market forces. In relationship marketing, especially in industrial markets, prices are set by a negotiation process that is part of the relationship. Price is determined by the process, not by the market alone, although the range of pricing alternatives is influenced by the competitive forces of the marketplace. This difference is critical to understanding relationship marketing: Price is an outcome of a negotiation process inherent in the relationship. Price is usually all wrapped up in a set of terms and conditions that are part of the total product offering. Price is a variable determined in the context of all other parts of the total (also negotiated) product offering.

## Adversarial Nature of Buyer-Seller Relationships

Even in the long-term buyer-seller relationship, however, as traditionally viewed by both parties, the relationship may still be essentially adversarial in nature. Price negotiations often expose the adversarial nature of the buyer-seller relationship. There are many illustrations in both consumer and industrial marketing.

The automobile purchaser expects to have to bargain hard for a favorable price and many customers probably regard the whole buying process as adversarial and distasteful. Only recently have some companies, such as Saturn and Dell Computer, begun to address the nature of the selling process as part of the product offering. With a focus on the quality of the relationship with the customer, Saturn encouraged dealers to follow a policy of adherence to low list prices and to avoid the high-pressure sales tactics that are characteristic of the automobile industry. Dell Computer uses the Internet and telephone sales representatives to help customers configure a system that fits their needs and to provide follow-up service for installation, applications support, and trouble-shooting. Each computer is custom built for the individual customer, and price determined accordingly. There is two-way communication, tailored to the needs of the buyer, not simply a one-way sales presentation.

In industrial marketing, the tough-as-nails purchasing agent is still a folk hero in many industrial companies and industrial sales representatives approach the selling situation as a jousting match. From the perspective of the 2000s, the shortsightedness of a focus on price is now evident. In the days before the quality movement had become a driving force, good purchasing practice was defined as developing tight specifications and finding several vendors who were willing to bid, thus assuring that the procurement could be based on low price. It was common for manufacturers to have multiple vendors for every item, on the assumption (often not warranted) that their products were interchangeable. The lowest price bidder was awarded the largest portion of the company's requirements, with other vendors receiving smaller orders to keep them interested as potential bidders and to keep price pressure on the main supplier. Multiple vendors also provided some insurance against an unforeseen interruption in supply due to equipment failures, strikes, natural disasters, or other unforeseen events.

Even though these business dealings meet our definition of a relationship, they were managed by the rules of the transaction. Most of the important information about a vendor's product offering was assumed to be contained in the price and the objective was to find the lowest available price. The result was often poor quality, poor service, production problems associated with changing vendors frequently, interruption in supply, and excessive inventories throughout the system. Lowest price usually did not mean lowest total cost.

In this purchasing environment, the marketing and selling process was just as adversarial as the buying process. Customers were given only the information that they demanded, which was usually an attempt to justify the price being quoted. The supplier treated its manufacturing process and product technology as proprietary information. Such negotiations as were necessary to determine the terms and conditions of transactions were conducted on the basis of "Win/Lose." If the buyer gained something, the seller lost something in return, often in the form of profit margin. Chapter 6 continues the discussion of relationship marketing in business markets. Adversarial, transaction-oriented buying and selling are still practiced in some industrial markets.

## *Relationship Marketing—A Matter of Attitude*

Before discussing the operational requirements for relationship marketing, it is important to point out that it is fundamentally a question of attitude. The customer isn't the enemy; he or she is a business partner. Under the new marketing concept, the company is called on to put the customer first, in all decisions, always. That means that the customer comes before the product. It also means putting the customer ahead of the sale. In fact, given that every company has limited capabilities, putting the customer first may require foregoing the sale. Some customers' requirements may be met only by compromising the firm's ability to satisfy other customers. Which customers come first? Those with which the firm has an ongoing, profitable relationship.

Under the new marketing concept, the relationship cannot be adversarial. It must be one of interdependence, trust, cooperation, and partnership. A very direct implication of this requirement is that the company must choose its customers very carefully. Not all potential customers are candidates for a long-term relationship, however. What can a relationship-oriented marketer do about a customer who is still committed to the old adversarial view of the world and really prefers to buy on a transactional basis?

## *Good and Bad Customers*

In relationship marketing, there are good and bad customers. The good customers are those who value what the company does well, who are attracted by its value proposition, who value the relationship they have with the firm as an asset in their personal life or business, and who are willing to pay fairly for the resources committed to solving their problems. The marketer has two potentially attractive options for addressing the fact that not all customers value a long-term relationship. One is to do business, on a relationship basis, only with "good" customers. This may require some customer education, selling the basic value proposition including the value of the long-term relationship to the customer. The benefits of doing business on a relationship basis may not be obvious to the customer who has always treated the sale as a one-time transaction.

The other option for the marketer is to develop a differentiated marketing strategy for distinct market segments, defined by the customer's preference for transactions or varying degrees of long-term relationship. The company that can learn how to deal profitably with customers who prefer a straightforward transactions orientation will find that they are not necessarily bad customers. However, they must be dealt with differently and very efficiently. In most consumer markets, it is very difficult for one company to have differentiated marketing strategies and to serve both transaction and relationship customers. The experience of the airlines confirms this: Low-price seekers who have discretion as to when they fly and business travelers with high service requirements and who must fly at specified times end up on the same airplane receiving more or less the same service although they pay very different prices. Business travelers have become increasingly vocal in their concern that these pricing practices are fundamentally unfair to them, reducing their perceived value of their relationship with a particular airline.

However, these distinctly different segments, transaction and relationship customers, may be served by different competitors in some markets. Low-price, no-frills carriers Southwest Airlines in the United States and Ryanair in Europe have been able to carve out market niches to compete effectively with higher price, full-service providers such as American and Lufthansa. Low-price convenience goods going through discount mass marketers, such as unbranded laundry detergents, might serve transaction-oriented customers while more expensive national brands sold through supermarket chains target a more quality- and performance-conscious relationship segment. In industrial markets, it is much more common for one firm to attempt to serve both types of customers, but with differentiated strategies. We develop this idea in Chapter 6, where we consider segmenting industrial markets based on the nature of the buying process.

To summarize, relationship marketing is positioned significantly along the continuum away from the pure transaction. Repeated transactions represent the beginning of a relationship based on trust. The simple relationship remains essentially adversarial, however, guided by the transaction-oriented rules of the competitive marketplace. Without the possibility of two-way communication or personal contact, it is not a true relationship.

A true, long-term buyer-seller relationship develops when the marketer knows the name and characteristics of the customer, including the history of transactions, and there is the potential for two-way communication. The marketer can direct communications at specific individuals rather than the anonymous consumer in the mass market. The potential customer can respond and the marketer can then tailor its response accordingly.

True relationship marketing requires a fundamental shift in attitude, toward viewing the customer as a partner, a business asset to be managed for long-term profitability. The sale isn't a conquest and it isn't the end of the marketing process. It is the beginning of the relationship with the customer. We must focus on the relationship, not the individual sale.

# IMPLEMENTING RELATIONSHIP MARKETING

For the consumer marketer and the marketer of services, a commitment to relationship marketing is essentially a commitment to developing a customer database and to using it for developing and implementing all phases of marketing strategy, including product, pricing, and promotion decisions. In the markets of the twenty-first century, there is a concomitant requirement for investment in an information system, including supporting technology. Information technology, including telecommunications, data storage and retrieval technologies, and the World Wide Web, have created a revolution that is shifting the firm's orientation from production efficiency back to customer needs.

Because it permits direct, personalized communication with the individual customer, "high-tech" marketing also becomes "high touch." It draws the customer closer to the company, builds a relationship, and reduces the probability that the customer will switch to a competitor. Companies now see their best profit opportunities in exploiting their customer base, selling more products and services to their existing customers rather than trying to find new customers for their existing products.[3] Relationship marketing moves companies from a product- and company-centric view of the business toward the customer-centric view advocated by the marketing concept. The purpose is not to sell what the company has made, but to offer products and services that are tailored more precisely to customer needs and wants.

Customer relationship marketing does not make sense in every situation. There almost certainly should be the opportunity for repeat purchases from the customer. The lifetime value of the customer must be high enough to support the marketing investment required. Also, the potential value of relationship marketing is a function of the relative ease of identifying and reaching the target customer. It helps if the purchase is planned rather than made on impulse and there must be a substantial degree of product differentiation.

Premium quality exterior paints and stains for houses would fit most of these definitions of desirable characteristics (planned purchase, differentiated and branded products, and high lifetime value). While it might be difficult to actually target potential customers before they have made their first purchase, magazine readership and household zip codes are good indicators. Likewise, expectant mothers are excellent relationship marketing targets, and are fairly easily identified through physician referrals. They have high lifetime value for products such as disposable diapers (estimated to be $1,400 per year per baby), which is usually a planned purchase as part of a shopping trip and a branded, differentiated product. Other illustrations of good opportunities for relationship marketing include cruises, hobbies such as coin collecting and photography, educational materials and seminars, and automobile racing.

## Interactive Marketing

The term *interactive marketing* is sometimes understood to be synonymous with electronic retailing and other forms of E-commerce, but that is not the only meaning. Interactive marketing is not just marketing on the Internet; interaction is the essence of relationship marketing. In its simplest form, interactive marketing has been around for a long time. The essential element of interactive marketing is, as noted earlier, the ability of the company to send messages to identifiable prospects, the message recipient's ability to respond, and the company's ability to then tailor messages and product offerings unique to that individual prospect. Many traditional marketing practices were interactive in this rudimentary form including, for example:

- Broadcast and print media advertising that offer a telephone number or mailing address permitting the recipient to contact the company.
- Direct mail addressed to a specific individual with a product offering or information on how to contact the company.
- Catalogs mailed to consumers or businesses in a list of addresses that contains information about the recipients' demographics and previous purchases.
- Outbound telephone marketing to lists of households whose names are known.
- Inbound telephone marketing permitting customers to place orders, obtain product or service information, or check on order status.

Before mass marketing, the type of marketing with which most people are most familiar, there was interactive marketing. Selling involved personal contact, by definition, as vendors hawked their wares, traveling salesmen covered their territories, and consumers knew their local retailers as members of the community. All personal selling is interactive marketing, but not all mass marketing is interactive.

The earliest form of mass marketing, the catalog, was interactive in that it solicited a direct response, namely mail orders, from the consumer. Mass marketing in the United States can be traced to the late 1890s and early

1900s. Although there had been catalogs before, including that of Richard Warren Sears' own jewelry, watches, and diamonds business, his new Sears, Roebuck and Company's catalog, aimed at rural midwestern consumers, started the general merchandise mail order business in 1893.

Mass media were not interactive to begin with. The first modern American mass circulation magazine, *The Saturday Evening Post* (the origins of which go back to Benjamin Franklin's *Pennsylvania Gazette,* founded in 1728), appeared from Curtis Publishing in 1897. Radio broadcasts to the public began in the United States on January 12 and 13, 1910, direct from the Metropolitan Opera in New York but the first commercial radio station was probably Pittsburgh's KDKA, licensed in 1920. Television broadcasts, the most revolutionary marketing medium up to that time, occurred in New York City in 1939, when NBC broadcast a program to the 400 homes having television receivers. World War II put a stop to further development until 1946, when there were 7,000 television sets in the United States. Only four years later, there were 10 million and the Television Age had begun. When print media began to incorporate telephone numbers and direct response cards and broadcast media solicited consumer response via telephone ("Call this number now!"), the beginnings of interactive marketing were in place.

In a fundamental sense, relationship marketing was also being used by any company with a salesforce that called on customers in their assigned territories on a regular basis. Customer information was routinely gathered by any company that had a field sales organization calling on regularly assigned accounts, as a way of controlling the efforts of the sales representatives, although the data may not have been carefully maintained and used effectively to develop relationships with those customers.

## Interactive Marketing Begins with a Database

In interactive marketing as it is found today, each customer is the subject of a record in a database that contains the prospects' or customers' names, addresses, and other contact information. The database may also contain information about these people's personal characteristics, media usage patterns, and purchase histories, including a record of previous contacts with the company. The content of the data file depends on the specific needs of the marketer and the type of business involved.

A fundamental shift has occurred, from mass marketing that sends messages about a standard product offering to anonymous persons, to personalized marketing with messages and offerings tailored to the specific individual. It is now possible to approach each customer as an individual with unique needs, preferences, and requirements, and as a unique business opportunity. Even mass media such as *Time* magazine can send a message addressed directly to an individual, by name, inside its magazine using inkjet printing technology, as well as unique advertising messages to individuals within given areas identified by postal zip code.

Interactive marketing is defined by the fundamental importance of *addressability*.[4] Each customer becomes known as a specific individual as the result of their first contact with the marketer. They might respond to an advertisement in a newspaper or magazine, dial an 800 number, go to the marketer's Web site, or receive a personal call from a sales representative. The consumer might join a buyer's club at the local supermarket or open an account with a bank, a car rental company, or a credit card company.

At that first contact, the marketer requests certain information, depending on the nature of the business, legal and credit requirements, and so on. That information includes at least name, address, telephone number, and possibly information about type of residence, place of employment, age, education, income, marital and family status, and more. The customer may also be asked to indicate which magazines, newspapers, and other media he or she used to become aware of the marketer, whether he or she likes to receive promotional offers such as cents-off coupons, which recreational activities he or she enjoys, and whether he or she would like to receive promotional offers from other companies. All of this gets entered into the database and becomes the basis for directing specific communications and product offerings at that particular consumer.

Each contact with the customer is noted in the database. The company will know which communications the customer has received and can subsequently judge whether they were effective, modifying its efforts over time to reflect what it has learned about the customer's interests and responses. When the customer makes a purchase, or requests information, that is entered into the database, so there is a record of *transactions* to accompany the record of personal information. Using statistical modeling techniques, the marketer can begin to develop analyses that will lead to increasingly efficient decisions about product offerings, pricing, and promotional activities.

Among the most familiar examples of interactive marketing are consumer credit cards of all kinds including banks and oil companies; catalog marketers such as L.L. Bean, Lands End, and Levenger; frequent flyer and frequent traveler programs such as American Airlines AAdvantage Program and Holiday Inns' Priority Club; Internet service providers such as AOL, and Internet retailers such as Amazon.com. In each instance, the customer is known as an individual with whom the marketer can communicate directly, sending specific promotional messages and product offerings tailored to that individual. Each transaction is entered into the database—every charge card use, every telephone, Internet, or mail order, every flight or overnight stay, every sign-on to the Internet and every piece of information accessed during that session. Every electronic communication device including telephones, automatic teller machines and cash dispensers, home computers, cable-access home televisions, and point-of-sale charge card reader has the potential to become a two-way terminal in an interactive marketing system.

Some of the most sophisticated systems for interactive marketing are found at the supermarket checkout counter where countertop and hand-held scanners record the details of every single transaction—each product by brand, size, price, and other characteristics—and enter that information into the database. The purchase information can be matched up with customers' personal files as they are identified by their credit card or buying club card presented at the time of purchase.

Either immediately or following the store visit, the marketer (through sophisticated modeling and decision rules) can offer the customer special buying incentives and rewards based on his or her purchasing behavior. For example, the computer might print out instructions for the cashier to give special discounts right on the spot. Or the consumer might be given coupons good for the next purchase. For example, Coca-Cola might offer a coupon good for a free quart of Coke to every consumer who has purchased a large Pepsi or Frito-Lay may send coupons for a free bag of Munchos to everyone who buys Fritos Corn Chips. Consumers are rewarded for their participation in these programs by receiving these discounts and special promotional offers.

Even more sophisticated are so-called "single source" databases that match up the customer personal data file and the transaction file with information about that customer from other sources such as cable television monitoring systems, newspaper and magazine circulation files, consumer credit files, and so on. Thus, the marketer may be able to target television ads to customers with very specific demographic and shopping characteristics and to subsequently evaluate advertising expenditures by noting the individual purchase responses by customers in the database. The possibilities here are mind-boggling.

## Segmentation Is Key to Customer Relationship Management

The significance of these technological developments and their implementation in relationship marketing cannot be overstated. They have made possible major steps toward creating a true customer-oriented, market-driven company. The marketer who is not using these tools to improve both the effectiveness and the efficiency of its marketing programs is almost certainly not going to survive. Increasingly demanding customers are able to achieve precise responses to their changing needs and wants, their changing definition of value. Companies are able to serve their customers more precisely and more efficiently, with better products and services at lower cost. Value for the customers is enhanced in terms of product performance, better service, and lower price.

The requirements for effective marketing strategy have not changed. Market segmentation, targeting, and positioning are the fundamental elements of sound customer relationship management. The database of customer information, combined with sophisticated analytical techniques, makes possible substantially better, more precise segmentation strategies. It is also possible to monitor changes in these segments over time, as old segments decrease in size while others grow and to estimate customer profitability, by segment, and to manage it as these segments evolve.

Some customers will be profitable because of the high volume they represent; others will be profitable because of high margins. These two market segments require very different marketing strategies to serve them profitably, not just different prices. Segmentation for relationship management means finding those customer characteristics that are associated with long-term profitability as they vary from segment to segment.

## Measuring and Managing Customer Profitability

Virtually every company knows that 80 percent of its revenue comes from 20 percent of its customers; digging deeper, it is also usually true that 80 percent of its profits comes from 20 percent of its customers, but these are not the same customers who produce 80 percent of sales. The largest customers are not necessarily the most profitable. Furthermore, many companies find that a significant portion of the profit earned from their best customers is squandered trying to serve customers that are not profitable and actually result in losses. It is not uncommon to find that as many as 30 percent of customers are unprofitable; in banking, it is known that the number can be as high as 45 percent. For specific lines of business, such as retail checking, the number of unprofitable accounts might be as high as 80 percent. Hopefully, these checking account customers are also users of other, profitable bank services.

The overriding objective of customer relationship management is to secure information about customers that can be used to target marketing effort more precisely and to manage value-delivery processes more effectively and more efficiently. The goal is to attract and retain loyal, profitable customers. Customer satisfaction is a means to that end, not an end in itself. Satisfied customers are not necessarily loyal and loyal customers are not necessarily profitable. Customer relationship management must benefit both the customer and the company. Otherwise, it cannot be a stable relationship. Determining the profitability of various market segments, and of individual customers within those segments, is crucial to the success of the customer relationship management program. Customer profitability must be central to the total business model, "the entire system for delivering utility to customer and creating sustainable value from those activities," in the words of one marketing expert.[5] Research has shown that increased customer satisfaction and loyalty can have a positive influence on long-term financial performance, so customer relationship management programs, properly executed can be justified in terms of profitability.[6]

Measuring customer profitability requires data that relate to both revenues and costs. Measures of revenue on a customer basis include the total volume of purchases, prices paid, and the profit margins on those purchases. Cost measures include not only the cost of producing the product or service itself but all of the associated costs of serving that customer such as order entry, inventory, packaging, transportation, applications and engineering assistance, selling time, credit, billing, postsale service, and product collection, repair, and disposal. It is usually easier to identify revenue measures than cost measures, given the difficulty of assigning the costs of many activities to specific customers, although it can be done.

With the interactive marketing capability in place, and with a customer database that is continuously updated and analyzed for new marketing opportunities, the company can place a specific value on a given customer. The value of that customer reflects the statistically determined value of the profit margins on a future stream of transactions with that customer. The data allow the firm to compute the frequency and size of purchases by that customer and the expenses associated with communicating with and serving that customer. Further analysis will place a value on the potential purchases of new products and services to be offered to the customer.

For the interactive marketer, the customer database becomes the single most important business asset, the most valuable part of the business. It is also its most important strategic resource. The product offering becomes a variable, changing to meet the evolving needs and preferences of the customers in the database. New products are a major tool for maintaining and enhancing the relationship with the customer.

Not every marketer is a candidate for a full-blown interactive marketing system based on sophisticated information technology. But the concept can be applied at a much more immediate level. While the most dramatic opportunities may exist for consumer packaged goods marketers who have the data available from millions of transactions every day that can now be recorded at the point of sale, virtually every business has the opportunity to learn the identity of its customers, develop a small amount of valuable information about them, and keep track of their purchasing history. Using that information, even the smallest marketer has the opportunity to tailor products, services, prices, and communications more efficiently.

Remember that the basic point of relationship marketing is one of attitude—treating the customer as a partner rather than an adversary. The opportunity is to enhance efficiency by focusing marketing effort on the existing customer base rather than using a shotgun to blast marketing dollars into the anonymous marketplace hoping that a few new customers may fall to ground. Interactive marketing binds the customer to the company and vice versa. It is an opportunity to increase revenues and prices obtained while simultaneously reducing the costs of marketing and serving customers.

Company experience generally shows that it is more profitable to commit additional resources to market segments that are already profitable than to spend them trying to make unprofitable customers profitable. In some cases, the major profit opportunity is that of devoting additional attention to customers where there is potential for higher sales volume. Increased frequency of sales calls or assigning individual account managers to high-value customers, as some banks do, can result in the sale of additional products and services. In other cases, the opportunity is one of increased prices where the customer is willing to pay more to obtain the enhanced service they value on an assured basis. In yet other instances, the real opportunities reside in the cost reduction area when analysis reveals that expensive service elements have little value for customers who would be happy to do without them if prices were somewhat lower. Modeling and statistical analysis of purchase records over time may produce better insights in this regard than attempting to ask customers directly what will cause them to buy or pay more.

## Frequency and Loyalty Reward Programs

Among the most commonly found techniques for enhancing customer profitability are programs that reward customers for frequent and loyal purchasing behavior. These take the familiar form of airline frequent flyer awards programs based on mileage flown, hotel guest awards based on nights stayed, credit card rebates based on dollar amount charged, grocery store dollars rebates tied to purchase volume, and so on. The rewards offered include free travel, merchandise gifts, and lower prices.

The objective of these programs is to retain profitable customers, to prevent them from switching to competitors, and to increase their rate of purchase. The rewards offered are intended to offer greater value to the customer and to increase the level of customer satisfaction, leading to heightened repeat purchase and loyalty. Assuming that the company has in fact identified its most profitable customers to whom these programs are offered, it is believed that increased satisfaction leads to increased loyalty, which in turn pays off with additional sales volume and greater profitability.

Loyalty programs have become so commonplace in some industries, however, that their value in terms of increases in customer loyalty and profitability can be seriously questioned. It is known, for example, that the typical business traveler belongs to four or five frequent flyer programs and several hotel guest programs. In mature markets where most marketers use such programs, it is likely that the net effect is lower revenues from the same customers due to discounts and free services with little if any impact on incremental revenue from new customers. Once initiated, they are hard to terminate and marketers get trapped in a classic "Prisoner's Dilemma" in which the search for individual advantage and failure to cooperate leaves all of the players worse off.

There can be significant benefits for the marketer when the conditions are right. In general, research has shown that higher levels of satisfaction can contribute to higher levels of customer loyalty and increased usage. However, there is always the possibility that increased use of a product can lead to *decreased* satisfaction if the results of heavier use are disappointing and do not meet the customer's expectations. For example, the more experience the traveler has with a particular airline, perhaps the less satisfied that traveler will be. Whether increased usage will have a positive long-term effect on profitability requires that the additional purchase experience produces positive results and in fact leads to greater satisfaction. One research study of a credit card loyalty program concluded that members were actually more likely than nonmembers to perceive positive aspects to their purchase experience, indicating a kind of "halo effect" associated with being a member of the program and a greater willingness to overlook disappointing service. These consumers had both increased usage rates and lower rates of cancellation that those card members not enrolled in the program.[7]

## Issues in Interactive Marketing

Interactive marketing systems, especially with the use of sophisticated telecommunications and electronic commerce technology, raise a number of important management issues including:

- Confidentiality and privacy.
- Security.
- Customer frustration.
- Cost and management complexity.

### Confidentiality and Privacy

Consumers and marketers both have become increasingly concerned about the issue of confidentiality and privacy. Consumers may not take kindly to marketers' having such detailed information about them. There are clearly opportunities for abuse, especially if there is unauthorized use of the information or if a careless information provider releases incorrect information, for example about a consumer's credit history. While these are very legitimate concerns, there is also evidence that most consumers enter into such marketing relationships with enthusiasm. A large majority of those offered participation in supermarket buying clubs, for example, elect to do so. Also, many customers may view interactive marketing as an attractive alternative to a flood of unsolicited junk mail and direct marketers' telephone calls during the dinner hour.

Marketers have become quite sensitive to these concerns. Consumers using the Internet are told when the information they are about to provide is not confidential and warned that it will become part of a permanent record, giving the consumer the opportunity to cancel the message. Consumers can now notify direct marketers, telephone marketers, and Internet marketers if they do not want their names and other information made available to other marketers. The ability to "opt out" is an important protection of consumer rights.

### Security

Fraudulent use of consumer information remains another major concern that has undoubtedly kept many consumers from buying on the Internet. Similar concerns exist any time a consumer offers his or her credit card, or a personal check, or other financial information to a seller, whether it is a waiter in a restaurant, a telephone marketer, a catalog ordering representative, or an offer on television. Companies have instituted sophisticated fraud-prevention programs and have limited the availability of personal identification numbers, for example, along with programs for limiting, in some cases to zero, the customer's obligation for fraudulent use of this information. Advanced computer programming methods are now being used to provide maximum Internet security for customer-provided information, and to protect privacy and confidentiality.

## Customer Frustration

Most consumers have now had fairly extensive experience with customer relationship programs, including interactive marketing in its various forms and loyalty programs. It is fair to say that their experience has not been uniformly positive and there has been some backlash reflecting their specific concerns about privacy, confidentiality, and security. More generally, there is frustration with the one-sided nature of much so-called relationship marketing.

For example, many frequent travelers have been angered by their experience in trying to redeem their miles, finding that there were few seats available at the times they wanted to travel and that certain dates, especially during school vacations and other peak travel periods, were blocked.

Many consumers perceive that marketers use the information the consumer has provided not to serve them better but to be able to sell it to other marketers who approach the consumer with unwanted solicitations. The average mailbox is full of unwanted "junk" mail targeted to persons of known reading habits, good credit standing, or identifiable lifestyles such as recreational and travel habits. At the same time, it is difficult to see that the company to whom information is volunteered has responded with superior value delivery or more carefully tailored selling messages.

The consumer response to this situation may very well be to stop providing the information that marketers have requested. The fundamental element of trust may be disappearing from many attempts at customer relationship management.[8]

## Cost and Management Complexity

Customer relationship marketing and interactive marketing programs are expensive. One source estimated that U.S. businesses would spend $20.4 billion by 2001 and \$46 billion by 2003 on customer relationship management.[9] These sophisticated information systems require huge investments in hardware, software, and modeling capability. They require large expenditures to generate and maintain databases, whether developed on a proprietary basis or purchased commercially from vendors such as Dun and Bradstreet, Citicorp, TRW, and Information Resources, Inc.

Establishing a solid customer relationship management program, including the installation of the necessary technological capabilities, can be a daunting task. Not every marketer has the management talent and time to do it. Fortunately, there are several excellent service providers now offering totally integrated customer relationship management solutions, such as IBM's Enterprise Interactive Marketing group.[10] Simply installing the system is not enough, of course. It must also be managed effectively, which requires the commitment of additional management resources.

Issues relating to management include the development of the necessary statistical modeling capabilities within the company to be able to exploit the potential of the database. It is fair to assume that most marketing managers do not possess the necessary educational and technical backgrounds. A staff of analysts and programmers, representing a significant ongoing expense, must support line managers. Then, accounting systems must be developed for providing necessary cost, revenue, and margin measures and managing the database as a strategic asset. Some of this analytical work can also be outsourced to consultants and other service providers, but internal resources are still needed to integrate this work into the development and implementation of sound marketing strategies for customer relationship management.

## Marketing Alliances

Out of a focus on relationship marketing (including but not limited to interactive marketing) comes another strategic development of the utmost importance under the new marketing concept: marketing alliances. It starts with the proposition that the firm's customer base is its most important and most valuable strategic asset. The question is how to develop and exploit that asset for maximum strategic advantage. Improvement and broadening of the product/service offering is usually the best way to offer additional value to customers and strengthen the relationship, binding the customer ever closer to the company and building the value of the customer base itself.

This brings us back to the fundamental shortcoming of the old marketing concept. Remember that the old marketing concept failed to recognize that a commitment to customer satisfaction must be matched up with the company's capabilities, an issue that was addressed by strategic planning. No company can be all things to all customers. How can we reconcile the need for continuous broadening of the product offering in order to serve the customer base better with the limitations that any firm faces in its ability to develop and deliver products and services? How do we integrate the concepts of distinctive competence, the value proposition, and relationship marketing?

There are two answers, and the first is not necessarily the best. The first answer is to *develop internally* the capability necessary to broaden the product line offered to the customer base. Thus, an airline may decide to start an insurance company in order to offer frequent flyer program participants death and disability coverage as part of the service they receive when booking on their flights. Or a catalog marketer may decide to manufacture certain products themselves, such as the L.L. Bean hunting shoe or the Lands End canvas luggage or the Orvis fly rods, to maintain control over the quality and availability of a key part of their product offering. Business marketers often partner with strategically important customers to develop new technological capabilities appropriate and necessary to those customers' businesses. In these high-tech businesses, developing the underlying technological capabilities is a necessary precursor to generating specific new products to serve those customers.

The danger to this do-it-yourself approach is that the company may *not* be able to develop the distinctive competences required to be a truly viable competitor in this new business or to attain the scope and scale of operations required to become an efficient producer. Airlines probably are not well equipped to begin insurance companies; catalog marketers probably have limited manufacturing skills; technology-based firms cannot become distinctively competent on all of the technologies converging on their markets.

Increasingly, *marketing alliances,* the second alternative, are seen as the most effective and least risky path for expanding the product offering for the customer base. The marketer looks for partners who can provide products and services that will enhance its relationship with its customer base. The customer base remains the focus of its strategic intent and the source of its distinctive competence. For example, Amazon.com has broadened its product offering for its customers by partnering with suppliers of musical recordings and toys. At the same time, Wal-Mart has partnered with Amazon to add Internet capabilities to its customer relationships. Exxon/Mobil Oil Credit Company regularly offers merchandise from a variety of manufacturers at favorable prices and credit terms to its credit card members.

Many U.S. airlines have entered into marketing alliances with foreign carriers to extend their routes around the globe. Delta Air Lines, for example, is a member of a global marketing alliance called SkyTeam, whose other members are Aeromexico, Alitalia, Air France, CSA/Czech Airlines, and Korean Air. In addition, Delta has code-sharing arrangements with Air Jamaica, British European, China Southern, El Al, LAPA, Royal Air Maroc, South African Airways, and French Rail, and also allows its passengers to exchange frequent flyer miles with Air Malaysia and United Airlines.

The relationship marketer has the opportunity to take multiple products and services, some of them actually produced by the marketer and the others purchased, and integrate them into a total system for the customer. This function is seen in the activities of so-called "systems houses" and "value-added resellers" in the computer field, for example. Notice that the distinction between a manufacturer and a distributor becomes blurred as the firm committed to relationship marketing is likely to perform both sets of functions. The focus is always on the customer relationship, not on products or manufacturing plants.

Strategic marketing alliances also take other forms beyond broadening the product offering. In a general sense, all marketing-related combinations with other businesses are marketing alliances. These include the hiring of an advertising agency, contracting with a market research firm, and long-term relationships with resellers of all kinds. We return to the subject of marketing alliances in Chapter 6 when we look at strategic alliances and network organizations. In the present chapter, we have considered marketing alliances as a specific tool for enhancing the ability of the firm to deliver a broader range of services and products to its base of customers. Marketing alliances are a logical result of a move toward relationship marketing.

## SUMMARY

The old view of marketing that focused on the next sale is being replaced by a new view that centers on the customer as a long-term business asset. The economist's concept of the transaction occurring in a perfectly competitive market has been replaced by the concept of a relationship between the company and its customer. The purpose of marketing is not to make the sale but to gain a customer who will provide higher revenues and profit margins at lower marketing costs over the life of the relationship. Customer relationship management has the objective of enhancing profitability by improving revenues and prices from carefully defined and targeted market segments while simultaneously reducing the costs to serve those markets. Marketing communications and product offerings can be more precisely targeted at these distinct segments.

In consumer marketing, customer databases and interactive computer systems now permit the development of precisely tailored marketing strategies aimed at individual customers, who can communicate back to the marketer. In the age of addressability, interactive marketing replaces mass marketing. Customer-oriented marketing is driven by customer needs, not products and production requirements. When the company sees its customer base as its principal business asset, it may be more effective to rely on marketing alliances for broadening its product offering to these customers than to attempt to produce them internally. Growth comes from serving customers better and concentrating on distinctive competence. Managing the product offering and the value-delivery system in a value-oriented concept of business strategy now frequently requires strategic partnering at multiple points in the value chain, not just with customers. In Chapter 6, we examine in more detail the nature of these strategic partnerships in the process of developing and delivering super customer value.

# 6

# Strategic Partnering and Network Organizations

*Put all your eggs in the one basket and—WATCH THAT BASKET.*

Mark Twain

*Pudd'nhead Wilson* (1894)

Just as consumer marketing has moved away from a strict transactions orientation to customer relationship management and interactive marketing in all its forms, so has industrial (business-to-business) marketing moved from a short-term, tactical, transactions-oriented approach toward longer term, strategic, buyer-seller partnering. At the same time, aided by the Internet and other advances in information technology, procurement strategy has also incorporated more aggressive price-seeking for some products through Internet-based reverse (i.e., buyer) auctions. Information technology is not the only driver. Intensive global competition, cost-cutting pressures, and the development of network forms of organization in the pursuit of superior customer value have all contributed to the dramatic changes taking place in buyer-seller relationships.

In this chapter, we focus on the marketing of products and services by businesses to other businesses and organizations. This is largely a matter of convenience and to avoid the confusion of slipping back and forth between consumer and industrial marketing. It is important to remember, however, that the forces and strategies that are discussed are quite widespread across all kinds of markets. Many of the following observations about business-to-business marketing apply to the purchasing and partnering activities of consumer products resellers such as wholesalers, mass merchandisers, supermarket chains, discounters, warehouse stores, and Internet retailers. Manufacturers of both consumer and industrial products face the same set of forces in their procurement strategies.

In the previous chapter, a continuum of buyer-seller relationships was presented, from pure transactions to complex network organizations. To manage the analysis, that chapter focused on pure transactions, repeat transactions, and long-term buyer seller relationships with special reference to consumer marketing of goods and services. In this chapter, we concentrate on strategic buyer-seller relationships, alliances (including joint ventures), and sophisticated network organizations in business-to-business markets. It will be seen that transactions and simple buyer-seller relationships are also of critical importance to many industrial marketers and in most industries. As each of these types of buying have evolved and taken on unique roles as distinct market segments in the total procurement picture, marketers have had to adopt much more complex, tailored, and sophisticated marketing strategies to respond. New levels of analytical and strategic sophistication are necessary for effective marketing management in the markets of the twenty-first century.

## Value Chain Management

Recall from Chapter 3 that value chain management is one of the three core marketing processes. (The other two are innovation management and customer relationship management.) The concept of the supply chain was broadened into that of the total value chain. The concept of supply chain management looks backward in the value chain to the flows of goods and services that are brought together in creating the firm's product offering. The concept of the value chain incorporates both "downstream" relationships with vendors and "upstream" relationships with resellers and end-users.

To maintain the necessary strategic focus on marketing as the process of defining, developing, and delivering superior customer value profitably, it is useful to use the broader concept of the value chain rather than the narrow concept of the supply chain. Our focal point for this analysis is the firm that has the strongest relationship with the end-user customer. If you drive a Ford car or truck, Ford can correctly define you as their customer. For some purposes, however, Ford should probably think of the dealer you purchased your vehicle from as its customer. The dealer certainly believes that you are their customer, not Ford's. The dealer had taken both legal and physical possession of your car and paid Ford Motor Company for it (probably through a credit arrangement).

Inside your car or truck are products produced by hundreds of suppliers such as Bose audio components, Lear seating and airbags, Eaton axles, Goodyear tires, Milliken carpeting, General Electric lamps, and Mobil motor oil and lubricants. Products purchased from outside vendors might account for as much as 80 percent of the value of the automobile. You are not the direct customer of these suppliers except in a very limited sense.

Ford's procurement strategy reflects their judgment that they can deliver superior value to you by buying, not making, these components. They must enlist each of these suppliers as strategic partners in their value-development and value-delivery processes. It is quite likely that these vendors were involved in the design stages for the model you purchased, that their manufacturing processes and costs have been carefully monitored by Ford, and that their logistics processes (including inventory management and transportation) are carefully integrated with those of Ford. Ford probably has a major voice in the relationships of these vendors with the vendors' own suppliers, and so on back down the value chain. Marketing into these complex supply chain arrangements is a very demanding and challenging process, one that frequently crosses national and industry boundaries. Ford's marketing and procurement managers have a common cause to provide superior value to customers. Supply chain and value chain management are at the heart of the value-delivery concept of marketing strategy.

## STRATEGIC BUYER-SELLER PARTNERSHIPS

Because of their central importance, we begin the analysis by looking specifically at strategic buyer-seller partnerships, which we can then use as a reference point to look back toward simpler transactions and forward to more complex alliances. The unique nature of strategic buyer-seller partnerships makes them specific to industrial marketing, where both of the partners are businesses or other types of organizations with *strategic intent*, a concept not highly relevant for consumers.

One key distinguishing feature is the strategic intent of both the customer and the marketer. From the buyer's perspective, responsibility for a key part of the value chain has been assigned to a partner upon whom the buyer will depend for the creation and delivery of value to its customers. These relationships have been called *value-adding partnerships*[1] to capture this essential notion of the vendor as an integral part of the firm's value creation and delivery process. The concept of partnership represents a significant shift away from the adversarial nature of most buyer-seller relationships.

Most strategic partnerships require that the marketer make investments specific to the relationship with this buyer and they typically represent a significant portion of the marketer's total production capability. Business between the parties is conducted on the basis of terms and conditions specific to the partnership. It is organized and managed by a different set of rules than those that apply in normal, market-based relationships.

The concept of vendor partnering developed in the 1980s as a direct result of the quality movement and total quality management (TQM). The preponderance of pressure to move in this direction came from the buyer's side of the relationship as manufacturing organizations attempted to export their quality programs downstream into their vendors' operations. For this reason, much of the following analysis comes from the customer's perspective.

In the value-adding strategic partnership, the vendor's operations become an extension of those of the customer and the boundaries between the two organizations and their operations become blurred. Instead of simply awarding a portion of its requirements to various suppliers based on price, the customer is likely to evaluate vendors using multiple criteria. The customer is interested in the vendor's total capability for providing solutions that involve both products and services. Rather than develop a tight specification and ask several vendors to bid against it, the customer will ask the supplier partner to assist in the design of the product and the development of those specifications, to take maximum advantage of the vendor's technical competence. The design process is guided by the customer's definition of value and draws on the distinctive competence of the vendor organization.

## Just-in-Time Supply Systems

Just-in-time supply systems are the epitome of the strategic partnership. Typically these consist of a single vendor for a given part (although there could be more than one supplier) who agrees to provide 100 percent usable product to the customer in specified quantities, usually just enough for one production shift. Furthermore, these quantities must be delivered on a very tight schedule, with delivery times specified typically with acceptable variation of no more than several minutes. A truck that arrives early, when previous deliveries are still at the dock, can be as big a problem for the customer's operation as a truck that arrives late, slowing production and delaying future deliveries. It is the combination of quality, quantity, and schedule that defines a just-in-time supply system.

Just-in-time systems were developed based on the model provided by the Japanese automobile industry, especially Toyota City, in what is called the *kanban* system. Toyota City was unique because the vendor built supply facilities very close to their customer. Some of the just-in-time systems developed in the United States by Japanese automobile assemblers also included new vendor facilities nearby. One unique feature of the Japanese *kanban* systems is the interlocking ownership patterns among customers and vendors, part of the larger *keiretsu* system of organization found in Japan. The simple idea behind *kanban* is to turn the operations of vendors and the customer organization into one large machine.[2]

Just-in-time systems have two inseparable objectives: lower inventories and better quality. Traditional production scheduling and inventory systems depended heavily on the presence of "buffer stocks" at several points in the production process to protect against the presence of defective parts and inconsistencies in the ordering and delivery of parts from several vendors. These buffer inventories were subject to shrinkage and deterioration over time from damage, theft, and exposure to the elements. Because not all vendors' parts were interchangeable and because designs might change during the production period, duplication and obsolescence were major costs. Under the old systems, it was common to talk in terms of "days" or "weeks" or even "months" of inventory on hand. In just-in-time systems, the measuring units are minutes.

It is said that Toyota's managers developed their ideas about just-in-time systems while visiting the United States. Much of the initial thinking at Toyota was stimulated by Eiji Toyoda's visit in 1950 to Ford's totally integrated River Rouge plant, although there was also a lot about that wholly owned-by-Ford operation that the Toyota people thought needed improvement.[3] Other Japanese production managers are reported to have drawn inspiration from the efficiency of the modern American supermarket. They were impressed by the fact that these large retailing facilities devoted virtually all of their store space to actual shelf display of merchandise, with very little inventory sitting in the backroom.

Quality and inventory control were totally interrelated in these new systems. In the old production systems, extra inventories were needed because of the presence of unusable parts as well as unreliable logistics systems. Quality levels were stated in terms of defects per hundred or per thousand parts delivered. Incoming inspection was a major part of the supply process, but it was seldom possible to do 100 percent inspection, thus some defective parts inevitably entered the production process. If an entire batch was defective and was not caught at incoming inspection, the problem was integrated into the production system resulting in a whole production run requiring rework at the end of the production process or else allowed to go into the field where customers would discover the problem.

Perfect quality, consisting of 100 percent usable product delivered on time in the necessary quantities, could eliminate the need for incoming inspection and substantially reduce the costs of inventory, production delays, rework, and end-user customer dissatisfaction. It was a basic lesson that had to be learned the hard way—from global competitors in the marketplace. While just-in-time systems in the United States were first developed in the automobile industry in response to market inroads by Japanese manufacturers, they soon spread out to the suppliers' suppliers and into other industries.

While strategic partnering has been most visible and most advanced in the automobile industry, it has also spread quickly into a broad variety of businesses. Among the companies who have spoken publicly about their strategic partnering activities are the marketers General Electric, IBM, DuPont, Monsanto, and Honeywell with customers that include American Airlines, Ford, Milliken, Procter & Gamble, and the federal government.

## Wal-Mart's Cross-Docking System

Similar innovations were brought into retail distribution by Sam Walton's Wal-Mart Stores, Inc. Founded in 1962, Wal-Mart is today the largest retailer in the world and the United States' largest multinational corporation with revenues exceeding $200 billion. In 2002, there are over 3,500 Wal-Mart stores in the U.S. and another 1,000 in other countries. Wal-Mart employs over 1,000,000 people; over 100,000,000 customers visit their stores every week. The key to Wal-Mart's success is not its in-store merchandising. Wal-Mart is able to deliver prices that are consistently as much as 30 percent lower than those of competitors because of the efficiency of its distribution operations.

At its many distribution centers, the central paradigm shift that Wal-Mart brought to the distribution of packaged goods and other consumer products can be observed. Wal-Mart operates its own fleet of trucks and also contracts with private motor carriers. Wal-Mart manages more than 1 million loads each year. When a supplier has a load ready for shipment, it calls Wal-Mart's "Backhaul Betty" system using either the Wal-Mart automated interactive telephone system, Electronic Data Interchange (EDI), or the Internet, for instructions on where to deliver. As trucks arrive from manufacturers' plants and back their trailers up to the warehouse docks, merchandise is taken from those trailers and moved directly into trailers with loads being assembled for delivery to specific stores. The truck tractor may then pick-up another loaded trailer to return to the area from which it originated, thus avoiding an empty backhaul. It is the exception if products are actually stored in the warehouse for any length of time.

Wal-Mart quite forcefully dictates the terms under which it will conduct business with its vendors and requires that they have capabilities for both EDI and sophisticated logistics management, as well as tight standards on product quality and cost. The operation is still guided by Sam Walton's three basic beliefs, which include "Service to Our Customers," based on everyday low prices and friendly service by Wal-Mart associates in the store.[4]

## Using Sole-Source Procurements

The requirements of just-in-time supply systems created a strong leaning toward sole-source procurements. The demands of the system for integrated design, production, and logistics activities call for total integration between the customer and the supplier. This interaction requires extensive communications and multiple interpersonal relationships between the two organizations. Product, production, and distribution/logistics decisions must be made jointly and in unison. The time horizon of the relationship is very long-term. The supplier is likely to have to make extensive investments in plant, equipment, information systems, and organizational arrangements that are specific to this single customer.

In return, the customer may also have to make relationship-specific investments, in tools and dies, in shipping and handling equipment, and also in information systems. The two companies' operations become totally linked and interdependent. There is substantial risk for both of them, but each trades off the risk associated with market-based uncertainty for the risk that comes with resource dependency. Both trade-off market control for administrative control over the buyer-seller relationship, which significantly increases their costs for executing and monitoring their transactions while reducing the costs associated with low quality, high inventory, price negotiations, production uncertainty, and market uncertainty.[5]

Underlying the entire relationship there is the fundamental requirement for *trust*. Sole-source strategic partnerships are very high risk for both parties. Each is totally dependent on the other for that part of their operation—the customer for an uninterrupted supply of a critical finished product for resale, subassembly, component, or raw material; the marketer for a substantial portion of its total revenue for which it has made a substantial investment.

### Sole Sourcing May Be Unstable

The experience of many companies has revealed some fundamental problems with sole sourcing. Perhaps the most obvious are risks of interruption of supply from unforeseen emergencies such as natural disasters or fire damage to the supplier's facility. There is also risk of work stoppage created by labor-management disagreements, work slow downs, and strikes. Problems in the supplier's relationships with *its* vendors can also create problems for the customer.

Pricing risk is another matter. While contract terms may specify the conditions under which prices will change over the life of the contract, both parties may come to question whether those terms are really fair. There may be provision for annual price increases in line with the change in the government's wholesale price index or a similar guide. Industry market conditions may change over time, such as the entrance or exit of competitors in the supplying industry or changes in the availability and pricing of critical raw materials, which call into question the previously expected price terms.

The fundamental problem in a sole source procurement is the absence of market forces to control the relationship from the perspective of both parties. Almost inevitably, over time the customer is likely to question whether the vendor is really providing the best possible pricing, products, and service. Suspicions will arise about the effort being put forth on the customer's behalf in such areas as product development and process improvement. The customer's definition of value is going to evolve; the question is whether the customer perceives that the vendor's offering has also evolved in response. It is the old question "What have you done for me lately?"

The view from the supplier's side is equally frustrating as customers begin to signal fears and distrust and to question the commitment of the marketer. This can lead to substantial uncertainty for the supplier and the need to spend substantial effort in trying to reassure the customer of the soundness of the relationship. Such concerns have led some marketers to steer away from sole-source supply relationships. One Sales and Marketing Vice President for a large chemical company told me: "I don't want to be a 100 percent supplier. I will be quite happy with 80 percent or 70 percent. When I have a competitor at the account, it keeps us on our toes, gives us information about market developments, and gives the customer a standard against which to compare our pricing and our performance. Everybody is better off. Without the ability to compare and evaluate our performance, the relationship inevitably breaks down over time."

With only one source of supply, the customer is eventually going to solicit other proposals to test the market. This will put serious pressure on the incumbent in terms of both pricing and performance. The relationship can quickly turn adversarial and the management of day-to-day dealings can deteriorate rapidly, resulting in reduced efficiency, higher costs, and lower profitability for both parties. Sole source procurements are by no means a panacea. Similar forces may be at work in any buyer-seller relationship where one party is highly dependent upon the other and becomes concerned about their ability to monitor performance.

## Managing Strategic Partnerships

A major source of risk inherent in strategic partnerships in their early days was the lack of experience in managing them in most American companies. Whether they were aware of it or not, most American purchasing, sales, and marketing managers were trained and educated under the assumptions of the old transaction-based, adversarial model. Company policies and procedures reflected these assumptions. Strategic partnering requires cooperation, win/win negotiation, and joint problem-solving, whereas the traditional sale-as-conquest approach calls for persuasion, bargaining and compromise (win/lose and lose/lose negotiations), and the protection of individual self-interest (profit margins and proprietary technology). Strategic partnering calls for a new set of marketing skills and attitudes not readily found in many industrial firms.

From the marketers' perspective the move toward strategic partnering with key customers is an important step forward in the implementation of the new marketing concept. It also calls for a new set of management skills and its raises a unique set of management issues. These issues begin with the problem of selecting strategic partners. The next set of issues comes in the structuring of the relationship with the strategic customer partner. Then there follows the challenge of managing the relationship as it evolves over time. Experience has shown that strategic partnerships are extremely changeable as the relationship matures.

### When to Partner: The Customer's Perspective

From the customer's perspective, the first problem is to determine when to rely on a strategic vendor for the majority or all of the firm's requirements for a given procurement. This decision depends both on the nature of the product being purchased and the availability of attractive partners for collaboration. The internal assessment would be based in the customer's quality management program and the clear opportunity to assign an important part of its value creation activities to an efficient specialist firm with the necessary capability and the willingness to make the commitment to this customer.

## Choosing the Partner: The Customer's Perspective

Once the decision has been made to seek a vendor partner, the problem shifts to selecting the proper partner. Almost certainly, the firm will already have an established relationship with the potential partners, although this would not be true if the product was being produced internally. If the vendor is known, much of the required experience will exist throughout the customer organization in the knowledge of those who have worked with this vendor. Some of the most important information will be subjective and qualitative, having to do with the management knowledge, skills, and attitudes of the vendor firm. Professor Robert Spekman has proposed a list of questions for evaluating a potential strategic supplier:

1. How early in the design stage is the vendor willing and able to become involved?

2. Does the vendor understand the level of commitment required to achieve the targeted gains in quality and does it have the resources required to sustain that involvement?

3. Will the supplier be able to grow with us and to continue to offer improved value in the future?

4. Does the vendor really have the necessary technical competence and will it be willing to contribute that expertise?

5. Does the supplier have a team approach to quality, purchasing, and production and a positive attitude toward cooperation and collaboration, including win/win negotiating?

6. Is the supplier's senior management committed to the processes of cooperation, collaboration, and conflict-resolution that are required for strategic partnering? What have they done to demonstrate that commitment?

7. How much future planning is the supplier willing to share with us? Are they willing to share the necessary proprietary information with us and, at the same time, treat our proprietary information in a confidential manner? Is there a fundamental level of trust in the relationship?

8. How well does the supplier know our business? Has it made the necessary investment of time and effort to become truly knowledgeable about our operation and our problems?

9. Has the vendor demonstrated its commitment in the past by willingness to make necessary investments in plant, equipment, and other resources? What has been the level of that commitment?

10. What will the supplier demand of us in return? What assurances and guarantees will be required as a condition of partnering?[6]

## When to Partner: The Marketer's Perspective

Strategic partnering calls for a significant investment in relationship building and management on the part of the marketer. The first requirement, however, is the commitment to a positive attitude toward relationship marketing, as called for by the new marketing concept and that fundamental willingness to put the customer first, always, that is its hallmark. The analysis of customer relationship management in Chapter 5 has shown that there is the opportunity for improved profitability in making the commitment to strategic partnering, from more efficient marketing expenditures and greater profit margins on sales to established customers. A balanced perspective includes the caution that not all market segments, and not all customers within those segments, are good candidates for strategic partnership.

## Segments Based on Buying Behavior

Segmentation analysis may reveal that customers differ in terms of their willingness and ability to become strategic partners. Such analysis often reveals three distinct types of segments in industrial markets:

1. *Transactions customers* who are interested primarily in low price and efficient ordering and delivery service.

2. *Relationship customers* who want the support of the vendor's broad capabilities for technical assistance and innovation, tailored inventory management and logistics, and other services.

3. *Strategic partners* who require integrated operations with their vendors including such things as the co-development of technologies, joint operation of facilities, assignment of personnel from one organization to the other, and so on.

In some cases, the marketer may take the initiative based on segmentation analysis and approach customers with a differentiated marketing strategy by segment. In other cases, the customer, not the marketer, often will make the overture about partnering. In the latter case, the marketer must decide whether to make the necessary investments and commitments. As a first order of business, the marketer must decide whether its wants to do *any* business on a strategic partnering basis. Before deciding on a partner, basic strategic questions must be answered, such as:

- Is partnering consistent with the firm's business strategy?
- Is partnering consistent with the firm's distinctive competence?
- Does the firm have the necessary EDI and logistics capabilities?
- Does the business model allow value capture from a large, powerful customer in a strategic partnering relationship?

An overture from an important customer may force the issue, but it must first be addressed at the strategic level. Examining the potential relationship with a customer who has raised the question of strategic partnering can be a useful first step in analyzing the general strategic issues, but they must be resolved in a strategic framework of market segmentation, targeting, and positioning.

A critical question is whether that particular customer is actually willing to make the long-term commitments required on its part. Unfortunately, some marketers report very negative experiences in this regard. The customer brought the vendor into a strategic partnering arrangement, often as part of its quality program, only to revert to old buying tactics to drive prices down severely once the vendor was irreversibly committed to plant, equipment, and systems that made it virtually dependent for its survival on that customer. It is a disturbing fact of commercial life that it is often easier for the customer to monitor and verify the activities and performance of its suppliers, in order to invoke contract penalties and rewards, than it is for the supplier to monitor and control the activities of its customers.[7]

As in the case of a customer looking for a vendor to partner with, detailed above, the marketer must ask a series of questions about the customer and the nature of the commitment he is being asked to make. The reader can easily turn that set of questions reviewed above into those that would be asked by a potential vendor partner about its customer, simply by substituting the word "customer" for "supplier."

In those cases where the initiative for strategic partnering will come from the marketer, there are two sets of decisions. The first is whether to pursue a relationship and partnership marketing strategy or to stay in traditional old-fashioned transaction-marketing mode. A decision to stick with transactions-oriented marketing might itself require substantial commitments of resources as the firm strives to achieve the efficiencies in production and transactions management required in the intensely competitive marketplace.

The second set of required decisions, given the decision to move toward relationship marketing as a strategy, is whether to treat all customers the same way or to define distinct market segments based important differences in the nature of the buyer-seller relationship across segments. There can be substantial difficulties in this regard as the firm must develop specific product offerings, sales approaches, and service delivery capabilities for each distinct segment. It may be especially tough to keep the defined segments distinct as customers in one segment become aware of and demand features and services of product offerings in other segments with different pricing structures.

For many industries, of course, relationship marketing is not new. Most industrial marketing is relationship marketing, at least to a degree, because the customers are known by name, location, and operating characteristics, there are probably multiple personal contacts between the companies, and their operations become interdependent to a significant degree. In commercial banking, for example, relationship marketing has been accepted business practice for decades, where a given client will depend upon the bank for a full range of banking services. Even here, however, there are customers who prefer to deal on an individual transaction basis and divide their business among several banks based on current pricing for cash management services and loans of various kinds. The interrelationships between customers and vendors in such industries as chemicals, paper, machinery, mainframe computers, and railroad transportation place them within the band of relationship marketing, rather than transactions, by definition. The preponderance of industrial marketing activity is relationship marketing. The real question is whether the marketer should move to the more advanced stage of strategic partnering with customers and its attendant commitments.

It is essential to look at the details of the nature of customers and competition in a given market segment. If there is little or no meaningful product differentiation, if multiple vendors are common, if prices fluctuate wildly depending upon supply and demand, if customers are known to follow aggressive, transaction-oriented purchasing practices, then there would not appear to be great opportunities for strategic partnering, even when customers request it. On the other hand, if buyer-seller relationships tend to be very stable, if service is an important part of the product offering, if there are substantial investments and other costs associated with switching vendors, then the potential for strategic partnering is great. Strategic partnering is also favored when the customer depends on the vendor for substantial portions of its technology, as in the relationships between airframe and jet engine manufacturers and between computer chip manufacturers and their equipment suppliers.

## Cautions about Strategic Partnering

Recent theoretical analysis suggests that, contrary to the popularity of the notion that strategic partnering is good business practice for both buyers and sellers, marketers should be very careful about entering into such partnerships. This analysis concluded that they make sense for marketers only when specific assets and uncertainty create the need for such practices. That is, if the vendor is required to make specific investments, if the customer is also required to make specific investments, if there is high uncertainty about both future market conditions, especially volume requirements, and technology, then there are incentives for both parties to develop a long-term strategic partnership.

Strategic partnerships are also favored when vendor performance requirements are both complex and ambiguous, in particular when many factors other than price are important, and when normal business practice favors long-term continuity. Finally, strategic partnerships make more sense when both parties benefit from joint forecasting and planning in R&D, engineering, and production.[8] Absent those conditions, strategic partnering may be a bad idea for the marketer, even when it is a good idea for the buyer.

Put simply, the marketer must protect its investment. Strategic partnering is going to make sense when the marketer has reason to believe that the customer will honor its commitments over a long period of time and be willing to engage in collaborative action and joint problem-solving. A field study of one manufacturer's collaborative relationships with a total of 46 supplier partners confirms this viewpoint. It was found that successful partnerships are based on substantial investments by one party that are specifically valued by the other. Each side must be convinced that the other faces high costs if it elects to exit the relationship. Also, each party must have access to alternative partners and strategies, so that it does not have "all its eggs in one basket," and so that it cannot be "held hostage" or threatened by its dependence on the other. Even then, however, each party must continuously reconfirm its commitment to the other in order for the relationship to remain productive and stable.[9]

## DEVELOPING THE PARTNERING STRATEGY

We noted earlier that not all customers are attractive candidates for relationship marketing, especially as the relationship progresses toward a true strategic partnership. One way to think about the problem of developing a partnering strategy has been proposed by James Anderson and James Narus.[10] Their approach integrates the issues of partnering that we have addressed above with the broader strategic considerations of market segmentation, targeting, and positioning. It also uses the concepts of the augmented product and of product bundling to provide a comprehensive view of the strategic challenges inherent in buyer-seller partnerships. Their framework has six stages that follow the general approach we have been advocating in the current and previous chapters:

1. Market segmentation, placing customers on the continuum from transactions to partnership.
2. Assessing the value of the product to customers in each segment.
3. Market targeting—selecting customers for specific types of relationships.
4. Developing relationship-specific product offerings (value propositions).
5. Evaluating relationship outcomes and reassigning accounts.
6. Updating the relationship offering.

### Market Segmentation

In every industry or market, customers will illustrate a wide range of preference and conduct when it comes to buyer-seller partnerships. Some will evidence a clear preference for low price and a transaction type of business relationship. Others will demand substantial service commitments from their suppliers, have a broader definition of quality, and expect to develop long-term relationships. The transaction customers will be interested in what can be essentially thought of as the core (generic or expected) product.

The relationship customers are interested in the augmented product. Partnership customers must also be interested in the potential product.

A marketer may face the full range of relationship possibilities in its served markets. A large paper manufacturer, for example, may have customers in several industries including retailing, newspapers, catalogues, magazines, book publishing, packaging, and envelopes. Within each of these industry segments there will be a broad variety of purchasing practices. In some industries, say envelopes, there may be primarily a transaction orientation; in other industries, say newspapers, the emphasis may be on long-term relationships; in packaging, the customers may tend to emphasize strategic partnerships that draw on the paper manufacturer's full technical capabilities. In other industries, say magazines, the paper manufacturer may see a full range from transactions to collaborative partnerships.

Within each customer industry or market segment, there are likely to be subsegments of customers with similar buying characteristics. The objective of the segmentation exercise is to identify customers for differentiated marketing effort, in terms of both the product offering and marketing communications.

## Value Assessment

The objective of strategic partnering for both buyer and seller is the same—superior value from using the vendor's products in the target application leading to improved profitability and enhanced shareholder value. At a given point in time, however, not all customers who are potential candidates for relationship or partnership marketing may be fully aware of the benefits. The marketer needs to assess their operations and their management to understand the opportunities that may exist above and beyond the current methods of doing business. The customer's definition of value, as we have seen, changes continuously. An enhanced product offering may be the key to moving the customer away from its transaction and price orientation.

Many of the points concerning customer profitability analysis in the previous chapter also apply here. Revenue potential, by segment, requires looking at the opportunity for both sales volume and value-based pricing. Cost estimates must include all elements of the cost to serve each customer segment and to reach them with effective marketing communications, as well as differences in the actual costs of producing the product.

An assessment of the potential for delivering superior value to a prospective customer should be based on a clear understanding of the customer's operation and its definition of value. What is the customer's strategy for making money? Is it trying to be a low-cost producer or does it go to market with a highly differentiated, high-quality product offering? Does the customer define cost in terms of purchase price for the core product or does it have a total-cost-in-use view that looks at the total product offering, including service? How can our product deliver superior value: By offering a low-cost, low price alternative—the core or expected product, or by offering an augmented product? To repeat, within a given market segment, there may be a wide or narrow range of vendor relationships that characterize that segment.

## Market Targeting

A critical management judgment is called for in deciding on the number of segments to be targeted. The marketer must assess its own capabilities in order to make this judgment. Do we have the capabilities required to compete in multiple market segments? Can we sell both a core/unbundled product and an augmented/bundled product offering? It may be very hard to keep products, strategies, and operations separate. Do we have the marketing communications skills and resources, especially the depth and breadth in our sales organization, to launch focused marketing effort at multiple market segments?

The most sophisticated marketers will lean toward a "portfolio" of relationships, from pure transactions to strategic partnerships.[11] They will recognize the potential, over time, for upgrading customer relationships into higher value-producing opportunities. They will see market segments that are relatively underserved by their competitors with less refined market segmentation, targeting, and positioning strategies.

Other firms, especially those in tightly focused market niches and possessing limited production and marketing resources, will elect to concentrate marketing effort on one or a few market segments where they can achieve unique and sustainable competitive advantage. These may be relatively small market niches that are not likely to attract larger, resource-rich competitors. With these focused segments, it is still possible to develop a range of relationships.

The last step in market targeting is to select specific customers for marketing effort. Once again, this calls for detailed analysis of each potential customer's use situation, production capabilities, definition of value, and relationship preferences. It is important to identify their existing suppliers and the nature of those relationships, in order to make a judgment as to whether they are likely to be strongly satisfied with their existing relationship.

## Developing the Product Offering and the Value Proposition

Having targeted market segments and individual accounts in those segments, the marketer still faces the difficult problem of developing its product offering for those customers and the core value proposition that will be the basis of all communications. Once the different types of customers' and their different definitions of value are understood, the company can refine its value propositions by segment, the reasons why each type of customer should do business with them rather than their competitors.

While there should be a strong bias toward relationship marketing and strategic partnering, where there will be an opportunity for enhanced value delivery and value-based pricing, it may also be that the best opportunities exist in unbundling the product, focusing on the core product, and offering the customer a very attractive price. If the supplier has the capability to be a low-cost producer, this can be an attractive alternative if the product is more or less commodity like and if the customer doesn't have a real need for the high-cost service enhancements being offered by competing suppliers. Today's transactions-oriented market segments may be just as sophisticated as their relationship-oriented counterparts. Market transactions must be conducted with extreme efficiency, typically incorporating the most advanced information technology including Internet capabilities for delivering product, pricing, and scheduling information as well as order-entry and tracking capabilities.

On the other hand, an enhanced service offering—giving the customer an augmented product rather than merely the expected product—is often the key to delivering superior value to the customer. In many industrial market segments, especially those with well established and limited competition, a new market entrant with a superior product offering may be able to change the key success factors by significantly increasing customer expectations.

If the marketer follows a strategy of differentiated marketing, as opposed to concentrated marketing in a single segment, the company will need to develop distinctive product offerings for each segment. Special care must be taken to insure that the market segments are in fact distinct and to offer product bundles that are unique in each segment. Service will be a critical part of the total product offering, along with unique product features, and is likely to be the most important basis for differentiation. Opportunities for differentiation based solely on superior product technology have become increasingly rare and, when available, short-lived.

## Organizing to Sell and Deliver the Relationship Product Offering

Equal in importance with the differentiated product offering, tailored marketing communications and distribution arrangements will be required for each segment. In relationship marketing, the sales representative and the distributor become part of the product offering. Some customers may be reached through direct selling, either by a geographic salesforce or by a salesforce organized for key accounts, a particular industry, or a specific product offering. Others may be served through the Internet or telemarketing or various types of resellers. If the company has identified multiple target markets with unique requirements, it will want to consider using several different types of marketing channels and sales approaches, in what has been called a "hybrid channel system."[12]

The salesforce is especially critical as a tool for implementing a relationship or partnership marketing strategy. A market segment characterized by a transaction approach, a limited core product, and low price will require a different type of selling effort than a partnership-oriented segment with an augmented product offering at a higher price. Separate sales organizations may be required. One approach identifies three types of selling:

1. Transactional sales.
2. Consultative sales.
3. Enterprise sales.[13]

*Transactional* customers may be reached through a nonspecialized geographic salesforce calling on potential customers in several target industry segments. These customers are buying the core, expected product and nothing more. They do not need or value the intangible product variables that the supplier might be able to offer. The selling task may involve mostly soliciting and responding to requests for quotation or taking orders from a standard product catalogue.

However, if that is all these customer require, it is likely that they can be served more efficiently and effectively by means of the Internet, EDI, or the telephone. Customers will not be willing to pay the price required to cover the costs of an inefficient and unwanted salesforce. Unless the sales representative adds true value for the customer, chances are their job should not exist. Wal-Mart, for example, refuses to meet with suppliers' salespeople, except when there are specific issues to be addressed.

Market segments receiving the standard product offering may be serviced through independent distributors who have the freedom to offer further price reductions to these transaction-oriented customers. The higher the value of the product offering in the customer's use, the more likely that customer should be targeted for relationship or partnership marketing and served direct through a product, market, and/or account specialized salesforce.

*Consultative* customers need and value the information and assistance that a marketer's sales representative can provide. They are buying more than the core product. They are buying the information and service that goes with it, and they value the assistance of the sales rep. Some of the customers identified as strategic partners are likely to require a key account sales organization, perhaps with several sales representatives and managers from several functions assigned to different locations of the account, carefully managing the relationship in a negotiated, collaborative approach to address customer problems with special engineering, manufacturing, logistical, and service solutions. Key account managers may be responsible for coordinating all of these activities with the purchasing activities of their customers on a global basis, providing the customer with the single point of contact that they are likely to demand.[14]

*Enterprise* selling is likely to be a top management responsibility with key executives working with top management from the customer on a regular basis to oversee, manage, and negotiate the terms of the relationship. These customers are looking for the new knowledge offered by their vendor partners to help them grow and shape their businesses. They want the supplier's resources to become an integral part of their value development and delivery processes. Some parts of the customer's operation may be handed over to the vendor for management. As one example, an oil refiner might turn over total responsibility for managing its refinery to an engineering, maintenance, and construction firm. Ownership of the facility itself might transfer to the technical specialist who would in turn lease back the facility to the refiner or perhaps contract to sell them the output of the process. It involves a complete redefinition of the boundaries between the two organizations and a blurring of the distinction between buyer and seller.

## Segmented Marketing and Hybrid Go-to-Market Systems

The investment and expense involved in maintaining multiple salesforces and distribution arrangements for distinct market segments are major reasons why the firm may decide to follow a focused strategy of concentrated marketing. Even if the firm has the resources for more than one approach, it may still decide that the complexity of maintaining distinctively different marketing strategies and organizations is a source of potential problems, especially if customers in one segment become aware of different pricing, product offerings, services, and sales coverage and distribution arrangements available to customers in another market segment. Most likely, customers in the augmented product, relationship segments will demand the lower prices of customers in the core product, transaction segments, while those enjoying lowest prices will demand higher service levels. Neither may be willing to give up what it is already getting, so simply reassigning them to another market segment may not be the answer. Customers don't always understand or care about the marketer's segmentation strategy!

Not all customers targeted for a given approach will be responsive to it. Stable relationships require that both parties be comfortable with the approach adopted by the other. There will be obvious mismatches where the marketer tries a relationship approach and the customer responds in transaction mode or *vice versa*. There will also be instances where the customer would prefer a stronger relationship orientation and an enhanced product offering with better service while the sales representative, through ignorance and insensitivity to the customer's needs, continues to behave in transaction mode, pushing price and looking for the next order rather than concentrating on building a stronger relationship.

In the latter instance, the real problem may be a poorly trained and supervised sales representative rather than a strategic failure. The marketing strategy won't count for much if the salesforce is not prepared to implement it in the field. The natural tendency of most industrial salespeople is to concentrate on getting the next order, and to assume that the lower the price the higher the probability of making the sale.

Other customers may respond positively at first and then modify their behavior over time. This is especially an issue in strategic partnering, where the vendor is required to make large initial investments and other resource commitments in order to become a strategic partner for its customer. Several studies have found that strategic partnerships remain viable to the extent that *both* parties have substantial and roughly equal dependence on the other. If the supplier has made the principal investment and committed a significant portion of its production capacity to the strategic customer while the customer has continued to maintain relationships with other vendors (perhaps on related product lines even if there is a sole source arrangement with the focal supplier), the relationship will be unstable, especially if the suppliers experience wide swings in their sales volume with this customer. On the other hand, sole source procurements can be equally unstable, as noted above.

## Cycles in Buyer-Seller Relationships

There appears to be a predictable evolution in strategic buyer-seller partnerships. After the initial courting period in which the parties make their mutual commitments and go through a "honeymoon" period, often characterized by public pronouncements about the path-breaking nature of the partnership, the collaborators settle down to do the work required in managing the partnership. There will be inevitable problems, misunderstandings, and disagreements, not all of which will be completely resolved to the satisfaction of both partners. This can lead to a period of growing dissatisfaction with the relationship, an active search for other partners, strained relations, and either reconciliation or dissolution of the strategic partnership.

This cycle can be anticipated and managed, in particular by knowing the signs of trouble to look for and having the necessary mechanisms in place for joint problem solving and conflict resolution. If the basic forces at work in the partnering cycle are ignored, problems are inevitable.

As noted in our brief discussion of the problems inherent in sole source procurements, the basic weakness in strategic partnering comes from the relative lack of "market control." This is the negative side of the move away from market-based transaction orientation. In a transaction type of buyer-seller relationship, the customer has the comfort of knowing that there are competitive product offerings and prices available. These are a handy reference for assessing the performance of the vendor (although, as noted earlier, it is harder for the supplier to monitor the customer's performance). Competitive bids are frequently solicited just "to keep the supplier honest." Similarly, the threat of a potential competitor can provide the necessary incentive for the vendor to strive to achieve cost improvements and product innovations.

As we move from transactions to strategic partnering, we substitute bureaucratic or administrative control for market control. The buyer's and seller's operations become linked as if they were part of the same organization and their relationship is guided by internal communications, negotiated agreements, policies, guidelines, and procedures as part of their joint understanding. Market forces have been largely removed from the relationship.

Experience suggests that this is a very fragile and tenuous arrangement, especially for the buyer who is accustomed to doing business in the adversarial transaction mode. How can he or she be sure that they are "getting the best deal" and being treated fairly by the vendor? How can the buyer know that the supplier is constantly exerting best effort to find cost reductions and to improve its product? What incentive does the supplier have to make the necessary investments in research and development? There may also be specific issues in the day-to-day relationship such as a quality problem, or an interpersonal conflict with the sales rep, or a late delivery, or a disagreement between personnel of the two organizations that will provoke an accusation of lack of commitment.

One way for the buyer to try to get answers is to explore the market and initiate discussions with other potential vendors. This is most likely to take the form of simply looking for a lower price, without necessarily getting into the details of the competitive product and service offering. This will not only reveal new options from other marketers anxious to establish a new relationship but it is also likely to introduce suspicion and distrust into the established collaboration. The buyer may decide to try to renegotiate the arrangements or may invite another vendor to provide a portion of the requirement. Sensing this possibility, the marketer may also be looking for new partners who will place a higher value on the commitments he has made to the production and service capabilities that are now being questioned by his existing partner. At this stage, the strategic partnership is in danger of breaking down as each side accuses the other of unfair dealing and violations of the agreement.

It is essential that the marketer committed to strategic partnering be sensitive to the issues raised by the absence of market control. The marketer must continuously monitor the relationship for signs of stress and have procedures that are clearly understood by members of both organizations for dealing with the inevitable problems and disagreements. The marketer must be sensitive to the buyer's need for frequent demonstration of satisfactory performance under the contract, and offer continuous improvements in the product and service offering.

In the final analysis, "What have you done for me lately?" is a legitimate question to ask of a vendor. As the customer faces changing requirements from its own customers, continued pressures for cost reduction, changing technology, and changing competition, it must depend upon its strategic vendor partners for new solutions, and better and better definitions of superior value.

Having said that, however, it isn't obvious that strategic partnerships should last forever or that transaction customers cannot evolve into relationship and partnership prospects. As the customer's situation changes, as their definition of value changes, so must the marketer change its approach.

## Updating the Relationship Offering

It was pointed out in Chapter 3 that continuous innovation is "the name of the game" under the new marketing concept. It follows logically from the commitment to putting the customer's interests first in all aspects of the business operation. If quality is defined as meeting and exceeding customer expectations, and if the customer's expectations keep increasing as the company improves its performance and competitors make promises of superior value, continuous improvement is an inevitable requirement for survival in the customer relationship. As product lifecycles evolve and markets mature, the customer expects more for less. As often noted throughout this text, offering the augmented product has the effect of educating the customer about the product and the market so that they can now concentrate more on finding the lowest price for the enhanced product offering. In a real sense, good is never good enough.

The marketer must systematically, from time to time, assess the adequacy of the product offering for a given market segment and adjust it accordingly. Given a thorough consideration of what is involved in the necessary improvement and upgrading, the marketer may decide that the cost of the next generation of product improvements is beyond the company's capabilities. The choices then are to exit the market or to unbundle the product and resegment the market. These may offer more attractive profit opportunities, especially for smaller firms following niche marketing strategies.

For example, consider a market in which a major competitor has made a huge investment in information technology. That competitor now offers every customer a computer terminal tied into a communication network that provides instantaneous information on product availability at multiple inventory locations, all pricing and credit terms, technical information on product features and use, electronic order processing, and overnight delivery anywhere in North America. Our marketer may correctly conclude that this has fundamentally changed the key success factors in the business. The best response for the smaller competitor may be to significantly reduce its technical service levels and prices and to focus on those customers in the nearby regional market who require standard products and are too small or otherwise unable to take advantage of the new technology. Our small marketer may be able to offer the benefits of nearby service and better prices in comparison with the larger competitor.

Modifications to the relationship offering should be considered in both directions as the market evolves. There is a never-ending cycle in which differentiated products regress toward commodity status while commodity-like products are differentiated with new product features and services. At any point in the cycle, the marketer's strategic choices should be made in the context of its relationship marketing strategy and guided by its strategy for developing and maintaining its distinctive competence. Market segmentation, targeting, and positioning remain as the essential strategic activities in developing the value proposition in relationship marketing. As the customer's definition of value keeps changing, so must the firm's value proposition. Value is defined in the marketplace, by the customer. That is the basic truth upon which the new marketing concept is based.

To summarize briefly this rather lengthy discussion of strategic buyer-seller relationships in industrial markets, the evolution from transactions toward strategic partnering is often driven by the customers' total quality management and cost reduction programs. The result may be better quality and lower cost for the supplier as well when the operations of buyer and seller are more carefully integrated with joint forecasting and planning of requirements. The opportunities for more profitable and more stable long-term strategic partnerships are balanced by the higher risks associated with interdependence. Only if the investments and commitments of the parties are in reasonable balance and if both recognize and value the commitments that each has made for the other will these relationships remain stable and viable.

Sophisticated marketers can think of a range of business relationships from transactions through increasingly complex buyer relationships to true strategic partnerships. Market segmentation, targeting, and positioning can yield highly differentiated marketing strategies for each of several distinct segments, taking full advantage of the different opportunities represented by customers who prefer to do business based on transactions, relationships, or partnerships. For all but the most sophisticated and resource-rich firms, the better opportunity may be to concentrate marketing effort on those market niches which are relatively underserved and where the company's distinctive competence can result in the best product offering.

We now broaden our analysis to include the whole range of strategic alliances that are available to the firm committed to delivering superior value to customers. These include not just traditional vendors but other partners who can help the firm complete its value offering. As the firm defines its distinctive competences and decides which to develop most aggressively, it needs to find strategic partners who can assist it with their own unique capabilities.

## Hierarchical, Bureaucratic Organizations Evolve into More Flexible Forms

For too long, bureaucracy, hierarchy, and multiple layers of middle management protected CEOs from their customers. Marketing processes were strictly controlled, but not integrated, in functional silos with poor communication and coordination across them. Customer relationship management was nonexistent from a strategic point of view. Messages from dissatisfied customers, containing information on the nature of competition and how customer definitions of value were changing, seldom if ever found their way to the policy and business strategy level of the organization in a timely manner. The new product development process, the lifeblood of any business, was slowed down by the need for reviews across multiple business functions and approvals at multiple levels of the hierarchy. Supply chain management was a foreign concept as the large company tried to achieve control and cost efficiency by making as much of the total product offering as possible and keeping suppliers at arm's length.

Hierarchies as an organizational form are governed by policies and procedures designed to preserve and protect the *status quo,* including managers and their departments. They tend to be internally focused, not externally driven. Values relating to entrepreneurship, flexibility, responsiveness, and innovation were not prevalent in most large, traditional, hierarchical, bureaucratic organizations of the kind that spawned the strategic planning process described in Chapter 2.

New, flexible organization forms began emerging in the late 1970s as large corporations searched for ways to defend themselves against more nimble global competitors who were winning the battle for the customers. These new organization forms, variously called virtual corporations, strategic alliances, network organizations, and other names, were shaped by the renewed importance of customer orientation, the quality imperative, the quickening pace of technological change, the convergence of multiple technologies in a given area, and the overriding need for responsiveness and flexibility in the intensely competitive global marketplace. They consisted of multiple strategic partnerships and alliances, joint ventures, and other temporary business relationships as well as wholly-owned subsidiaries and divisions of established corporations. Traditional organization forms were modified, supplanted, and integrated into the evolving new structures. Much publicized processes of downsizing, de-layering, and mergers and acquisitions affected such corporate giants as General Motors, IBM, Boeing, Sears Roebuck, Eastman Kodak, Xerox, and United Technologies, to name a few.

These flexible organization forms did not appear out of thin air. In many industries, such flexible arrangements among multiple partners have been a characteristic way of doing business for decades. Design, engineering, and construction firms, aerospace and defense contractors, oil drilling and exploration companies, and movie producers are among the many examples of companies that typically did business with flexible forms of project management organization, tailoring the relationships and resources to the unique requirements of each large-scale project.

As these flexible, network forms of organizations have become common ways of doing business, they have serious implications for the role of marketing in the organization. With only the rudiments of traditional bureaucratic forms of coordination and control, how can a firm keep the entire enterprise focused on the customer and develop and manage market segmentation, targeting, and positioning strategies to deliver maximum value to customers?

Network organizations represent a fulfillment of the twin mandates of the marketing concept—customer orientation and innovativeness. In contrast to the old marketing concept, however, they address specifically the strategic issue of matching up customer needs with the firm's distinctive capabilities. Network organizations are constantly redefining how the company can participate with multiple partners in the development and delivery of superior value to customers. They are defined by their customer base and their knowledge and skills, not by their factories and offices.

## STRATEGIC ALLIANCES

We have already examined two types of strategic alliances in this and the preceding chapter: strategic partnerships with major customers (or with vendors, from the buyer's perspective) and marketing alliances in which the firm seeks a partner in a related business who can help complete the product offering or who can offer a needed marketing skill, such as advertising creativity, distribution, or marketing research. Other types of strategic alliances include partnerships with real or potential competitors for the development of a new product, R&D partnerships focused on achieving a desired technical breakthrough (usually involving two distinct but related technologies), or manufacturing joint ventures to own a facility to produce products that will be sold separately by the partners. Strategic alliances among airlines from different regions and countries have been formed to give each carrier a broader reach beyond the markets it has traditionally served and to make travel arrangements easier for their customers. Unfortunately, ongoing disagreements among nations with respect to airport access and the weak economic condition of many airlines have caused short life spans for many of these alliances.

One of the most familiar forms of strategic alliance is the joint venture in which the partners combine resources to produce some tangible result such as a new product. Joint ventures are the most complete and complex form of strategic alliance, usually resulting in a new company which can itself begin to enter into other types of strategic alliances. In contrast to other forms of strategic alliances, joint ventures have their own capital structure, with the partners as owners.

Strategic alliances are a tool for achieving the strategic objectives of the partners. Strategic alliances can be defined formally as a strategic collaboration among partners involving the commitment of assets and management resources with the objective of enhancing the partners' competitive positions. Each element of this definition is important. The collaboration must have the strategic intent of enhancing the partners' competitive positions. There must be a commitment of assets, in the form of investments or facilities. And there must be a commitment of management time and personnel to the venture.

Among the most common objectives for strategic alliances are exploitation of the potential inherent in related technologies, new product development, building an efficient production facility, entry into a new market—either a foreign country or a new industry, increasing global service capabilities for global customers, and outsourcing manufacturing to a more efficient competitor. To illustrate the many forms that strategic alliances can take, the following examples have been widely publicized:

- General Mills combined with PepsiCo, Inc. to create a joint venture to market their snack foods in Europe. General Mills also formed a 50–50 joint venture with Nestlé to sell General Mills cereals everywhere but in North America.

- Ford Motor Company teamed up with Mazda Motors Corporation, with initial 25 percent ownership that increased over time, to create ten new cars including the Ford Explorer/Mazda Navajo, built by

Ford; the Ford Probe/Mazda MX-6; a new version of the Ford Es-
cort/Mercury Tracer; the Festiva; and the Mazda 323. A new Mazda
pickup truck was built by Ford. When Ford built its Hermosillo
(Mexico) assembly plant, said to be the most efficient in the world, it
modeled it after Mazda's Hofu (Japan) plant. Ford also partnered
with Volkswagen to create Autolatina to produce cars in Brazil, a
venture that was ultimately unsuccessful.

- IBM and Apple Computer entered into an extensive agreement to
  collaborate in developing new products in several areas including
  hardware, software, and networking. The agreement called for two
  new companies to develop multimedia software and a new operating
  system, cross-licensing of technology, and shared facilities and personnel. IBM has historically had many hundreds of strategic alliances, especially with software developers, whom it calls "business
  partners."

Strategic alliances are often the best answer to the strategic problem of
entry into a foreign market, as a means for overcoming political and cultural barriers. Most strategic alliances involve the sharing of technology,
either product or process technology and often both. Very often these are alliances between partners who are also competitors. By allowing the partners
to share and jointly develop technology, a strategic alliance can speed the
new product development process and substantially reduce the cost. Strategic alliances are a virtual necessity for the firm that wishes to compete in the
global marketplace.[15]

Strategic alliances are not without their problems. Many studies, by
both academic researchers and management consultants, have found that
the chances of a strategic alliance succeeding are less than 50/50, where success is defined as meeting the partners' objectives.[16] The problems usually
result from inter-organizational conflicts between the partners, including
incompatible expectations, often rooted in very different corporate cultures.
It helps if the firms are of roughly equal size. It has also been found that alliances between a strong firm and a weak firm have a lower probability of
success; they should be based on mutual strengths rather than being intended to overcome a strategic weakness. The strategic rationale for the alliance usually proves to have been sound, however, even if the alliance fails.
That is, most alliances fail because of bad implementation and management, not because they were bad ideas in the first place. As more companies
gain experience with strategic alliances, and as their experiences become the

basis for more research and writing on the management of alliances, the chances for success have improved.[17]

The point of our analysis is not to assess the management issues involved in strategic alliances but to recognize their strategic importance, the way they are changing the shape of many organizations, and the new requirements for marketing management that result from these organizational arrangements.

## THE VALUE CHAIN REVISITED

In Chapter 3, we introduced the concept of the value chain, that set of linked activities from raw material to end use by the consumer that is involved in developing and delivering value. Earlier in this chapter, buyer-seller relationships were positioned in the context of the total value chain. It includes the extraction of the raw materials and their processing, research and development activities, the design and production of goods and services, the assembly of products, their promotion and distribution, the combination of products and services into systems, pricing, customer service, and all of the support functions such as advertising, sales promotion, market research, transportation, credit and financing, and public relations and publicity required to bring goods and service to customers. (See Figure 6.1.) Today, the concept of the value chain must also go beyond customer use and look at the consequences of that consumption and the activities necessary to deal with them, including recycling, recovery, and reclamation of waste products.

Obviously, no single economic actor is able to perform all of the functions along the value chain efficiently without help from other organizations and economic actors. One important contribution of the value chain concept is that it looks at the firm from the outside, as part of a total value-delivery process, not as a separate entity isolated from the rest of the competitive world. The fundamental strategic issue for the firm is how to get the necessary functions performed most efficiently.

Every firm makes a number of strategic choices about those parts of the value chain that it will perform internally and those for which it will rely on outside suppliers and other partners. Given the need for flexibility in responding to a changing competitive environment and the customer's continuously evolving definition of value, many firms have shifted their bias from owning production facilities and making most of their products

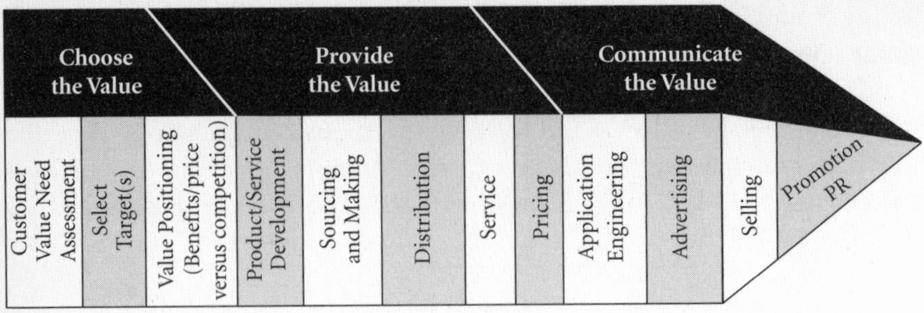

| Choose the Value | | | Provide the Value | | | | | Communicate the Value | | | | |
|---|---|---|---|---|---|---|---|---|---|---|---|---|
| Customer Value Need Assessment | Select Target(s) | Value Positioning (Benefits/price versus competition) | Product/Service Development | Sourcing and Making | Distribution | Service | Pricing | Application Engineering | Advertising | Selling | Promotion PR | |

Notes:

Value = Benefits – price

Benefit = Attribute(s) desirable to customer (in customer's eyes).

Price = Total costs to customer (as perceived by customer).

Superior perceived value = Customer believes buying/using the product or service gives a net value superior (more positive) than alternative's value.

**FIGURE 6.1** The marketing value-chain. *Source:* Cathy Anterasian and Lynn W. Phillips, *Discontinuities, Value Delivery, and the Share-Returns Association: A Reexamination of the "Share-Causes-Profits" Controversy,* Research Program Monograph, Report No. 88-109 (Cambridge, MA: The Marketing Science Institute, October 1988), 8. Reproduced with permission.

themselves to leasing or sharing assets and buying products and services from others with stronger capabilities. As the firm tries to define its distinctive competences and to develop its unique value proposition for the customer, it must make a conscious strategic choice about those activities it will perform itself and those for which it will depend upon others. For most firms, this now means becoming much more focused on a small set of activities where it is, or has the potential to be, the best in the world.

## Defining the Firm's Position in the Value Chain

Every company must be clear about the functions required to create superior value for customers, where it has the competence to do something at the quality level of the best competitors in the world, and where it must depend on other partners for their distinctive competence, now and in the future. Prahalad and Hamel have developed the concept of "core competence," which we have been referring to as "distinctive competence," and its relationship to strategy.[18] An understanding of the firm's core competence is fundamental to the development of a strategy for delivering superior value to customers and as the basis for forming strategic alliances for creating and delivering superior value. Prahalad and Hamel make the point this way:

> Nor is it possible for a company to have an intelligent alliance or sourcing strategy if it has not made a choice about where it will build competence leadership.[19] . . . How can a company make partnerships intelligently without a clear understanding of the core competences it is trying to build and those it is attempting to prevent from being unintentionally transferred?[20]

Certain strategic alliances will be based on the need to "import" the partner's distinctive competence, one that the firm does not have and does not wish to develop itself, in order to have an up-to-date and complete product offering. This might lead to a strategic alliance with a vendor of a critical component, for example, such as the laser for a computer printer, or with an independent distribution organization in a foreign country. In this type of strategic alliance, the partners are operating at different points in the value chain, and we can call them "vertical" alliances.

Other strategic alliances are created for the co-development of a technology that is central to the distinctive competence and strategic commitment of both parties.[21] These can be called "horizontal" alliances. In this instance, both partners are operating in the same range on the value chain. They are competitors, at least potentially. Both parties are committed to achieving and sustaining competence in that area and see the alliance as the best vehicle for maintaining it. In such alliances, developing terms for sharing the new technology poses one of the larger challenges in forming and managing the alliance.

One of the reasons for strain in strategic alliances is that, over time, horizontal alliances may begin to look more vertical as a partner who was joined because of its competence at a different point in the value chain begins to move into the firm's position in the value chain. A specific illustration is provided by the American firm that formed a marketing alliance with a Japanese distributor. Over time, the Japanese company gained familiarity with the American firm's product technology and became interested in manufacturing products for sale in Japan. At the same time, the American firm began to develop its own sales and service organization in Japan, creating the distinct impression that it was planning to compete with its partner. The strategic alliance ended with both firms as competitors. In general, it is not unusual for a company that has partnered to provide a technical component to a product assembler to become an assembler itself and begin competing with its former customer partner.

# MARKETING CHANNELS AS STRATEGIC ALLIANCES

Marketing channels are a well-known example of strategic alliances. Here is another illustration that strategic alliances and network organizations are not new. Partnerships between manufacturers and distributors have been around for centuries, beginning in the United States when Cyrus Mc-Cormack created a network of dealers for his mechanical reaper. The extension of similar partnership arrangements to other types of companies in the value chain is a strikingly new idea, however. It is common now to find strategic partnerships with multiple parties as several stages of the value chain, reaching backward to raw materials, core technologies, and component parts as well as forward to the last stages of distribution and the end-user. In bringing its bovine growth hormone, Protiva, to market, Monsanto partnered with Genentech for the recombinant DNA technology and manufacturing, Federal Express for distribution, Boatman's Bank for credit and collection, Waste Management for collection and disposal of used needles and syringes, and several thousand veterinarians to support farmers in the field.

Marketing channels provide a prototype for strategic alliances between partners at different points in the value chain. With very few exceptions, American and European firms have tended to be specialists in either manufacturing or distribution. Automobile, farm equipment, and truck manufacturers, for example, have always relied on independent dealers while large retailers such as Montgomery-Ward, J.C. Penney, and Wal-Mart have rarely owned their own factories, relying instead on manufacturers, over whom they were often able to exercise considerable influence and control. The integrated petroleum companies provided something of an exception as many that owned their marketing and distribution organizations, but these were separate companies, many of which have now been sold off or shut down.

Services companies provide a more complicated situation. Insurance companies, for example, tend to be divided between those who sell their products through independent agents and those who go to market through their own sales organization. Airlines, car rental companies, hotels, and cruise lines rely heavily on travel agents to market their products but at the same time maintain their own reservations, sales, and marketing organizations. Strategic marketing alliances have become very common in the travel industry, bringing airlines, car rental firms, cruise lines, and hotels together to offer packaged product offerings to the traveler.

# DEFINING THE CUSTOMER IN A NETWORK ORGANIZATION

Defining the customer becomes a key strategic issue for the players in a network organization. Who is Procter & Gamble's customer: Wal-Mart or the shopper who buys the diapers? Can it be both? These are critically important questions, given the basic principles of the new marketing concept:

- Customers define the business.
- Customers define value.
- Customer-orientation should be the driving force in every business.
- Marketing must move from a transaction- to a customer-relationship-orientation.
- Information about customer needs, preferences, and buying patterns is the most important input to all business decisions.
- The firm should be committed to continuous innovation to offer superior value to customers.

The definition of the customer in a network organization must be found in the concept of partnership. From the manufacturer's perspective, the brand name represents a promise to the consumer or end-user, a promise of consistent product quality and performance. Because that has value for the consumer, it also has value for the reseller. But, as discussed in Chapter 5, if the consumer is not known to the manufacturer, there is no possibility of a relationship between them. If there is no brand identification, the question is moot; if the customer can't identify the manufacturer, there can be no relationship. On the other hand, a well-known manufacturer's brand is a major source of strength in the manufacturer's relationship with the reseller.

Even if the end-user customer is not known to the manufacturer of the branded product, the customer is frequently known to the reseller. Some retailers such as Sam's Club (an affiliate of Wal-Mart), are "for members only" and charge an annual membership fee. Others such as J.C. Penney establish a relationship with the customer through a credit card and charging privileges. Buying clubs are the basis for relationship building in supermarket chains that have adopted scanner technology and built customer databases. In these instances it is the reseller who "owns" the customer and who has the principal relationship with that customer. The manufacturer is a partner with the reseller in delivering superior value to the customer, embodied in the branded product and supported by efficient systems for order-processing, delivery, and in-store stocking.

Partnership is the key concept. All of the partners in the network organization must share a common commitment to delivering superior value to the end-user customer and the work of each partner is not done until the end-user is satisfied. Whose customer is it? There are two answers:

1. The customer "belongs to" the company with the customer database and therefore the opportunity to build a relationship. With that ownership of the customer goes the awesome responsibility for keeping the rest of the network organization informed about the customer's evolving definition of value.

2. The customer "belongs to" the entire network organization. He or she isn't really "our" customer or "your" customer. Rather, all firms in the network are engaged in the joint pursuit of satisfying the customer by delivering super value. Anyone who is not committed to that basic objective cannot be an effective partner. Once again, adversarial, transaction-oriented thinking is out of place.

For the manufacturer of consumer packaged goods, the most important relationship is with its resellers. The reseller company and its buying and operating personnel are the names in the manufacturer's database, the customers with whom it is in daily contact, the ones who tell it what it must do to be an effective partner in the relationship.

For the industrial supplier, the manufacturer-customer is the focal point, but here too the vision of the total network organization must extend to the consumer end-user. The manufacturer of textile fibers must look beyond its immediate customer—the fabric manufacturer. It must be able to look out past the garment designer/manufacturer, through the fashion retailer, to the consumer who wants durability, color fastness, easy laundering, moisture wicking, and quick drying, and a subtle look of worn-out elegance, as it tweaks molecules and extrusion processes to create its yarns!

## THE "BOUNDARYLESS" ORGANIZATION

A network organization, then, is a set of interlinked, interdependent companies, each concentrating on a fairly narrow set of economic activities where it strives to achieve best-in-the-world performance, collaborating with the other partners to deliver superior value to end-user customers. The partners deal with one another through long-term commitments and relationships supported by contractual agreements and facilitated by processes for mutual problem solving and conflict resolution. These relationships are collaborative rather than adversarial, focused on maximizing the long-term value of the relationship to both parties rather than the value of each individual transaction for each of the partners. Each partner, ideally, understands its distinctive competences and is committed to maintaining them while relying on the partners for their distinctive competence, constantly challenging them to do a better job.

The network organizations that have evolved in the United States are in some respects similar to the *keiretsu* organizations found in Japan. These are interlocking networks of companies from multiple industries, often linked primarily through buyer-seller partnerships and distribution arrangements. The keiretsu are usually headed by a large bank or manufacturer, which often serves as a source of "patient capital" for other companies in the network. Among the best known keiretsu are those of Mitsui (which includes Toyota), Mitsubishi, Sumitomo, Sanwo, and Dai Ichi Kangyo. These long-term relationships among companies are typically supported by linked ownership, with each partner owning a small number of shares, usually less than one percent of the total, in the other partner. The objective of share ownership is to symbolize the mutual commitments within the keiretsu, not to exert any kind of control. The keiretsu usually functions on the assumption that the partners will not do business with competitors outside the network.

The American network organizations differ in a number of important ways from their Japanese counterparts:

- Banking regulations keep banks separate from manufacturing in the United States.

- The American networks have much more limited share ownership among the partners, although in some instances a major firm may buy interest in a smaller supplier in order to provide the capital necessary for the latter to finance a major R&D project or plant expansion required to become a just-in-time supplier.

- The power of the leader of the network to dictate terms and to control the operations of its suppliers is much more limited by both law and culture than is the case in Japan. Supplier firms in the United States may be both as large and as innovative as their industrial customers, whereas in Japan the leadership on technical innovation may be provided by the large parent/customer company.

American firms could benefit from learning the attitudes and behaviors of cooperation and collaboration that are characteristic of Japanese business if they want to be effective participants in network organizations.

These network organizations that continue to evolve among American companies are really a new and distinct organization form, neither hierarchies nor markets.[22] Prices are determined not by the impersonal market but as an outcome to processes of negotiation and joint problem solving focused on delivering superior value to customers. Price is an output of, not an input to, the buyer's and seller's decision processes. But, unlike hierarchical organizational structures, the partners maintain their freedom and flexibility for dealing with those economic actors who are most efficient and most responsive to changing market conditions. Decision makers can focus on externally driven definitions of value and efficiency, not internal mandates of policy, procedures, and protocol designed to protect the hierarchy and defend the status quo.

## The Demise of Hierarchy

While elements of hierarchical organization forms will remain in most companies for the foreseeable future, it is the modifications and transformations of hierarchies that should attract our attention. In the words of Jamie Houghton, former Chairman and Chief Executive Office of Corning, Inc., "the age of the hierarchy is over."[23] It has become common to refer to such networks as "boundaryless" organizations.

Once again, General Electric Company led the way with a new concept of management and organization, as it did with the original marketing concept, strategic planning, and the PIMS studies. Although General Electric management would certainly not claim to have created the concept of the boundaryless organization from scratch, it appears to have coined the term and has been its most vocal advocate. In General Electric's 1990 Annual Report, former Chairman and CEO John F. Welch commented:

> In a boundaryless company, suppliers aren't "outsiders." They are drawn closer and become trusted partners in the total business process. Customers are seen for what they are—the lifeblood of a company. Customers' vision of their needs and the company's view become identical, and every effort of every man and woman in the company is focused on satisfying those needs.

> In a boundaryless company, internal functions begin to blur. Engineering doesn't design a product and then "hand it off" to manufacturing. They form a team along with marketing and sales, finance, and the rest. Customer service? It's not somebody's job. It's everybody's job.[24]

As Mr. Welch points out, the concept of the boundaryless company as part of a network has clear implications for the traditional functional form of organization. Functional specialization and autonomy are relics of the past. Separate departments and staff functions, the well-known functional "chimneys" or "silos" of management, with their hierarchical reporting and approval processes, are simply too slow and too complicated for the new organization. Decisions take too long to get to the required levels of authority for approval and then communicated back down and out to those parts of the organization that will have to implement the decisions.

In place of functional organizations, teams of people with the knowledge and skills necessary to address and resolve a particular problem are created, managed, and then disbanded as problems are resolved and new opportunities and challenges emerge. In Chapter 3, we saw that teams were a key part of total quality management. Teams can bring the relevant skills from multiple disciplines into a coordinated response to a customer's problem. In network organizations, the team members may come from several companies. Such cooperative endeavors are the essence of network organizations.

Within General Electric, a process called "Work Out" was employed for several years with the objective of breaking down traditional functional barriers and hierarchical decision processes and creating flexible, team-based mechanisms for customer-focused problem solving. The process at General Electric was guided by a value-delivery concept of strategy, focused on understanding customer needs, with a goal of becoming the most efficient producer in the world in its chosen businesses.[25]

With this strong focus on customer needs and creating superior value for customers, network organizations represent a fulfillment of the promise of the original marketing concept. Profit is a reward for creating a satisfied customer, for having matched a set of customer needs with the firm's unique resources and skills. Strategic partnering and relationship marketing configure the firm's capabilities with those of other economic actors to create the best, most efficient, solutions to customer problems in a competitive marketplace.

Consistent with the value-delivery concept of strategy, the shared problem for all of the players in the system is to keep focused on the customer and his constantly changing definition of value. This poses a fundamentally new challenge for marketing management in the context of network organizations.

## THE ROLE OF MARKETING IN NETWORK ORGANIZATIONS

The network organization is centered around the firm at the hub, what we call the core firm, the leader of the network (Figure 6.2). The core firm is defined by its core competences and its customer base. Its knowledge of its customers, its relationships with them, and their trust in the company define one of its core competences. To the maximum extent possible, this competence should be databased, embedded in a customer information file that is computerized and available to all participants in the network. The network organization consists of the core firm plus its resellers, customer partners, vendor partners, joint ventures, and other strategic alliances as well as its more traditional divisions and other strategic business units. The

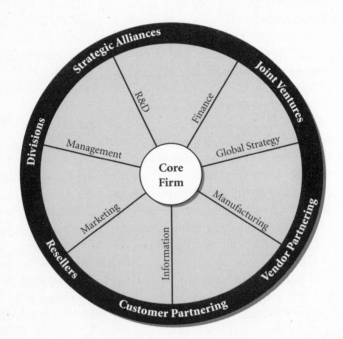

**FIGURE 6.2** The network organization. *Source:* Frederick E. Webster, Jr., "The Changing Role of Marketing in the Corporation," *Journal of Marketing* 56 (October 1992), 1–17, at p. 9. Reproduced with permission of the American Marketing Association.

traditional management functions are the knowledge and skills that hold the network together—marketing, finance, manufacturing, information management, and general management. These management functions represent knowledge and expertise but the boundaries between them become permeable and the organization functions as a team. The functions are bound together by a strategy that defines markets globally and is built on sound information about customers and competitors.

The essential role of marketing in a network organization is to keep all of the partners and business units focused on customers and their changing definition of value in the competitive marketplace. Marketing's responsibility can be thought of as that of being "expert on the customer." Marketing's principal activity is providing information to decision makers throughout the organization, and this is the main justification for maintaining marketing as a separate and identifiable business function. The marketing function needs to be supported by a highly competent management information capability and the appropriate investments in information technology. The overarching objective of all marketing activity should be continuous assessment of customer needs and the company's product offering compared with those of competitors, defining new ways to deliver superior value to customers.

A related responsibility for marketing management, in conjunction with top management of the corporation and of individual business units, is to be an advocate for the customer throughout the organization. It will be recalled that one of the shortcomings of the original marketing concept was that it was frequently not supported by top management, who continued to put the interests of shareholders ahead of the customers'. Chapter 7 considers in more detail the problem of developing an organizational culture that is customer oriented, and traces its positive impact on profitability.

## Marketing at the Corporate Level

At the corporate level, which is to say at the hub of the network and from the point of view of the core corporation, the strategic problem is to define what business the company is in and to determine the mission, scope, and structure of the firm, specifically its position in the value chain and its distinctive competences. As part of corporate management, the basic responsibilities of the marketing function fall in five areas:

1. Customer advocacy.
2. Market structure analysis.
3. Positioning in the value chain.

4. Professional development.

5. Strategic partnering.[26]

## Customer Advocacy

As just noted, marketing must be an advocate for the customer. Marketing managers must take the lead in making sure that all business decisions take the customer's point of view as the starting point. This requires that the very best customer information be available throughout the network so that there can be organizational consensus about those performance variables that are important to the customer and those attributes of the product offering that will serve his interests best. At the top management level, corporate leaders must be able to explain to other constituencies, especially owners and suppliers, why their interests are also ultimately best served by putting the customer's interests first.

## Market Structure Analysis

Marketing should also be responsible for market analysis as the key input to strategic planning. At the corporate level, the central question is what businesses (product/market combinations) to be in. The marketing task is to understand the structure of the market in terms of strategic market segments defined by sets of customers with common needs and buying patterns and sets of competitors who are serving those segments with differentiated strategies. The market positions, resources and skills, and distinctive competences of each of the major competitors must be analyzed in detail. As a prelude to a decision to enter or to exit a business, it is essential to understand the key success factors in that business. How do customers define value and how do competitors provide it? Can our firm establish a leadership position in this market with a distinctive and superior product offering? Of particular importance is developing an understanding of the strength of the relationships between competitors and major customers in their served markets.

## Positioning in the Value Chain

Although the development of the value proposition is a strategic problem that must be addressed at the level of the business unit, a prior set of issues needs to be addressed at the corporate level, namely establishing the firm's positioning in the value chain. Marketing plays a key role here because the task must be approached from the perspective of the customer. The customer's definition of value must be translated into specific capabilities and activities. The performance of those activities requires specific skills and resources that the firm must develop and maintain internally or which must be developed through strategic partnering. Where in the value chain will the firm attempt to establish a unique and sustainable competitive advantage?

## Professional Development

At the corporate level, and in conjunction with human resource management, the marketing manager must insure that there are programs for recruiting, developing, and deploying professional marketing management talent throughout the organization. As a starting point, marketing management must be recognized as a distinct and important management competence, not simply as a reward for a successful sales management or strategic planning performance—although such experience can be helpful. Marketing people must be selected for their analytical skills and their understanding of the marketplace, especially customer needs and buying patterns, relationships with distributors and other key partners, and competitors' business strategies and product offerings. In a large corporation, marketing management at the corporate level, again in conjunction with the human resources professionals, should also have responsibility for developing and delivering marketing training programs to nurture an understanding of marketing and of the marketplace throughout the organization, across all disciplines and functions, at all levels of management.

## Strategic Partnering

At the corporate level, marketing management should have central responsibility for designing, developing, and managing strategic partnerships with key customers, resellers, and vendors. These partnerships are a direct outcome of the definition of the firm's position in the value chain. Contractual relationships with these partners should be designed specifically in ways that ensure maximum value for customers, including clear statements about new product development activities and responsibilities, expectations about cost- and price-reductions, and criteria for assessing performance. In most companies, it should be expected that marketing management would be the repository of the highest levels of experience and skill in designing and managing strategic partnerships, including the necessary skills in negotiation.

In the traditional sense, marketing management does not "do market-ing" at the corporate level. Rather, the function of marketing at the corpo-rate level is that of advocating for the customer, representing the customer's viewpoint in the strategic planning process, positioning the firm within the value chain and creatively defining its distinctive competences, developing marketing management competence throughout the organization, and de-veloping the firm's strategic partnering arrangements.

In network organizations, marketing management has a critically im-portant role to play with dimensions that differ significantly from tradi-tional corporate responsibilities. Defining the firm's position in the value chain and guiding the development of strategic alliances to offer superior value to customers are unique responsibilities in network organizations. Marketing management's fundamental and essential responsibility is to keep the whole network focused on the customer by designing a corporate-level strategy, and organization structure and culture, appropriate to the firm's value-delivery mission.

This task does not call for a large marketing staff at the corporate level. Rather, it requires experience, expertise, and sophistication in understand-ing customer needs and communicating this understanding throughout the organization. It would be a mistake to have marketing become a bureau-cratic enclave, but it would be equally disastrous to skimp on commitment of resources necessary to attract and retain the most competent marketing management personnel.

## Marketing at the Business (SBU) Level

At the corporate level, the strategic question was "What business are we in?" At the level of the individual business unit, the strategic question is "How should we compete?" The tasks for marketing management at this level are:

- Market segmentation, targeting, and positioning.
- Developing the value proposition for the business.
- Developing the partnering strategies for the business unit.

The value proposition becomes the basis for communicating with cus-tomers and for focusing the entire organization, including strategic part-ners, on delivering superior value to customers. Once again, the key responsibility for marketing management, this time at the business unit level, is to be expert on the customer and to communicate that knowledge throughout the organization.

## Market Segmentation, Targeting, and Positioning

The analytical work of marketing managers at the corporate level concentrated on understanding market structure, the clustering of customers and competitors into market segments. At the business unit level, the problem is to understand each of those segments in detail, to select those segments which the firm will focus on—a task which usually calls for some resegmentation of the market and presents the opportunity to define new segments, and to develop the firm's positioning relative to competition in those segments. The discussion of these subjects in Chapter 4 was aimed primarily at this management level.

## Developing the Value Proposition

The value proposition summarizes the firm's business strategy at the business unit level. In a network organization, it performs the essential function of focusing all of the partners on common definitions of value for the customer and coordinating their efforts in the work of delivering superior value. This can be a very difficult task when the partners in the network have very different corporate cultures making the creation of a common set of values and beliefs about the customer to support the value proposition a major challenge. Managing a culture of customer orientation is the focus of the next chapter.

## Developing Partnering Strategies

As the individual business unit defines its distinctive competences (a subset of the distinctive competences of the larger corporate/network organization), and specifies its position in the value chain, it identifies the need for partners to deliver a superior product offering to customers. Those partners include resellers of various kinds, partners for the co-development of technology and new products, critical vendors for goods and services that help to complete the product offering, and partners with related product offerings that can be packaged into larger systems of solutions to customer problems. A defining characteristic of a network organization is that virtually every activity, function, product component, and service is analyzed in terms of whether it should be provided by the core firm or by a strategic partner. The "make versus buy" question—whether something is to be obtained through transactions, relationships, alliances, or internal production—is part of every strategic decision and is recognized as an option for the performance of every step in the value chain. This analysis includes all of the services performed by the marketing organization, including advertising, sales promotion, personal selling, distribution, package design, and publicity, as well as all product components and materials. Marketing management guides the search for answers to that question by defining the customer's best interest for all of the parties involved, by looking at the product offering through the eyes of the customer, and by knowing the competitive options that are available to customers in the marketplace.

## Marketing at the Tactical Level

At the tactical level, we are back to the traditional role of the marketing function—decisions about product, price, promotion, and distribution required to implement the business strategy. This is the level of *functional* strategy as distinct from corporate and business level strategies. At this level, the organization requires functional specialists in the individual business units including sales managers, product managers, pricing specialists, sales promotion experts, advertising managers, and so on, to decide on and deliver the specific product offering for the customer. They too must be "expert on the customer" and guided by the overarching value proposition. They can also be controlled and evaluated by specific budgetary objectives and other quantitative and qualitative measures of customer satisfaction and business performance, including sales volume, market share, and profitability. Their mandate is to obtain maximum returns from the financial resources that they are given as part of the budgeting process.

Even at the tactical level, however, marketing takes on new forms in network organizations. The focus shifts from transactions to relationships and alliances with customers. Long-term goals and measurements become more important relative to short-term gains in volume. Marketing managers do more of their analysis using the customer database that is developed as part of relationship marketing, providing the opportunity for analysis with real customers about the possible impact of virtually every marketing action.

Regis McKenna, a well-known marketing consultant, author, and lecturer, has articulated the changes in marketing management in a fashion which fits nicely with Jack Welch's concept of the boundaryless organization:

> The marketer must be the integrator, both internally—synthesizing technological capability with market needs—and externally—bringing the customer into the company as a participant in the development and adaptation of goods and services. It is a fundamental shift in the role and purpose of

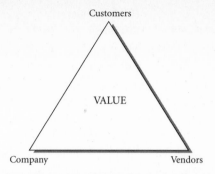

**FIGURE 6.3**   Partnerships in a value-delivery concept of strategy.

marketing: from manipulation of the customer to genuine customer involvement; from telling and selling to communicating and sharing knowledge; from last-in-line function to corporate-credibility champion . . .

The relationships are the key, the basis of customer choice and company adaptation. After all, what is a successful brand but a special relationship? And who better than a company's marketing people to create, sustain, and interpret the relationship between the company, its suppliers, and its customers?[27]

An important detail in McKenna's comment is that marketing is equally responsible for guiding relationships with suppliers as well as customers, as part of its responsibility for value delivery. The vendors become part of the company's product offering and part of the relationship with the customer. Under a value-delivery concept of strategy, the relationship between the company, its suppliers, and its customers is seamless. (See Figure 6.3.) Marketing is the management function responsible for defining, developing, and delivering superior value to customers. Some companies now give responsibility for procurement strategy to their marketing executives as a way of ensuring that suppliers are fully integrated into the company's value-development and value-delivery processes. Marketing and buying have common objectives.

## SUMMARY

Organization forms are evolving rapidly, from hierarchical, bureaucratic divisionalized pyramids into networks of strategic partnerships along with more traditional business units. The objective of this organizational evolution is to respond more quickly and effectively to changing customer needs. The new organization forms offer more flexibility and help the firm to focus on its distinctive competence while it depends on partners for their distinctive competence as necessary to complete the product offering to the customer.

Providing superior value to the customer is the purpose of the network organization. In network organizations, the most important business asset is the customer base and the on-going relationship with those customers. Customers define the business because they define value. As their definition of value changes, so must the business change.

Within these new organization forms, the role of marketing must be redefined. At one level, marketing is no longer a functional specialty because the entire organization and all of the individual actors must take responsibility for delivering superior value to customers. However, a set of professional marketing managers is necessary at both the corporate and business unit levels to provide information and expertise about customers and to implement the firm's business strategy with product, pricing, promotion, and distribution strategies and policies. Marketing strategy must guide the sales function.

The key marketing function in the network organization is to manage the relationship between the firm and its customers (and information about them) and to keep the entire network focused on the customer's definition of value. Marketing represents the customer to the company as well as the company to the customer. At the corporate level, this calls for advocacy on behalf of customers; analyzing market structure to determine which businesses to be in and how to position the business within the market; defining the firm's distinctive competence; developing a partnering strategy for delivering value; and developing competent marketing management throughout the network organization.

At the business unit level, the strategic role of marketing shifts to that of developing and managing strategic partnerships, including long-term relationships and alliances with customers, suppliers, and technology providers; market segmentation, targeting, and product positioning; and developing and communicating the firm's value proposition throughout the network. At the tactical level, marketing managers within the business unit must design and implement the marketing mix (product, price, promotion, and distribution), with a focus on long-term customer relationships as appropriate.

In the network organization, the boundaries separating the company from its customers, suppliers, distributors, and even its competitors (as potential partners for the development of technology) break down. Likewise, within the organization, old functional boundaries give way to cooperation and teamwork, focused on finding the best solutions to customer problems, reducing the time and cost required to create and deliver a complete product offering. Network organizations are a tool for achieving customer orientation and represent a fulfillment of the marketing concept.

# 7

# Organizational Culture and Customer Orientation

*We exist to provide value to our customers, which means that in addition to quality and service, we have to save them money.*
*I know most companies don't have cheers, and most board chairmen probably wouldn't lead them if they did.*

Sam Walton

*Made in America*
Doubleday, 1992, pp. 10 and 157

The new marketing concept calls for putting the customer first—always. At its heart, the marketing concept is a statement of corporate or organizational culture, a set of values and beliefs relating to the importance of serving the customer. To repeat, from Chapter 1, a statement by the father of the original marketing concept, Peter Drucker:

> [Marketing] encompasses the entire business. It is the whole business seen from the point of view of its final result, that is from the customer's point of view.[1]

Adoption of the marketing concept as a management philosophy is a shared recognition that everything that happens within the company must be focused on creating satisfied customers and maintaining a commitment to continuous improvement on behalf of the customer. This notion of a shared viewpoint is at the heart of most definitions of organizational culture. Following a definition proposed by Stanley Davis,[2] we can think of organizational culture as *the pattern of shared values and beliefs that help the members of an organization understand its functioning and provide them with norms for behavior in the organization.* Thus, implementation of the new marketing concept calls for understanding corporate culture and managing it with the objective of focusing everyone's attention on their role in delivering value to customers.

# THE CONCEPT OF CORPORATE CULTURE

In the 1980s corporate culture became something of a fad among business commentators and management experts. The concept of culture was simultaneously applied to nations, companies, and groups within organizations. Japanese companies in particular were said to derive some of their competitive edge in the global marketplace from unique characteristics of the Japanese national culture, including cooperativeness, commitment to the larger group, and a strong work ethic. While national or "background" culture is clearly an important consideration, it is distinct from the concept of organizational culture.

At the corporate level, the successes and failures of companies as diverse as Apple Computer and IBM, Wal-Mart and Sears, and Reynolds Metals and Bethlehem Steel were attributed by some observers to their underlying organizational cultures. It has now become popular to explain the failure of corporate mergers such as that of EDS with General Motors in terms of unresolved conflict between two competing corporate cultures. Yet, it is an open question whether all organizations have clear strong cultures, and whether the culture as expressed by the values of the founders is the same as the culture practiced by current organizational members. Many authors, such as Wilkins and Ouchi[3] and Martin[4] have argued that a strong corporate culture is an exception rather than the rule and that multiple cultures may exist in any organization, often in conflict with one another.

Some experts argue that strong culture is more often found at the level of the work group, in what might be called "clan" or "group" culture. For example, a strong professional identity shared by a group of functional specialists in a field like engineering or chemistry or actuarial science may be thought of as a type of organizational culture. Within a given company, the superior performance of a particular department, project, or team is often believed to reflect the presence of a strong subculture shared by the group that makes it distinct from other groups within the organization. Such attributions abound in stories of successful new product developments, encapsulated in phrases like "skunkworks," and in the mythology of superperforming districts within a salesforce.

Culture means different things to different people. The literature on the subject of corporate or organizational culture contains many different and even conflicting concepts of culture, making it difficult to test some of the basic assertions about the relationship between organizational culture and business unit performance. Only recently has significant progress been made in understanding how organizational culture, and customer orientation as part of corporate culture, relates to such measures of performance as profitability, rate of sales growth, and market share.

In this chapter, we first consider the relationships among business strategy, organization structure, and culture in the implementation of the new marketing concept. We then review several different views of corporate culture. While recognizing that the argument about the correct definition of corporate culture is far from resolved, we examine a view of culture as organizational knowledge or "cognition" that has proven to be helpful in assessing differences in the extent to which a firm is focused on its customers and how that, in turn, relates to performance. Finally, we look at some research studies that have produced interesting evidence of the connections between corporate culture, customer orientation, and business performance.

## How Strategy, Structure, and Culture Relate to the Marketing Concept

Implementation of the new marketing concept requires management attention at three levels: strategy, structure, and culture. Previous chapters stressed that the company's business strategy must be focused on creating customer satisfaction through delivering superior value. The structure of the organization must be designed to implement the business strategy and to work with business partners to create and deliver superior value. Finally, the underlying values and beliefs of the entire organization must put the customer first in all organization activities. Studies of business success and failure have strongly suggested that it is culture that is often at the roots of strategic outcomes, and that of all of the variables, culture is the hardest to manage and change.

At the *strategic* level of the new marketing concept, the challenge is to develop a business strategy that is built around market segmentation, targeting, and positioning, one that clearly defines the value proposition of the company and its unique competitive advantage over the competition. The definition of market segments and target customers and the requirements for satisfying those customers, including investments in innovation, distribution, and promotion, should be at the center of the business plan. Financial goals should be seen as outcomes of successfully meeting market-oriented objectives, not as objectives in themselves.

Organization *structure* is the second element in the implementation of the new marketing concept. In traditional, hierarchical organizations, the marketing department was a separate marketing function responsible for product, pricing, promotion, and distribution policies. Such a view of the marketing function within the business is obsolete under the new marketing concept. Even in traditional, hierarchical organizations (which are, after all, still common), the marketing function must be decentralized away from the corporate level and out into the operating units of the business. At the business unit level, marketing responsibility and sensitivity must be dispersed through the organization so that everyone knows that customer satisfaction is the overriding goal of their job.

In the new network organizations, the challenge for the marketing professionals at the hub of the network is to be expert on the customer, providing customer information to decision makers throughout the organization. Marketing management must also take the lead in advocating for the customer with business partners throughout the network. The overriding objective is to keep all efforts focused on the customer, putting the customer's interest ahead of those of *all* the other resource providers, including owners/shareholders, management, suppliers, and the employees themselves. It is the customer's willingness to pay that ultimately determines the value created for the owners of each of the individual business units and the welfare of the other claimants on these firms and their resources.

Every manager is familiar with the mandates of strategy and organization structure. Organizational *culture* is a less familiar concept. While everyone talks about organizational culture, there is seldom any depth of understanding of its sources, components, and influence. It is hard for managers to make organizational culture explicit and to discuss it analytically because it is pervasive and elusive, multifaceted and intangible. These characteristics are at the heart of the very nature of organizational culture.

This essential feature of culture, its simultaneous ambiguity, pervasiveness, and intangibility, has been captured in the definition of culture as "the things people take for granted," the underlying set of common assumptions that make all other forms of interaction, social exchange, and joint action possible. One of the most significant challenges in implementing the new marketing concept, then, is to make the assumptions of corporate culture explicit, to be sure that everyone understands and is committed to the importance of putting the customer first. In this sense, the problem is to make the "intangible" values of a customer-oriented culture tangible in the form of specific words, symbols, behaviors, processes, and other actions.

## Culture as Integration, Differentiation, or Fragmentation

Looking at organizational culture in different perspectives helps demonstrate the depth, complexity, and richness of the subject. Scholarly researchers, struggling to develop a reasonable definition of the concept that will facilitate studies of the formation and functioning of organizational culture, have followed several different research traditions from the fields of anthropology, sociology, and social psychology in addressing the problem. Martin, for example, identified three very different concepts of culture as *integration, differentiation,* and *fragmentation* and then examined the same company using these different perspectives, in a manner reminiscent of the fable about the blind men and the elephant.

In the *integration* perspective, culture is what people share, implying that there is an organizational consensus about certain important issues. The integration perspective would seem most appropriate for considering culture at the corporate level, from the point of view of top management. The new marketing concept requires that such a perspective be developed— that a commitment to customer orientation, value delivery, and quality be accepted as a basic set of norms throughout the organization, at all levels of the organization and across all functions.

In the *differentiation* view, culture is what makes people different from one another and can be the source of conflict within an organization, as seen in the tension between business departments such as marketing and engineering. Those using this perspective find it not surprising that top management often has a different set of values and viewpoints than people at lower organization levels. They are supported by the researchers who argue that a strong corporate level culture is more the exception than the rule. *Sub*cultures may be much stronger within the organization. In this sense culture, or more accurately subcultures, can be a problem for the manager committed to the new marketing concept because it is likely that different business functions and management levels will disagree about the value of putting the customer's interests first. The marketing people, advocates for the customer, may have to battle a top management committed to putting the shareholders first, R&D managers who want to pursue technology for its own sake, and manufacturing managers who want to produce large runs of standard products with cushions of a large order backlog and work-in-process inventories.

In the *fragmentation* perspective, culture is multifaceted and ambiguous, neither a monolithic shared consensus nor a distinct set of well-defined viewpoints. Rather, in the fragmentation viewpoint, culture is a dynamic concept reflecting changes in group composition, organization structure, and the external environment. People may be members of multiple subcultures within the organization and their self-concepts are likely to change rather constantly. The agenda of the organization changes continuously as the firm senses changes in the external environment and responds to them. This pattern of organizational behavior may be very helpful in a rapidly changing market environment and would suggest a relatively weak corporate-level culture. Coalitions form and dissolve as people address the changing set of issues, and organizational culture changes accordingly. The ability of researchers to track and understand organizational culture is very limited in this view. Ambiguity is seen as *the* defining characteristic of culture. The fragmentation perspective would distrust studies of organizational culture that focus on those areas where there is consensus, arguing that these may be less important and of little use to organizational actors who are trying to deal with real, pressing, immediate problems they face in their jobs.[5]

These three different views of culture are interesting indeed, but each seems to offer only a partial view of culture, based on limited aspects of the overall concept. Furthermore, the attempt to make them relevant at all levels of the organization, rather than differentiating among the corporate, group, and subgroup levels, may create something of a straw man. If we wish to understand an organization in depth, it is probably useful to employ all three points of view, using the integration perspective to analyze the total organization as viewed by top management and employing the precepts of the differentiation and fragmentation perspectives to analyze conflict and disagreement at lower levels.

Implementation of the new marketing concept calls for an integrated perspective, a top management commitment to putting the customer first. This commitment must pervade the organization. Overcoming barriers to its acceptance requires understanding the conflicts and ambiguities that exist at the operating levels of the business, guiding people away from traditional functional management viewpoints toward a shared consensus that puts the customer's interests first. The integration perspective on corporate culture should be the goal in implementing the new marketing concept—a single, pervasive commitment throughout the organization, guided from the top, that gives primacy to satisfying customer needs and expectations. The differentiation and fragmentation perspectives define the problems to be addressed by managers pursuing the goals of customer orientation. The latter two viewpoints can be useful management tools, however, sensitizing management to the issues that must be resolved in developing customer orientation throughout the organization.

# FIVE PERSPECTIVES ON ORGANIZATIONAL CULTURE

From the point of view of top management policymakers, there are many different ways to think about organizational culture.[6] Using our earlier terms, each of these is primarily an integration perspective. Each comes from a different research tradition in the social sciences and is potentially useful for understanding a set of issues important to marketing managers. Smircich has offered a very good summary of five different ways of looking at organizational culture:[7]

1. Comparative management.
2. Contingency management.
3. Organizational cognition.
4. Organizational symbolism.
5. Structural psychodynamics.

These five perspectives differ in terms of whether culture is seen as external or internal to the firm, whether it is an input to organizational decisions and actions or an outcome of them, and whether it sees culture as a part of the organization and a variable that can be measured and managed, or as a metaphor for the organization itself. Thus, we can characterize each viewpoint as to whether it sees culture as external or internal, input or outcome, variable or metaphor.

## Comparative Management

For many managers, the comparative management view of organizational culture is the most familiar. It was popularized, especially in the 1970s and 1980s, by a number of books on Japanese management and other studies of cross-national differences in company performance and competitive effectiveness.[8] This perspective treats national culture as a major determinant of corporate culture; it sees culture as *external* to the firm. Culture is an input to the firm's decision-making processes and a major influence on the behavior of organizational actors, and it is a variable that can be studied by academics and consultants although not controlled directly by managers.

Students of Japanese management have been impressed by the extent to which Japanese firms seem to focus on the customer although marketing departments as they are known in the United States are virtually unheard of in Japan. The Japanese language *kanji* characters for the word "customer" literally translate to "honored guest." If Japanese companies are characteristically customer-oriented, it may be because Japanese customers are notoriously demanding in terms of quality and service. Long-term customer relationships are extremely important in the Japanese culture.[9] Perhaps one of the unique features of corporate culture in Japan is that it is so strongly influenced by national culture. It is an open question whether national culture exerts an equally strong influence on organizations in other countries. It is clearly inappropriate, however, to equate national background culture with the unique culture of an individual organization.

A recent study of the relationship between national and corporate culture and their influence on company performance has helped to address this issue. Deshpandé, Farley, and Webster examined organizational cultures in five countries: England, France, Germany, Japan, and the United States.[10] Using a model of national culture developed by Hofstede's studies,[11] over a 25-year period, these authors identified four dimensions that differentiate national cultures:

1. Uncertainty avoidance—The preference for structured situations.
2. Power distance—The extent to which inequality between individuals is viewed as normal.
3. Individualism—Stressing individual rather than group action.
4. Masculinity—Valuing assertiveness, performance, and success.

To illustrate the use of these dimensions: France is high on the uncertainty avoidance and power distance dimensions and low on the masculinity dimension. Japan is high on uncertainty avoidance and masculinity and low on individualism. Both the United States and England are high on individualism and uncertainty avoidance, medium on masculinity, and low on power distance.

Deshpandé, Farley, and Webster (hereafter referred to as DFW), looked for relationships between these national culture types, organizational culture types, and business performance. We delay for a few more pages the description of the DFW organizational culture types, but we can say here that they found no strong or systematic differences in the relationship between national and organizational culture types in impact on business performance. While national culture types are different, the impact of corporate culture is surprisingly similar across national cultures. For example, as expected based on differences in national culture, Japanese businesses had more cooperative (clan) type organizational cultures while French firms had more power-based (hierarchical) cultures. Most importantly, no differences were found across countries in the impact of their national cultures on actual business performance. In other words, the effectiveness of a particular organizational culture did not depend on the national culture. Successful firms appeared to transcend national cultural differences in developing common patterns of effective business strategy. In this study, corporate culture proved to be more important than national culture in understanding differences in business performance.

## Contingency Management

Like the comparative management approach, the contingency management perspective also treats culture as a variable that can be measured and as an input to management action. However, in contrast to the comparative view, it sees culture as *internal* to the firm, something that managers can direct and influence, if not strictly control. In this view, culture develops within the firm and is unique to it. It is called a "contingent" perspective because it sees performance outcomes as dependent on cultural variables. Culture is defined as a set of values, beliefs, commitments, and meanings shared by the members of the organization. This viewpoint was captured in such well-known books as Peters and Waterman's *In Search of Excellence*[12] and Deal and Kennedy's *Corporate Culture*.[13] Successful companies are characterized by such cultural attributes as teamwork, customer focus, employee empowerment, and a commitment to excellence.

In both the comparative and contingency management perspectives, culture is seen as a tool that can be taken into account and managed, at least to a degree, in ways that enhance organizational performance. In both cases, the management task is to find consistency among strategy, structure, and culture. A concern for finding the proper fit of culture, strategy, and structure created a boom industry for management consulting in the mid-1980s.[14]

### *Managing Culture: Lou Gerstner's Reign at IBM*

In 1993, IBM hired Louis Gerstner from RJR Nabisco to replace John Akers as Chairman and CEO. Never before had the company hired its top executive from outside the ranks of IBM. This radical departure was said to be necessary to bring about a needed change in IBM's embedded culture, as a fundamental step in restoring the company to profitability after its losses of over $16 billion in three years. Gerstner was highly regarded for his ability as a strategic thinker, nurtured by the years he spent at McKinsey & Company.[15]

When he announced his retirement in 2002, Gerstner was widely credited with achieving one of the largest turnarounds of a company's fortunes in corporate history. As noted in Chapters 2 and 3, this was based in part on redefining IBM as a service business, not a hardware business. More basically, Gerstner refocused the entire organization on its customers. Shareholder value increased more than 800 percent during his tenure, further evidence of the link between customer value and shareholder value. Given the pervasive, complex, and ambiguous nature of corporate culture, it takes more than a change at the CEO level to change the culture, but that can be an important and symbolic beginning. Gerstner's successor Sam Palmisano is a 28-year IBM veteran who had been one of the leader's of Gerstner's customer-focused revolution. Palmisano was quoted as saying "The culture change in any large institution, when you are trying to drive a winning scenario, never stops."[16]

These first two views of corporate culture, the comparative and contingency management perspectives, treat culture as a variable to be considered and, if possible, manipulated, in developing business strategy and organization structure. Culture is seen as one part of the organization.

In the next three perspectives on organizational culture, culture is treated as a *metaphor* for the organization itself, another way of thinking about what the organization really is. A metaphor is a figure of speech (such as "our distributor relationship is a time bomb") or a symbol (a profitable business as a "cash cow") applied to something that it does not literally denote, to suggest a meaningful comparison and to further our understanding of the concept. At first glance, this approach might appear to be a bit silly, but given the ambiguity and complexity of organizational culture, the metaphorical approach has real value. Three different perspectives have been identified in which culture is a metaphor for the organization. In these views, culture isn't a *part* of the organization, it *is* the organization.

## Organizational Cognition

Organizations can be viewed as systems of meaning and knowledge. In the organizational cognition model, organizational culture is the shared knowledge, rules, and understanding that provide direction for members of the organization. Culture defines what constitutes appropriate and inappropriate behavior, what it means to be a "good" member of the organization. Culture also describes what is unique about the organization, how it defines itself as distinct from other organizations. It helps members understand why things happen the way they do in the organization.

The organizational cognition view of culture has been used to study and classify different types of organizations, such as "entrepreneurial," "scientific," and "humanistic," and to compare them with one another.[17] The concept of organizational knowledge systems also recognizes that firms are more than the sum of the individual members' knowledge, values, and beliefs. For example, no one person has all of the knowledge necessary to launch and recover a space shuttle, but the NASA organization can now do it routinely. Organization knowledge, skill, attitudes, values, and so on persist while its membership changes. This notion helps to get at the pervasive nature of organizational culture and how it is "handed down" from one generation of management to the next.

The view of organizations as systems of "shared cognitions" is also captured in the concept of managers' "thought worlds," an idea used by Dougherty to explore the conflict between marketing and R&D departments within companies.[18] Here the organizational cognition model is applied to subcultures. As we have noted in earlier chapters, even when various departments share a commitment to the customer, they may have vastly different definitions of what constitutes the customer's best interest. These managers live in fundamentally different "thought worlds," with different values, beliefs, cognitions, and rules for behavior—that is, different cultures. The organizational cognition view can be a useful tool for studying organizational conflict.

The organizational cognition perspective also helps to understand a very basic attribute of culture: It is a mechanism used by organization members to resolve conflict. At the same time, this view recognizes that there might be multiple "types" of cultures within an organization, not all of them shared with equal loyalty by all of the members. We can characterize organizations by their *dominant* organization type without saying that it is the only type. We will be using an organizational cognition perspective when we look in more detail at a "competing values" model of organizational culture later in the chapter, when reviewing the DFW study of the relationships among corporate culture, customer orientation, and business performance.

## Organizational Symbolism

A second metaphorical view of organizational culture sees organizations in terms of their prevalent symbols and rituals, as systems of symbolic discourse among their members. This view of organizational culture is especially clear in companies that have strong, long-standing cultures and familiar and easily observed behavior patterns. The presence of a strong dress code, company songs, even characteristic ways of speaking, come to identify members of the organization.

Language is the most obvious symbol system. To quote an article in *The Wall Street Journal*, "Like other tribal entities, corporations develop their own dialects as a way of linking members of the tribe and delineating their ranks." Walt Disney Company, the entertainment giant, was cited as an excellent example. Disney employees refer to one another as "cast members." They see themselves as "onstage" while working and "backstage" when on a break. Something positive that happens is called "good Mickey" while the opposite is "bad Mickey." Cheering up an unhappy child in a theme park is called "sprinkling pixie dust." Disney management obviously sees the strong culture and its symbols as an essential determinant of the quality of their product and the success of their business strategy.[19]

Most organizations have myths, rituals, and symbols that are important to the members and create a strong sense of belonging. Many companies consciously teach their members these aspects of culture through orientation sessions, seminars, regularly scheduled meetings, and social gatherings of all kinds. Company songs, cheers, slogans, and conventions for behavior are highly visible aspects of organizational symbolism, the patterns of symbolic discourse that provide the background against which members organize and interpret their experience within the organization. Conscious attention to organizational symbolism is undoubtedly helpful to managers trying to create a customer-oriented enterprise.

## Structural Psychodynamics

Many companies have been described as virtual extensions of the personalities of their founders and early Chief Executives. Walt Disney, Henry Ford, Mary Kay, Edwin Land of Polaroid, Thomas Watson of IBM, and Sam Walton of Wal-Mart are among the most familiar examples. This view of corporate culture is captured in the structural psychodynamics perspective, which is routed in the disciplines of anthropology and the study of social structure and transformational organization theory.[20] It sees an organization as a metaphor for the unconscious mind of the founder, an extension of his or her presence throughout the organization, as if people always ask, "How would Mr. X expect me to approach this situation?"

How does a manager or a researcher identify, observe, and take a measure of an "extension of the personality of the founder"? The structural psychodynamic perspective is the hardest to understand and to make operational as a method for studying organizational culture. The most common attempt to use a structural psychodynamic perspective is one in which researchers record the myths that are told by organization members about the founder. In one well-known company, managers shared a perception that there were two distinct cultures—one comprised of people who were hired by and worked with the founder and the other shared by those who came later. Recall that the first two paradigms treated culture as a variable that could be measured and managed; clearly, the structural psychodynamic perspective is least easily translated into things that can be measured and managed and it is therefore of most limited usefulness.

## Comparing the Five Perspectives on Organizational Culture

Each of these five perspectives on organizational culture offers a unique insight into the nature of the concept. For the manager interested in developing approaches for implementing the new marketing concept within a company, each viewpoint provides something to think about:

1.  What is the influence of *nationality* on the willingness and ability of my organization, with its global subsidiaries and business partners, to focus on customers and a value-delivery concept of the business? (Comparative management)

2.  How is the performance of my business units influenced by *differences* in their cultures? What are the predominant values in those units and how does customer orientation fit into those values? (Contingency management)

3.  How do different business units, functions, and levels of the organization view customers and their demands relative to those of other stakeholders? How do different organizational actors process and respond to information about the changing market environment? What are the basic *conflicts and disagreements* among different parts of the organization and how do they work themselves out into some form of organizational consensus about delivering value to customers? (Organizational cognition)

4.  What are the important *symbols and rituals* in this organization? How do they help people find meaning in their work and develop shared understandings? How can those symbols and rituals be used

to create a customer-focused, market-driven business? (Organizational symbolism)

5.  What is the *legacy of the founders* and of earlier generations of management? How does their historical presence influence the ability of managers to respond to a changing market environment? What things are held to be most important and why? Are these the correct values for this company in the competitive marketplace? (Structural psychodynamics)

These are only a few of the many productive questions raised by the five perspectives. The basic point is that organizational culture is important in designing and implementing business strategies that are consistent with the new marketing concept. Against this background consideration of the nature of organizational culture, we now come back to the specific question of how corporate culture, and customer orientation as part of the company's culture, influences profitability and other measures of business performance. The following section examines the theoretical construct of "customer orientation" and how it relates to corporate culture.

## CORPORATE CULTURE, CUSTOMER ORIENTATION, AND INNOVATIVENESS

The original marketing concept stated that every business had only two basic functions: *marketing* and *innovation*. Marketing was defined as the process of listening to customers, understanding and satisfying their needs and wants, and putting the customer at the center of all of the firm's planning and operations. The marketing concept *describes* a corporate culture, a basic set of values and beliefs that puts the customer first, always. But in defining and describing the concept of organizational culture, we have seen that it is ambiguous, complex, and multifaceted. It is time to make a clearer distinction between customer orientation and corporate culture.

Corporate culture is a much broader concept than customer orientation. Customer orientation is the business of putting the customer first in everything the company does and organizing all activities around the basic objective of delivering superior value. It is easier to define customer orientation than to measure it. It begins with a set of values and beliefs, subscribed to by members of the organization, that recognizes the primacy of the customer's interest. As part of the company's value system, it is part of the company culture. However, there can be strong corporate cultures that do *not* put the customer's interests first.

One of the most important questions we can ask is:*Does it make any difference if a company is customer oriented?* Does customer orientation translate into enhanced business performance, especially in terms of profitability, growth, and market share? A related, but different question, is: *Does the type of company culture influence business performance?* There is also a related question of the extent to which customer orientation is consistent with, or a part of, various types of corporate culture.

## Defining and Measuring Customer- or Market-Orientation

Despite its central importance, until recently there was surprisingly little effort to carefully define and measure the *customer orientation* construct. The phrase *market orientation* was often used interchangeably, although there was much inconsistency in the usage of the two terms. Significant research was undertaken in the past decade to clarify the meaning of these terms. Four studies are reviewed next that had the objectives of defining and measuring customer and market orientation and examining its relationship to business performance.

Kohli and Jaworski set out to understand the construct of *market orientation,* its causes, components, and outcomes, and to develop a set of testable propositions about them.[21] They wanted to know the meaning of market orientation, the factors that foster or discourage it, the consequences of it, and situations in which it might be more or less important. They began by reviewing the literature on the subject and concluded that there was a consensus among authors in the field that market orientation had three distinct components:

1. Customer focus, or customer orientation.
2. Coordinated marketing, an integrated marketing strategy.
3. Profit orientation—managing for profitability, not sales volume.

Earlier chapters have presented these as key ideas in the marketing concept and parts of a sound business model.

The researchers next developed an interview guide to explore how managers view these elements of market orientation and how they turn them into practice. In-depth interviews were conducted with 62 managers in four cities. The respondents unanimously concurred that customer focus was the central idea in a market orientation. Customer orientation is a part of market orientation, but not the same thing.

Managers felt strongly that customer focus is more than a philosophical commitment. It requires information about customers, about their needs and preferences. Even that is not enough, however. Using current customer opinion to determine what is to be produced and sold is incomplete and inadequate. These managers advocated a broader strategic concept of market intelligence that included going beyond customer opinion to a deeper understanding of customer needs and wants, anticipating how those will change in the future, and analyzing the impact of a changing market environment. This finding is consistent with the notion that the customer's definition of value is constantly changing.

The concept that Kohli and Jaworski labeled "coordinated marketing," is similar to our concept of integrated marketing, the assertion of the marketing concept that each element of the marketing mix—product, price, promotion, and distribution policies—should be managed in the context of the strategy whole. However, their manager-respondents saw it somewhat differently, as the proposition that all parts of the business had to be customer oriented and to conduct their activities in ways guided by market intelligence. It had to be actionable. It is significant that it was the managers, not the researchers, who pushed the concept in this direction. Coordinated marketing is nothing more nor less than the application of market intelligence to decision making throughout the organization, making sure that all functions are guided by the customer.

A similar conclusion was reached with respect to profit orientation. The researchers presented profit orientation as the objective of a business guided by market orientation, the notion of managing for profitability rather than sales volume. Again, managers saw it differently. Without exception, managers saw profit as a *result* of market orientation rather than as part of it. In fact, the managers' interpretation would appear to be loyal to the original statement of the marketing concept by Peter Drucker that profit is a *reward* for creating a satisfied customer. Thus, the concept of profit orientation, like that of coordinated marketing, devolves back to the fundamental concept of customer focus, with an emphasis on market intelligence and management response to changing customer needs and preferences. This central tendency was captured by Kohli and Jaworski in their summary definition: "Market orientation is the organizationwide *generation* of market intelligence pertaining to current and future customer needs, *dissemination* of the intelligence across departments, and organizationwide *responsiveness* to it."[22]

With their definition of the market orientation construct pinned down, Kohli and Jaworski then developed a total of 25 propositions to guide future research. These research propositions included hypotheses about the influence of senior management, interdepartmental dynamics, and organizational systems on the development of market orientation, how it is influenced by structural factors on both the demand and supply side in the market, and how a market orientation influences customers, employees, and business results. Using two mail surveys, one covering 222 strategic business units (most of which were each represented by two respondents) and another involving 230 managers, the researchers found strong evidence that market orientation is strongly correlated with:

1. Visible top management support for market orientation.
2. The use of reward systems that tie compensation to effectiveness in tracking and responding to market needs.
3. The connectedness of departments within the organization.
4. Decentralized decision making.

Both top management risk aversion and interdepartmental conflict had a negative impact on market orientation. Management risk aversion tended to slow responsiveness to market information but not its dissemination. Interdepartmental conflict hindered both the dissemination of market intelligence and organizational responsiveness. A strong market orientation had a positive impact on employees' morale and increased their commitment to the organization. The researchers also found a positive relationship between market orientation and business performance, across a broad spectrum of markets in terms of competitive intensity, market turbulence, and technological turbulence.[23]

The Kohli and Jaworski research validates the basic proposition that customer orientation is the key idea in the marketing concept and helps develop understanding of its causes and consequences. It provides evidence that market orientation has a positive result in terms of business performance. It confirms the importance of top management support and organizational systems that track and reward market orientation. It also reinforces the idea that implementation of market orientation boils down to managing market intelligence. This supports our assertion that the principal responsibility of the marketing department, and the only justification for maintaining it as a separate business function, is to be "expert on the customer."

## Effects of Market Orientation on Profitability

Research by Narver and Slater has contributed to our understanding of the relationship between market orientation and profitability.[24] Like Kohli and Jaworski, their first challenge was to develop a valid measure of market orientation. Based on a thorough review of the literature and the opinions of a panel of academic experts, the researchers identified five core constructs of market orientation:

1. Customer orientation.
2. Competitor orientation.
3. Interfunctional coordination.
4. A long-term horizon.
5. A profit focus (see Figure 7.1).

Using a questionnaire containing several statements related to the possible dimensions of market orientation, a panel of leading academic experts

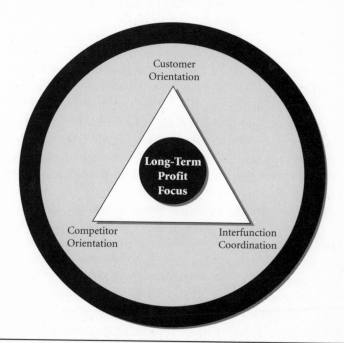

**FIGURE 7.1**  The components of market orientation. *Source:* John C. Narver and Stanley F. Slater, "The Effect of a Market Orientation on Business Profitability," *Journal of Marketing* 54 (October 1990), 20–25.

was asked to assess the relative importance of these dimensions to a definition of market orientation, and to suggest additional items. This revised set of items was submitted to a second group of three academic experts. Those items considered by this group to be consistent with a market orientation were included in the final questionnaire. The resulting questionnaire was used with a sample of manager-respondents in the forest products operations of a large western corporation who were asked to indicate the extent of their agreement or disagreement with each statement. Narver and Slater initially approached managers in 140 separate business units, including distribution businesses (paper merchants), specialty products such as cabinets, doors, and roof truss systems, and commodity products such as dimension lumber, plywood, wood chips, and logs. The final data analysis was based on the responses of more than 400 managers from more than 100 of these business units.

The most reliable measurements of market orientation were those relating to what the researchers called the "behavioral" components of the construct—those that imply specific management behaviors or activities: customer orientation, competitor orientation, and interfunctional coordination, with customer orientation proving to be the most reliable measure. This is very reassuring as it indicates that customer orientation is indeed a valid and important part of the market orientation construct. Competitor orientation and interfunctional coordination were also highly reliable. However, items relating to "long-term horizon" and "profit emphasis" were below the minimum acceptable statistical levels for reliability and were excluded from the analysis. A given business unit was assigned a score for market orientation based upon an average of the scores of each of the manager-respondents from that unit on each of the three measurements: customer orientation, competitor orientation, and interfunctional coordination. Table 7.1 indicates the specific components of each of the three constructs.

In comparison with the Kohli and Jaworski study, Narver and Slater's work found that *interfunctional coordination* and the idea that marketing is a *companywide responsibility* are key parts of market orientation. Both studies place heavy emphasis upon the customer information or market intelligence dimension. Narver and Slater's view of market orientation is somewhat more consistent with a value-delivery concept of strategy, with its integration of competitor orientation into their measures, recognizing implicitly that customers define value by comparing the company's product offerings with those of competitors.

The results of the Narver and Slater investigation of the relationship between market orientation and business profitability are interesting but

**TABLE 7.1**  Items Used to Measure the Construct of Market Orientation

**Customer Orientation**

    Customer commitment.

    Create customer value.

    Understand customer needs.

    Customer satisfaction objectives.

    Measure customer satisfaction.

    After-sales service.

**Competitor Orientation**

    Salespeople share competitor information.

    Respond rapidly to competitors' actions.

    Top managers discuss competitors' strategies.

    Target opportunities for competitive advantage.

**Interfunctional Coordination**

    Interfunctional customer calls.

    Information shared among functions.

    Functional integration in strategy.

    All functions contribute to customer value.

    Share resources with other business units.

*Source:* John C. Narver and Stanley F. Slater, "The Effect of a Market Orientation on Business Profitability," *Journal of Marketing* 54 (October 1990), 20–35, adapted from their Table 1, p. 24.

complicated. Profitability was defined as the performance of the business unit in comparison with that of its major competitor in its principal served market, as judged by the unit's top management team, on return on total assets, return on net assets, and return on investment. Measuring business unit performance relative to the largest competitor is consistent with the method used in the PIMS studies, discussed in Chapter 2.

The overall general result of the Narver and Slater analysis can be stated first: Market orientation *does* have a significant, positive impact on business profitability. For the noncommodity businesses (including distribution and specialty products), the relationship was "monotonic"—as market orientation increased, profitability increased. For commodity businesses, the relationship was more complicated: All businesses with a high market orientation score were on the high end of the profit measure. However, not all of the more profitable businesses had high market orientation scores; some of them had low scores on market orientation. For firms with market orientation scores at the median level or below, there was no consistent relationship with profitability.

Interpretation of this result suggested that it might be a case of the well-known "stuck-in-the-middle" idea that the least profitable businesses are those that have neither a differentiated, market-niche strategy nor a low-cost, low-price strategy.[25] According to this view, differentiation and low price are two generic strategies that can produce above-average profitability. Firms that have neither a differentiation strategy nor a low-cost strategy have below-average performance. The commodity businesses that were above average in profitability appeared to be those smaller businesses that had successfully positioned themselves as suppliers to large customers and were benefiting from long-term relationships and good records of customer retention. This result underscores the assertion in Chapter 6 that it is usually more profitable to serve existing customers well than to devote major resources to finding new ones. It also refutes a popular belief, consistent with the old adversarial model of buyer-seller relationships, that large customers with more buying power over the marketer produce less profitable results. Rather, it appears that a small, responsive supplier of a commodity product (who may be very service oriented, a source of differentiation), can achieve above-average profits even when working with large and powerful customers.

Narver and Slater recognized that profitability reflects many factors, not just market orientation. Among the other variables they examined were:

- The size of the business in terms of total sales volume.
- Its market share and cost position relative to its major competitor.
- Industry structure variables including rate of market growth, industry concentration, entry barriers, buyer and seller power, and rate of technological change.

One interesting finding was that the smaller commodity businesses tended to be more profitable when the market was growing rapidly in the short term. This appeared to create an opportunity for small businesses that were responsive to their markets. Larger businesses, low in market orientation, suffered decreased profitability when their markets were experiencing short-term growth, reflecting their inability (or perhaps management unwillingness) to respond to changing market conditions. This finding of the importance of responsiveness is consistent with the Kohli and Jaworski definition of market orientation that includes responsiveness to market intelligence.

Although Narver and Slater had no specific measures of company or business unit culture, they used the concept of culture to interpret some of their results. They made a distinction between those businesses that had a strong market orientation and those that were dominated by what they termed "product/technology-oriented culture." They saw the latter type of culture as a barrier to the adoption of a market orientation. One of the positive aspects of their research is that by focusing on a single corporation they could control for the effects of corporate-level culture. However, they could not assess its impact. It made sense to equate differences in market orientation to differences in business unit and department "subcultures," but they could not do so rigorously, given their research design. We must be cautious about projecting their results to other companies and other industries.

The distinction between customer orientation and corporate or organizational culture must be remembered. Culture, as we have seen, is a broader concept. The strength of customer orientation is one dimension of an organizational culture. Given that there are multiple types of organizational cultures, it remains an open question whether customer orientation is more consistent with some types of cultures than others. Do both customer orientation and corporate culture have an influence on business performance and do they work together or separately? This was the line of questioning pursued in the following study.

## How Customer Orientation, Innovativeness, and Corporate Culture Affect Performance

Deshpandé, Farley, and Webster (DFW), in a study introduced earlier in this chapter when we considered the influence of national background culture, were also interested in understanding the fundamental relationships among customer orientation, corporate culture, and business unit performance. In addition, their conceptual model incorporated innovativeness, picking up the other dimension of the marketing concept. Like the previous two research teams, DFW developed a scale for measuring customer orientation. But they went further and developed and used a model of corporate culture to help understand the relationship between customer orientation, innovativeness, and profitability.

### The Customer Orientation Scale

DFW saw customer orientation as a combination of market intelligence, a focus on customer service and operational measures of service levels, responsiveness to the customer, and acceptance of the proposition that the customer comes first. Table 7.2 indicates the statements used to measure customer orientation. These nine items are a subset of a larger group of 30

**TABLE 7.2** Items Used for a Customer-Orientation Scale

1. We have routine or regular measures of customer service.
2. Our product and service development is based on good market and customer information.
3. We know our competitors well.
4. We have a good sense of how our customers value our products and services.
5. We are more customer-focused than our competitors.
6. We compete primarily based on product or service differentiation.
7. The customer's interest should always come first, ahead of the owners'.
8. Our products/services are the best in the business.
9. I believe this business exists primarily to serve customers.

One version of these questions was used with two managers from the marketer company. A modified version in which the first person pronoun (we, our, I) was replaced with the phrase "The supplier," etc. was used with two managers of a customer company.

questions originally tested in a small sample of firms. The nine measures used are those that proved to be statistically most reliable as measures of customer orientation. They were combined into a summary measure used to describe the customer orientation of each firm studied.

Deshpandé and Farley subsequently took this scale, along with the scales developed by Kohli and Jaworski and Narver and Slater, and used measures of statistical association to combine them into a single 14-item scale to measure market orientation. This new scale consists of three sub-scales for customer orientation, competitor orientation, and interfunctional coordination. Any researcher continuing this research tradition will likely want to use this comprehensive, statistically validated scale.[26]

## A Quadrad Design

The DFW study used a unique "quadrad" design. Two managers from a supplier company were interviewed. They were asked to indicate three important customers. On a random basis, one of these customer organizations was contacted and two purchasing managers from the customer organization were interviewed using the same measures as used with the supplier firm's managers. Customer respondents were asked to evaluate the supplier's organization, not their own. Thus, for each subject firm there were a total of four managers' responses—two from the firm itself and two from the customer organization. These two pairs of respondents or "dyads" were combined into a "quadrad." This design permitted DFW to compare a firm's assessment of its own customer orientation with that of a major customer. Which measure, the firm's assessment or that of its customer, would you expect to have a stronger association with profitability, sales growth, and market share?

Professional market research companies were hired to interview managers in Japan, Germany, France, England, and the United States. A total of 148 marketer firms (dyads) were examined with a total of 592 managers interviewed. Appropriate care was taken in preparing questionnaires for use in each country, using back-translation to ensure that consistent meanings were maintained in all countries.

## The DFW Innovativeness Scale

This study also measured the innovativeness of the firm as one determinant of its performance. The researchers borrowed a scale from an earlier study.[27] On a five-point scale from "Never" to "Always," respondents were asked to indicate:

> In a new product or service introduction, how often is your company:

- First to market with new products and services.
- Later entrant in established but growing markets.
- Entrant in mature, stable markets.
- Entrant in declining markets.
- At the cutting edge of technological innovation.

A single innovativeness score for each supplier firm was created by averaging the responses of the dyads. The resulting innovativeness score was very high on a statistical measure of reliability giving the researchers confidence that they had a good measure.

## The "Competing Values" Model of Organizational Culture

The DFW study was the first to use rigorous modeling and measurement to study organizational culture within the field of marketing. To measure culture, they used a scale developed by Cameron and Freeman[28] and Quinn,[29] researchers in the organizational behavior area, based on an organizational-cognition type model of organizational culture. This model, shown in Figure

7.2, is called a "competing values" model to stress the fact that competing sets of values, or cultures, can be found in the same organization. It looks at the culture of the organization as a mechanism for processing, and acting on, information about the changing market environment. It uses two fairly simple dimensions that can be thought of as the extent to which the organization tends to be more *internally or externally focused* and whether its responses to change tend to be *flexible and spontaneous or tightly controlled and orderly.*

| ORGANIC PROCESSES (flexibility, spontaneity) | |
|---|---|
| Type: Clan<br>Dominant Attributes:<br>  Cohesiveness, participation,<br>  teamwork, sense of family<br>Leader Style:<br>  Mentor, facilitator, parent-figure<br>Bonding:<br>  Loyalty, tradition, interpersonal<br>  cohesion<br>Strategic Emphasis:<br>  Toward developing human resources,<br>  commitment, morale | Type: Adhocracy<br>Dominant Attributes:<br>  Entrpreneurship, creativity,<br>  adaptability<br>Leader Style:<br>  Entrepreneur, innovator,<br>  risk taker<br>Bonding:<br>  Entrepreneurship, flexibility, risk<br>Strategic Emphasis:<br>  Toward innovation, growth,<br>  new resources |
| INTERNAL MAINTENANCE<br>(smoothing activities, integration) | EXTERNAL POSITIONING<br>(competition, differentiation) |
| Type: Hierarchy<br>Dominant Attributes:<br>  Order, rules and regulations,<br>  uniformity<br>Leader Style:<br>  Coordinator, administrator<br>Bonding:<br>  Rules, policies, and procedures<br>Strategic Emphasis:<br>  Toward stability, predictability, smooth<br>  operations | Type: Market<br>Dominant Attributes:<br>  Competitiveness, goal achievement<br>Leader Style:<br>  Decisive, achievement-oriented<br>Bonding:<br>  Goal orientation, production,<br>  competition<br>Strategic Emphasis:<br>  Toward competitive advantage and<br>  market superiority |
| MECHANISTIC PROCESSES (control, order, stability) | |

**FIGURE 7.2** A "competing values" model of organizational culture types based on the work of Cameron and Freeman. *Source:* Rohit Deshpandé, John U. Farley, and Frederick E. Wester, Jr., "Corporate Culture, Customer Orientation, and Innovativeness in Japanese Firms: A Quadrad Analysis," *Journal of Marketing* 57 (January 1993), 23–37, at p. 25. Reproduced with permission of the American Marketing Association.

Using this simple two-by-two matrix, it defines four types of organizational culture: Clan, Adhocracy, Hierarchy, and Market.

A *competing values* view of an organization's culture is consistent with the *differentiation* view of culture, described earlier, in which culture is the basis on which groups within the organization differentiate themselves from one another. However, an *integration* view is also achieved in this model by combining these multiple viewpoints into a kind of organizational consensus around what types of values are likely to be dominant in a conflict situation. The model sees culture as a mechanism for resolving organizational conflict. Culture becomes an influence when members disagree about what action to take, expressing itself in statements like "That is not the way we do things around here!" A simple example of such a situation would be one where a contingent of managers argues for protecting the employment status of department members and rewarding their loyalty (a "Clan" type culture) while others argue for reorganizing the department and moving quickly to respond to the changing market (an "Adhocracy" type culture). Thus, cultures can be thought of as linking competing viewpoints, balancing internal and external forces in ways that guide people in making the difficult choices that they face in the normal course of business decision making. Virtually every organization faces the challenge of finding the proper balance between stability and change, the need for order and continuity on the one hand and for flexibility and responsiveness on the other. Because it captures this tension, the competing values model has a good measure of "face validity" in the real world of management.

The information-processing approach of the competing values model of organizational culture is entirely consistent with the Kohli and Jaworski definition of market orientation, with its focus on market intelligence—the gathering and dissemination of market information and the organization's responsiveness to it. We would expect to find some consistent relationship between organizational culture type and extent of customer orientation.

The four types of organizational culture are defined by the members' shared beliefs about four characteristics of the organization:

1. Its dominant attributes as an organization (e.g., cohesiveness, entrepreneurship, orderliness, or competitiveness).
2. Its leadership style.
3. Its bonding mechanisms.
4. Its strategic emphases.

Each of the four types of organization is described by a set of adjectives on each of these four dimensions. Respondents were instructed to divide 100 points among four statements about their organizations on each of these four dimensions. For example, on the leadership dimension, respondents were asked to distribute 100 points among these four statements:

(A)   The head of my organization is generally considered to be a *mentor, sage,* or a *father or mother figure.*

(B)   The head of my organization is generally considered to be an *entrepreneur,* an *innovator,* or a *risk taker.*

(C)   The head of my organization is generally considered to be a *coordinator,* an *organizer,* or an *administrator.*

(D)   The head of my organization is generally considered to be a *producer,* a *technician,* or a *hard-driver.*

Similar types of statements were offered for each of the other three dimensions: dominant attributes, bonding mechanisms, and strategic emphasis. A sum of all of the points assigned to the A responses provided a score for the Clan-type culture, the B responses for the Adhocracy, C responses for the Hierarchy, and D responses for the Market-type culture, according to the individual respondent. The scores of both members of the dyad were averaged to produce a score for the supplier. Customer purchasing managers were administered the same questionnaires, with appropriate small changes in language to make it clear that they were evaluating their supplier's organization, which were scored and summarized in the same fashion.

## The Four Culture Types in the Competing Values Model

*Clan*-type cultures are focused on the internal maintenance of the organization but tend to make flexible and spontaneous responses to the changing environment. Leaders are facilitators and mentors, parent figures for organization members. The bonding mechanisms of the organization emphasize loyalty, tradition, and cohesiveness. Strategic emphasis is on developing the human resources of the organization and maintaining employee commitment and morale. Journalistic accounts of the Apple Computer organization suggest that it fits this type of culture, with its popcorn machine in the lobby, Friday afternoon beer fests, open lounge-type offices, and casual dress. Clans value cohesiveness, teamwork, a sense of family, and participative decision making.

*Adhocracy*-type culture also values flexibility and spontaneity but is more focused on the changing external environment. The strategic emphasis shifts from human resources to products, innovation, market and sales growth, and the requirements of the changing marketplace. Leaders exhibit entrepreneurship and innovativeness and are risk-takers. The bonding mechanisms likewise emphasize entrepreneurial skills, risk-taking, and innovation; members who exhibit these characteristics find mutual affinity. General Electric reportedly has achieved this type of culture, through its "workout" program with its emphasis on entrepreneurship and risk taking, a conscious move away from the competing values of the hierarchy culture.

*Hierarchy* is internally focused and deliberate and cautious in its response to a changing environment. Hierarchical values compete with those of the adhocracy. These will be competing values within the organization. General Motors has provided a good example of a dominant hierarchical culture, one that its top management has been trying to change. Hierarchies place an emphasis on rules, order, policies, and procedures as their dominant attributes and their bonding mechanisms. Traditions and past practices provide strong guidelines for behavior. The organization rewards people for being "good soldiers" or for what one manager referred to as "attendance rather than achievement." Leaders are coordinators and administrators; risk taking is not rewarded and might even be actively discouraged by the strategic emphasis on stability, predictability, and smooth transitions. Hierarchies are least responsive to a changing environment, internally focused, and valuing control over flexibility.

*Market* culture combines an external focus with a planned, coordinated, and controlled response. It provides competing values to those of the clan culture. Market cultures value competitiveness, goal setting, and achievement over cohesiveness and teamwork. It is *not* by definition necessarily customer-oriented. The leaders are decisive and achievement-oriented rather than mentors and process-oriented facilitators. Members bond through striving for productivity, goal achievement, and competitiveness. The organization is focused strategically on maintaining its competitive advantage and market superiority. PepsiCo has been described as a market-type culture, one in which managers are encouraged to be aggressive and competitive and guided by rigorous goal-setting and evaluation processes.

This brief review of the four types of culture underscores the idea of a competing values approach by noting that the diagonals of the matrix in Figure 7.2 point to competing frameworks that might exist within a given organization. No organization will exhibit only a single type of culture. The determining factor is the relative strength or saliency of each set of values, especially as it is expressed when the organization faces a dilemma that must be resolved.

## The Organizational Climate Scale

The research questions asked of managers in the DFW study also included items to measure organizational climate. Culture and climate are related but distinct concepts (although some scholars argue that this is a distinction without a meaningful difference). Organizational climate is the way in which culture is expressed, the ways in which managers make operational the themes of the underlying organizational culture. Climate is expressed in the behavior that gets rewarded, encouraged, supported, and expected by the members. Organizational climate can be thought of as the answer to the question "*What* happens around here?" whereas culture is the answer to the question "*Why* do things happen the way they do?"[30]

The scale used to measure organizational climate was one that had been developed and tested before, in the same study that provided the DFW innovativeness scale.[31] It consisted of the eight items in Table 7.3, to which respondents indicated their agreement or disagreement, using a five-point scale.

Organizational climate captures a firm's decision-making style. It is concerned with the extent to which people feel encouraged, supported, secure, trusted, independent, and yet involved in the organization. If the members see these attributes as prevalent, they are more likely to engage in entrepreneurial and risk-taking types of behavior. Thus, we would expect organizational climate, like customer orientation and innovativeness, to have a positive impact on business performance.

---

**TABLE 7.3**    Items Used to Assess Organizational Climate

1. Our organization has a strong tendency toward high-risk, high-return investments.
2. We are always trying out new ideas.
3. Excellent performance is rewarded in our organization.
4. In our organization, there is excellent communication between line managers and staff people.
5. People trust each other in this organization.
6. Decision making in our organization is participative.
7. A friendly atmosphere prevails among people in our organization.
8. In our organization, people feel they are their own bosses in most matters.

---

## *The Measure of Business Performance*

Like many other researchers who have attempted to analyze the determinants of business performance, DFW measured it *relative to the largest competitor.* Managers were asked to assess their own company's performance on four dimensions—sales volume, market share, profitability, and growth rate—in terms of whether it was greater, equal to, or less than that of the major competitor. The measures on these four dimensions were summarized and averaged for the two managers who responded for each supplier firm to produce a single index of business performance.

The large amount of information gathered by DFW presented a major analytical challenge. They had measures of organizational performance, innovativeness, customer orientation, four types of organizational culture, and organizational climate from almost 600 managers in five countries. There is also the fundamental problem of determining whether a given variable, such as customer orientation, has its influence on business performance directly or through its affect on one or more other variables, such as organizational climate or innovativeness. The results provide some very provocative and interesting suggestions about the relationship between customer orientation and business performance.

## Performance Is Related to Organizational Culture

The unique concern of the DFW research was to understand the influence of organizational culture on business performance. Using the statistical technique of discriminant analysis, businesses were divided into high-performing and low-performing groups. The researchers had expected that the best performing culture type would be Market, followed by Adhocracy, Clan, and Hierarchy. For the whole sample, involving all supplier businesses in the five countries studied, the best-performing cultures were Markets followed by Adhocracies. The worst-performing cultures were Clans, not Hierarchies. Adhocracy and Market cultures had positive impact on performance, whereas Clan had negative impact, and Hierarchy was surprisingly neutral.

As a test of the basic validity of the "competing values" model, these results are positive. In the model, the competing cultures are the Adhocracy versus the Hierarchy and the Clan versus the Market: external focus and flexibility versus internal focus and control; or flexibility and internal focus versus control and external focus. Indeed, the statistical results show that Adhocracy and Hierarchy are strongly negatively correlated, as are Clan and

Market. However, Adhocracy and Market cultures are also strongly negatively correlated, indicating that they are not likely to be found in the same company. Mechanistic processes for maintaining order, stability, and control would appear to be antithetical to flexibility and spontaneity, even when there is a common external orientation. This conjecture is supported by a weak negative correlation between Hierarchy and Market cultures.

## The Impact of Organizational Culture Does Not Depend on National Culture

One important and general conclusion is that organizational culture does make a difference, and in the predicted direction. It had been expected that the impact of a given type of organizational culture would depend on its interaction with the national background culture. This did not prove to be the case. There were no significant differences across countries in the impact of corporate culture on performance. All we can say is that some types of corporate culture are somewhat stronger in some countries than in others. As noted, strong clan cultures were found more frequently in Japan and England and strong Adhocracies were found more frequently in France and Germany; but Clans were always negative in their impact and Adhocracies were always positive, regardless of the country.

Looking only at corporate level culture is a useful exercise, but it is preliminary and incomplete. The external orientation of the Market and Adhocracy cultures produces positive results on performance whereas the internal focus of the Clans and Hierarchies has a negative to neutral impact. This can be interpreted as a strong vote in favor of a market orientation, which is, by definition, external. This interpretation would be consistent with both the Kohli and Jaworski definition of market orientation, with its emphasis on organizational responsiveness, and the Narver and Slater conclusion that market orientation has a positive impact on business performance.

## The Relationship between Customer Orientation and Business Performance

This should not be interpreted as showing a strong relationship between customer orientation (as distinct from the broader concept of market orientation), as measured in this study, and business performance. In fact, there was no statistically significant relationship. Customer orientation by itself had only a minor, insignificant impact on business performance, and it had no specific relationship with any particular type of organizational culture.

When added to the regression equation with the other variables, it had some minor positive impact, but the difference was not significant.

There were differences across countries in the strength of customer orientation. The highest scores were found in Germany, followed by Japan and the United States (similar scores), France, and England when measured from the customer's perspective. From the marketer's own perspective, the rankings are the same for Germany and the United States, but England ranks third, followed by Japan and France. In every country, marketers assessed their own customer orientation at higher levels than their customers did. Customer orientation is positively related to business performance, but not as strongly as expected and not strongly enough to be statistically significant. The relationship to performance was a bit stronger for suppliers' own assessment of their customer orientation than for the customers' assessment.

## Innovativeness Has the Strongest Impact on Performance

Of all of the variables tested, innovativeness had the strongest influence in discriminating between high- and low-performing companies. This result was strong and consistent across countries and for all countries taken together. In relationship to the other statistically significant measures, the influence of innovativeness was stronger than the positive influence of Market-type culture and almost as strong as the negative influence of Clan-type culture. Organizational climate also had a significantly positive influence on performance.

One simple conclusion from these findings might be that actions speak louder than words, that the new product development activities of the business and the decision-making and risk-taking propensities of its management count for more than the philosophical nuances of customer orientation. It might just be that customer orientation is a necessary but by no means sufficient condition for above average business performance. Customer orientation when added to the regression equation strengthens the prediction, but only in the context of the impact of the four statistically significant relationships. Perhaps it goes without saying that innovativeness must be customer-focused and market-driven.

## Implications of the Study of Corporate Culture

We have learned that corporate culture can make an important difference in business performance, especially in terms of the responsiveness of the business to a changing market environment. But responsiveness is only one part of a broader concept of market orientation, and it is distinct from the simple idea of customer orientation that was the hallmark of the old marketing concept. Customer orientation by itself has little strategic value; it must be coupled with innovative response to the customer's changing definition of value, the central idea of the new, value-delivery concept of marketing strategy.

The Deshpandé, Farley, and Webster study shows the importance and relevance of trying to understand organizational culture in order to improve business performance in the marketplace. The significant analytical results using data from five of the most developed economies show that the competing values model of organizational culture provides a useful and valid framework for marketing researchers. It offers a model that can be used in a global context and suggests that the general model of culture types can be universally applied even though there will be important differences across countries.

The overriding conclusion from the DFW study is that an external, market orientation produces superior performance, not an internal focus on the cooperation, coordination, and control mechanisms of the organization itself. Advocates of the new teamwork models of management would be well advised to be sure that the team's efforts are guided by market intelligence, customer- and competitor-orientation, and a value-delivery concept of strategy.

Managers need to manage customer orientation, corporate culture and climate, and innovation simultaneously. It is undoubtedly a mistake to concentrate on only one of these important ingredients in business success, although we need more research to understand their complex interactions and interdependencies.

## SUMMARY

Customer orientation describes a corporate culture, a set of values and beliefs that focus on the customers' needs and expectations and their satisfaction. But customer orientation is only one aspect of a corporate culture. After examining several different views of corporate culture, we settled on one that looks at organizations as knowledge systems, the *organizational cognition* model that is concerned primarily with how organization members gather and respond to information about a changing external environment. This view of organizational culture is consistent with a definition of market orientation that focuses on the gathering and use of market intelligence to guide all parts of the business in developing and delivering value to customers.

The concept of market orientation is broader than a focus on the customer and proves to be more powerful in predicting business performance. Customer orientation must be combined with competitor focus and interfunctional coordination if it is to enhance profitability. The firm doesn't just need customer focus; it needs to respond to the customer with strategies and product innovations that are responsive to changing needs and preferences, and changing competitive conditions.

A specific model of organizational culture, the "competing values" perspective, a type of organizational cognition model, was used to examine the relationships among customer orientation, corporate culture, innovativeness, and organizational climate. Using two dimensions—external versus internal orientation and flexible versus controlled response to information about the changing market environment—four types of organizational culture were defined and examined in detail: Adhocracy, Market, Clan, and Hierarchy.

Culture, climate, innovativeness, and customer orientation all proved to have an influence on relative profitability, market share, and sales growth. Businesses with organizational cultures having a strong external orientation tend to be the best performers across all five countries studied. Usually, it is the combination of external focus and flexible response that pays the biggest dividends. Customer orientation has a positive impact on performance, especially when found in combination with an entrepreneurial approach to decision making and a record of innovation on the part of the company. However, customer orientation as a set of values, without the follow through on specific action that serves the customer and responds aggressively to competition, has little direct impact on company performance. Nonetheless, it may be the basic set of values and beliefs, the fundamentals of the corporate culture, without which no positive action is possible.

# 8

# Developing a Customer-Oriented, Market-Driven Company

*Consumption is the sole end and purpose of production and the interest of the producer ought to be attended to only so far as it may be necessary for promoting that of the consumer.*

Adam Smith

*The Wealth of Nations, 1776*

As the marketplace evolves under the converging pressures of changing demographics, global politics, economics, technology, and social mores, so do organizations change along with the nature of competition and cooperation among them. As organizations change, so must the role of marketing within those organizations. When corporations emerged as a major social innovation in the late nineteenth century, major businesses were organized for a world of transactions conducted in a competitive marketplace between large, divisionalized, bureaucratic organizations and their customers. Today, the world has moved toward a pattern of economic activity based on exchanges in a context of long-term relationships and partnerships among economic actors in the loose coalitional frameworks of network organizations. As a result of these shifts in organization forms and marketplace structure, as noted by Srivastava and his colleagues, "traditional marketing perspectives almost certainly contain within them the seeds of marketplace failure."[1]

Equally important as a driver for change in the marketing paradigm is the rapid development and deployment of information technology, especially personal computers and networked workstations, the Internet, large databases, telecommunications capability, and information storage and retrieval technologies. In a report on a conference on the future of interactive marketing held at the Harvard Business School in 1996, John Deighton commented that: "The boom in direct and database marketing, the dawning of electronic commerce, new ways to automate salesforce management, and the sudden blossoming of the World Wide Web all suggest that the (marketing) discipline is under pressure to reshape."[2]

To survive in the future, every business will have to be organized around information and knowledge, not physical or natural resources, and be customer-focused, market-driven, global in scope, networked, and flexible in its ability to deliver superior value to customers who are continuously modifying their definition of value. Strategic thinking has recognized that future business success will depend first and foremost on customer focus, organizing the business around a flow of information from the marketplace, and developing efficient processes for responding to customer needs and wants. In this chapter, we summarize the assertions and conclusions of the analysis in earlier chapters into an integrated framework for thinking about the new marketing concept in this new environment.

The new marketing concept, a value-delivery concept of marketing strategy, has evolved out of the old marketing concept by way of long-range planning, portfolio selection theory, strategic planning, competitor analysis, total quality management, the theory of distinctive or core competence, and a new value-delivery concept of strategy. This evolution is summarized in Figure 8.1.

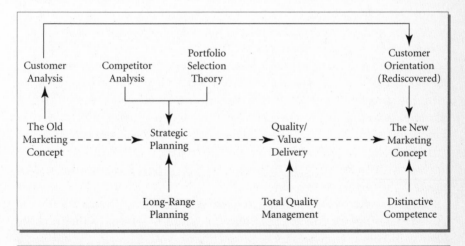

**FIGURE 8.1**    The evolution of the new marketing concept.

# MARKETS AND MARKETING PAST AND FUTURE

The economic environment that spawned the original marketing concept in the 1950s was one of postwar economic growth and pent-up consumer demand. America was rebuilding socially and economically, transforming a wartime economy into a consumer society. The marketing concept focused companies on the need to capture this increasingly affluent and demanding customer, who would be able to choose among a broader variety of competing product offerings. The average age of the population would be trending downward as the postwar baby boom accompanied an increased rate of household formation and laid the basis for the mass consumption and production. Companies faced two fundamental challenges—building the productive capacity to satisfy demand for goods and services and stimulating demand for what their factories could produce.

Europe and Japan were rebuilding physically as well as politically, recovering from the effects of the most devastating war in history that had ended with the advent of the Nuclear Age. The Cold War began almost as soon as World War II ended, as the United States formed alliances with European, Asian, and Latin American countries to counter the aggressive military moves of the Soviet Union under the dictatorship of Joseph Stalin. The phrase "The Cold War," first used by Bernard Baruch in 1947, defined a political, and potentially military, contest between the United States and its allies on one side and the Union of Soviet Socialist Republics and its mostly involuntary satellite countries on the other. The Western bloc, that included Japan, was held together by its focus on a common enemy. The battle between two fundamentally different economic systems, capitalism and communism, was to continue for almost 50 years. The Soviet Union began to unravel in the late 1980s as the smaller states pulled away without provoking Soviet military response and occupation. The Cold War officially ended with the final collapse of the Soviet Union in December 1991 when Ukraine, Russia, and Belarus declared their independence and the Soviet Parliament went out of business. The experiment with centrally planned socialism following the Marxist model had failed. Capitalism had won the contest. A difficult struggle to restore a market-based capitalistic system began in the former Soviet republics.

In 1950, the world's population stood at about 2.5 billion, with the United States population at 151 million or about 6 percent of the total. By 2000, world population was more than 6 billion, with China representing 20 percent and India 16 percent. (India is growing faster and is expected to be the largest country in the world, with a population of over 1.5 billion by the year 2050.) Most European countries are experiencing a decline in total population. The United States with a population of 281 million now represents less than 5 percent of the world total. World population is galloping toward a predicted 7.85 billion in the year 2025, of which Americans would be perhaps 335 million or 4.3 percent. Eighty percent of the world population is in the developing world, only 20 percent in the industrialized nations, but the developed nations' population is growing at an annual rate of only 0.1 percent compared with 1.6 percent for the developing world. The American population is getting older (average age is 35), a trend also seen in Europe and, to a lesser degree, throughout the world as health care improves (although the AIDS epidemic significantly reduces the younger age groups in some countries, especially in Africa). The aging population creates major shifts in the demand for goods and services. Population growth in the developing world will be a major driver of global market development, even as the industrialized nations continue to account for the largest share of consumption expenditures for the foreseeable future.

As we enter a new millennium, the world has changed faster, by almost any criterion, in the last half century than at any earlier time in history. We are living in a time that has variously been called the Information Age, the Knowledge Economy, and the Age of Discontinuity.[3] A predominantly resource-based economy has been supplemented by one based primarily on knowledge and information. The service economy, with information and information technology at its core, now accounts for more than half of employment and of consumer expenditures in virtually all of the developed countries. In the United States, services account for almost 60 percent of consumption expenditures and more than 75 percent of employment.

Worldwide economic and political conditions at the beginning of the twenty-first century were a cause for concern. The major American, European, and Asian economies were all in recession at the same time, underscoring the fact of the globalization. Political and economic turmoil from Afghanistan and Argentina to the Middle East and Zimbabwe cast a cloud over the global economy. The United States had been shocked by the collapse of a large portion of its Internet start-ups, followed by major declines in the stock market and the advent of the first economic downturn in more than a decade. The American public was made even more uneasy by the terrorist attacks of September 11, 2001, the bankruptcy of the nation's second largest retailer, Kmart, and of Enron Corporation, the sixth largest company in the country, which resulted in investigations into accounting practices of many of the largest corporations and their auditors. While economic recovery was widely expected, no one anticipated a return to the impressive and stable growth statistics of the 1990s. The ongoing worldwide war on terrorism, heightened security at airports and public gatherings, a nervous traveling public, and a return to basic consumer values relating to family and community were certain to bring permanent changes to marketing practice. It was certainly a different world than the one that spawned the original customer-oriented marketing concept.

## MARKETING TO THE GLOBAL CUSTOMER

The old marketing concept grew out of the need to serve customers created by the conditions of post-World War II affluence and population growth. The 1950s consumers would be the beneficiaries of aggressive competition among domestic producers, with new entrants in many industries as firms adjusted from military to peacetime production and entrepreneurs were attracted by the prospect of unprecedented growth in consumer expenditures.

Marketers in the 1950s faced the necessity of becoming truly knowledgeable about and responsive to a consumer with increased discretionary spending power who was informed, demanding, and confident about the future. Mass production and mass consumption of products with high symbolic value characterized the era of the Consumer Society, dubbed "The Affluent Society" by John Kenneth Galbraith.[4] It was an age of "conspicuous consumption," where products were often purchased based on what they conveyed about the self-concept and lifestyle of the consumer as much as for the specific performance benefits they delivered.

A new marketing concept is required for today's global customer who can choose among a much larger variety of products and services from efficient producers located throughout the world. In the developed countries, consumer needs are much less urgent than those that characterized their grandparents. Today's consumers have more discretion in terms of both buying motivation and choices available. Their purchases are more easily postponed and they are much more likely to judge products and services in terms of basic value, defined simply as the ratio of benefits to cost/price, including costs-in-use. The concept of customer value is at the heart of the new marketing concept and must be the central element of all business strategy.

The global customer learns quickly about the wide range of choices of products and services available, through modern telecommunications technologies of many kinds giving virtually instant access to cultural events, political news, fashions, and economic developments throughout the world. The Cable News Network (CNN) broadcasts political events and military actions around the world as they are happening. It was estimated that as many as three billion television viewers around the world watched at least some part the 2002 Winter Olympics from Salt Lake City. The traveler can view CNN 24 hours a day in hotels and airports almost everywhere in the world. The Internet gives first-hand exposure to global products and services of all kinds, creating informed, sophisticated, and demanding customers. Global media and news coverage, movies, music videos, satellite broadcasting, the World Wide Web, and international travel all help to spread current fashions and homogenize consumer wants and preferences as well as to create the demand for global products and services. Coca-Cola, Microsoft, Levi's, Ford, McDonald's, Intel, Inter-Continental Hotels, Caterpillar, IBM, Hertz, Hermes scarves, Colgate, British Airways, Kodak, Rolex, Sony Walkman, Heineken, Disney, Nokia, and Britney Spears are everywhere! For consumers in the developed countries, there are more than enough options to choose from in virtually every category of product and service.

The global customer faces a fundamentally different economic scenario than the consumer of the 1950s. Instead of scarcity, optimism, and growth, the market environment in the developed countries today is one of material abundance and excess productive capacity, pessimism, and stagnation. Economic uncertainty and political instability combine to create low consumer confidence and a high degree of caution. For the near- to intermediate-term future, the outlook is for little or no real economic growth, a continued high level of unemployment, increasing taxation, and widespread job insecurity resulting from the attempts of employers in both the private and public sector to control costs and eliminate employees wherever possible.

The global customer is also concerned about the natural environment in fundamentally new ways and increasingly considerate of the effects of the purchase and use of products on the depletion of natural resources and the pollution of air, water, and soil that often result. Government regulations often intervene in the production and consumption of goods and services with the intent to reduce environmental impact. The customer may expect the manufacturer or reseller to assist with the recycling or disposal of the spent product and its packaging. The prices of products must reflect the additional costs of responsible product manufacture, use, and disposal, heightening the consumer's sensitivity to both value and price. Companies wishing to do business on a global basis find that they must design products and services for the highest, not the lowest, common denominator in areas such as product recovery and recycling (where Germany, with its "green" political movement, appears to be setting the world standard). Whereas horsepower and tailfins impressed the automobile customer of the 1950s, today's customer is looking for fuel economy, safety, ease of handling and parking, and lowest total costs of ownership. The financial package may be as important as style, with leasing a very important option for many buyers.

While manufacturer brands remain important and global brands become more dominant, in most product categories there are more store or "own" brands promising the customer greater value. In many product categories, merchants and their brands have become equally or even more powerful than manufacturers in the marketing channel. Although retailing is still primarily national in scope, it has also become increasingly global. Wal-Mart is expanding aggressively beyond the United States while European retailers have moved into North America with acquisitions. The Brussels-based Delhaize Group owns the Food Lion chain of 1,200 supermarkets in the Mid-Atlantic and Southeastern United States, for example. Southland Corporation's "7-Eleven" convenience stores originated in the United States, expanded to Japan, and then were acquired in the United States by their Japanese partner. Other large retailers with a growing international scope include Staples, Home Depot, and Price Club/Costco and fashion merchandisers such as Louis Vuitton, Jaeger, and Chanel. Retailers from around the world also now have access to customers in other countries via the Internet, although logistics will continue to be an issue for global Internet retailing.

## THE VALUE-DELIVERY CONCEPT OF STRATEGY

A value-delivery concept of strategy is a necessary response to an increasingly informed, sophisticated, cautious, and value-conscious global customer. We saw earlier, in Chapter 2, how a focus on customer value grew out of the PIMS analysis showing that quality, not market share, was the major driver in the performance of the most profitable companies. Market share and profitability were both shown to be the result of delivering superior value to customers. By the late 1970s, strategic planning was shifting away from a definition of markets as collections of competitors back toward an emphasis on customers and their definition of quality. The total quality management (TQM) movement helped to focus the operations of many companies on the concept of customer-defined quality, which is to say value. Now, in many companies with successful quality programs, such as Motorola, where a concern for customer-defined quality has permeated the organization, separate quality departments are disappearing. Quality, like marketing in general, is too important to be left to a specialized department.

## Value Delivery and Distinctive Competence

The value-delivery concept of strategy helped to bring customer-orientation, as called for by the old marketing concept, back into the forefront. But it also added the fundamental notion that the firm's value-delivery strategy must be based on some distinctive competence, a source of unique and sustainable competitive advantage. More often than not, this distinctive competence is based on intellect and knowledge, which is to say people, not physical materials, plant, and equipment. In his paradigm of "the intelligent enterprise," James Brian Quinn proposes:

> At their core, most successful enterprises today can be considered "intelligent enterprises," converting intellectual resources into a chain of service outputs and integrating these into a form most useful for certain customers. . . . [M]ost of the processes that add value to materials derive from knowledge-based service activities.[5]

It was proposed in Chapter 3 that every business, even manufacturing companies, should define themselves as service businesses; customers buy benefits, not products. Usually, the physical product itself is only one part of the total value-delivery system for the customer; customer expectations are defined by the service aspects of the product offering. Information has the ability to turn any product into a service and into a customer relationship. For example, a package of Procter & Gamble's Crest toothpaste offers a toll-free telephone number (800-699-3974) that a customer can call with questions or comments. The caller's name and address are entered into a database and the consumer can request information about dental care. Even a simple product such as toothpaste can become a service and a two-way relationship between the marketer and the customer, who is buying improved dental health, not just a physical product.

The ability to command natural resources, technology, and capital as sources of competitive advantage is becoming relatively less important strategically while the ability to control knowledge and information becomes more important. The value-delivery concept of strategy is based on the fundamental assumption that value is defined in the marketplace, not in the factory, by customers who are continuously assessing competitive product offerings and their own needs and preferences, which change as the customer learns.

## Customer Knowledge as a Source of Competitive Advantage

The core of the successful business of the future will be its knowledge about customers, their characteristics, needs, and preferences, supported by information technology that makes this information instantly available to decision-makers throughout the organizational network. Customer knowledge is the essence of the marketing concept. Information about customers becomes the critical strategic resource for the business because customers define value in their own terms. Through their definition of value, customers also define the business itself by the demands they place upon it. In a business world increasingly characterized by network organizations, coalitions of firms bringing together their distinctive competences to create customer value, customer knowledge is the link that holds the network organization together and defines its shared objective and common purpose.

Customer knowledge is only one of several distinctive competences necessary for survival and by itself it is inadequate to differentiate the firm from its competitors. The firm must also have other knowledge-based competences, especially those related to technology and other dimensions of the product offering, that allow it to design, develop, and deliver superior customer value, solutions to customer problems. Coming back to the customer-knowledge dimension of competence, there is a prior question to be answered: Knowledge about which customers?

## Customer Selection: The Critical Strategic Choice

Customers define the business by placing a set of demands on it for delivering superior value. Customer selection—the market segmentation and targeting decision—thus sets up the criteria by which the firm will be judged in the marketplace. Every firm (and every network organization) is limited in its competences; the firm committed to a strategy of value delivery must therefore limit the customers it proposes to do business with. The selection of those customers becomes the critical strategic choice, the polestar for everything that happens in the business and most especially the development of the product offering. The product is a variable; it is the customer that is the given.

Under both the old marketing concept and the new, market segmentation, market targeting, and positioning are the central requirements for effective strategic planning. In the new marketing concept, however, the focus is sharpened by adding the idea of the "value proposition." The value proposition is the verbal statement that matches up the firm's distinctive competences with the needs and preferences of a carefully defined set of potential customers. The value proposition is a communication device that brings together the people in the organization and its customers, concentrating their efforts and expectations on those things that the company can do best in a system for delivering superior value to customers. The value proposition creates a shared understanding that is the necessary basis for a long-term relationship that meets the goals of both the company and its customers.

To maintain its strategic focus, its commitment to its customers and to developing its distinctive competence, the firm must be selective. Opportunism and "the siren song of sales volume" must be avoided; the essence of market targeting and positioning is the willingness to recognize that, in the case of certain customers, both the firm and customers will be better off if competitors serve those customers. Losing a customer can be the best thing that can happen to a business if that customer cannot be satisfied at a reasonable cost to the company. Not all customers are valuable customers. However, those customers who value those things the firm does well must be attracted and retained as the critical strategic resource for the business. In today's slow-growth markets, the key to survival for most firms will be retaining the customers that the firm already has rather than attracting hordes of new customers.

## MANAGING CUSTOMER LOYALTY

Under the old marketing concept, the objective of marketing was to make a sale. Under the new marketing concept, the objective to create and keep customers and to develop customer relationships. The sale is only the beginning. The customer is seen as a long-term, strategic business asset. As customer relationships and strategic buyer-seller partnerships replace transactions and simple repeat purchases as the objective of marketing activity, a new definition of customer loyalty emerges.

Under the old marketing concept, we talked about "brand loyalty," usually defined as the portion of a customer's purchases concentrated on the brand. It was a definition based on statistical characteristics of a string of purchases by an anonymous customer. Brand loyalty was specific to a given product, within a given category (e.g., loyalty to Pepsi-Cola within the carbonated soft drinks category). The brand loyal customers were defined by their demographic characteristics (e.g., age, education, occupation, and income). Customers were defined by statistics describing averages and central tendencies within a population, not as individuals.

## Customer Loyalty: A Two-Way Street

Customer loyalty replaces brand loyalty in the new marketing concept. It is a two-way street: Customers remain loyal to the companies and brands that serve their needs and preferences with a total set of related products and services. In return, companies demonstrate and maintain their loyalty to customers by becoming knowledgeable about them and responding to them with enhanced product offerings. The commitment to deliver superior value to customers contains an explicit commitment to managing customer loyalty.

Customer loyalty has meaning only within the context of relationship marketing. Relationship marketing is only possible when the company knows the customer as an individual, not as a statistical phenomenon, and can address communications and specific product offerings to her. In this way, the customer also develops a relationship with the company, not just a product or brand.

In Chapter 5, we explored the reasons why a repeat customer may be much more valuable than a new customer:

- Multiple purchases from the same customer.
- Lower costs of serving known customers.
- The likelihood that the loyal customer will pay a somewhat higher price.
- The opportunity to sell other products and services.
- The benefits of favorable word-of-mouth.
- The avoided costs of finding and attracting new customers.

It was also noted that price-oriented customer promotions often have the effect of attracting the "wrong" customers, those who are interested only in the low price, thus reducing both loyalty and profitability.

With a commitment to relationship marketing, the objective is to retain loyal customers by offering them superior value, defined as the ratio of benefits to cost/price. There is a positive trade-off between spending money to retain customers versus spending promotional dollars to attract new ones. The assumption being made in any customer retention program, which must be carefully tested, is that the customers in danger of being lost are in fact worth retaining. This is only true if the business has carefully and strategically selected the correct customers in the first place, namely those who value the things the firm tries to do well. The most serious mistake is to use low price to retain unprofitable customers.

This observation underscores the critical importance of the market segmentation and targeting decision. Customers selected should be those for whom the company can deliver superior value. Value-based pricing should be used as part of the process by which customers and companies select one another, not as an indiscriminate tool for attracting as many customers as possible, good and bad. Then the company should commit the resources necessary to retain those good customers by offering them a broad range of related products and services that will keep them loyal as their needs change and evolve over time.[6]

## Innovation and Customer Retention

Retaining customers requires keeping them satisfied and that requires innovation. While everyone remembers that customer orientation was the central theme of the old marketing concept, few recall that innovation was given equal importance.

In the 1950s and 1960s, the word innovation was synonymous with new product development. That was entirely consistent with the growth markets of the time and the opportunity to exploit technology, much of it developed as part of military and space exploration programs, for the consumer society. The objective was to invent products that could be produced in large quantities at low cost, allowing the low prices required to create mass markets.

The concept of innovation for mass production contains an interesting paradox. Innovation implies dynamic change whereas mass production calls for an unchanging product and a stable production process. As firms saw the huge growth in consumer markets, it was implicitly assumed that the key to profitability would be efficient production of large quantities of standardized products that would permit economies of scale.

The idea of mass production for mass markets was not new. Cigarettes were probably the first mass-produced product, with Buck Duke's American Tobacco company producing two million a day in the late 1880s, supported by $800,000 per year in advertising.[7] Henry Ford's dream in the early

1900s, beginning with the Model T, was to produce a car that was cheap enough that the people who made it could also afford to buy it. The phrase "Fordism" became a general term applied to the system of mass production and mass marketing. In the 1950s and 1960s, the concept of market segmentation moved industry well beyond the days of the Model T and "any color you want as long as it's black," but the standard model of production efficiency remained that of large-scale production of standard products. Once product designs were set, it was marketing's job to generate the necessary volume. Mass marketing was the handmaiden of mass production. Thus, marketing could quickly revert to a sales orientation, and it often did.

The quality movement of the 1970s and 1980s expanded the definition of innovation to include continuous improvement in both products and production processes. Commitment to finding new and better solutions to customer problems is another hallmark of the new marketing concept. In Chapter 3, we saw that the dynamic mechanism of customer expectations means that the definition of quality keeps changing. The augmented product becomes the expected product. As customers' expectations are met, they are revised upward. Competitors likewise respond with improvements and innovation, adding another stimulus to the firm's own innovation.

Continuous improvement represented a dramatic shift from the ideology of mass production, where the emphasis was on getting an optimum design and manufacturing process and then maximizing the volume being run through that process. Continuous improvement applied more to processes than products, although product improvement was also often a by-product. The new concern for process improvement was closely related to the realization that the supporting service bundle is often at least as important as the physical product in defining customer value and in the redefinition of the business as a service business.

## Process Improvement and Reengineering

The commitment to continuous improvement led to the development of the relatively new discipline called "reengineering," defined as a fundamental, radical rethinking of the business from the ground up.[8] To improve the level of customer service and to find and eliminate unnecessary costs, many companies have engaged in in-depth studies of the processes involved in developing and delivering customer value. Reengineering requires looking at the company and its processes of value delivery from the customer's perspective and redesigning those processes and their related organization structure "from scratch." Nothing about the company can be taken as "given" in a true reengineering effort. Today, reengineering is a major part of the practice of many consulting firms. One of the most common results of reengineering is to eliminate layers of bureaucracy, enhancing the ability of the business to respond to customer needs and marketplace developments and bringing top management closer to the customer.

Reengineering has been integrated with information technology in the latest development in total quality management called *Six Sigma*, a term referring to statistical variation around a mean value. Goals should be related to customer satisfaction, concentrating on a performance parameter known to be important to customers. A firm that achieves Six Sigma quality in a process is meeting its goal 99.9997 of the time, meaning that there are only 3.4 defects in the process per billion opportunities to mess it up. This latest development in quality is believed to have its origins in a quality improvement initiative in the early 1990s at General Electric Company led by the company's chief information officer. It was an integral part of General Electric's efforts to introduce information technology throughout the organization.[9] Six Sigma quality programs have been adopted throughout the business world, often as the result of business customers requiring them of their suppliers.

Reengineering and Six Sigma offer the twin benefits of cost reduction and higher levels of performance on process dimensions critical to customer satisfaction. Both are keys to improving and delivering customer value.

## From Mass Production to Mass Customization

The old marketing concept evolved in a world of standard products, mass production, and mass marketing. Traditional methods of marketing research were built around survey methodologies that had the objective of finding the common denominators of customer needs and preferences, the characteristics of the "average" consumer. Once that profile was established, perhaps for multiple market segments in the case of the more sophisticated marketers, a standard product was designed for maximum customer appeal, to be promoted using mass communications to attract and persuade the largest possible number of potential buyers.

Mass marketing, using the mass media and especially the new medium of television, provided the sales volume necessary to support the large factories that would deliver the economies of scale in production necessary for low cost and profitability. The legendary mass marketers, such giants as General Motors, Procter & Gamble, Anheuser-Busch, R.J. Reynolds, General Foods, Gillette, and General Mills, also achieved economies of scale in marketing with their superior ability to purchase hugely expensive television, radio, and magazine advertising time and space on a national basis at lowest possible prices. Mass production and mass marketing depended on highly standardized products and standardized messages that would appeal to the maximum number of potential customers.

Today's customers demand more precise and more complete response to their needs and preferences. With domestic and foreign producers aggressively competing for their patronage, customers can be demanding. They can ask for a larger variety of products and products tailored specifically to their needs and wants. And they can get them! We have moved from the age of mass production to mass customization, made possible by the impact of information technology on the processes of order entry, product design, production scheduling, manufacturing, inventory management, product delivery and distribution, and customer feedback. Marketers can now assemble and deliver product and service offerings as complex and diverse as automobiles, computers, online networking, portable communications, and factory process control systems tailored specifically to the demands of individual customers.

Researchers at IBM led the way in developing a theoretical framework for thinking about the move from mass production to mass customization.[10] The concept of mass customization was originally put forward in 1987 by a leading academic management authority, Stanley Davis.[11] If an increasingly demanding customer is the primary force pulling mass customization into being, the primary driving force is information technology, essential to the development of the low-cost, flexible production systems that make mass customization feasible. IBM has more than passing interest in the trend toward mass customization because it has great strategic importance for both its own products and its customers.

The IBM researchers conceived of an evolutionary process that begins with invention. By its very nature, invention is a dynamic process and the product remains a dynamic concept during the development process. To develop a commercial product, both the product and the manufacturing process must become as stable as possible. In the traditional paradigm, the next step after invention was the development of a stable mass production process that would insure a low-cost standardized product of consistent quality. This product was aimed at a homogeneous market where mass-marketing methods could be used to manage and stabilize demand. Stable product, stable process, and stable demand were all required for mass production. A series of product improvements and added features were developed over time to extend the product lifecycle and the life expectancy of the plant and equipment that had committed to the product. Product development cycles were long and expensive as the firm moved cautiously to avoid prematurely making its investment in old products and processes obsolete and to insure that the new product would have maximum appeal. In the days of pent-up demand, time-to-market for new products was not a priority.

Instability in demand levels, caused by economic cycles, changing customer demographics, and competitive moves, resulted in swings in inventory and rates of production and introduced major inefficiencies into a system that had been built on a basic commitment to stability. Large inventories were a buffer between inequalities in supply and demand and they were extremely costly. Further instability could be introduced by product and process technology shocks, as competitors brought innovations to market or achieved a lower cost position with a new production process. Another cause of inefficiency was found in the fact that most markets were not as homogeneous as assumed and that customers often demanded changes in the product to better suit their needs. A standard product was a sitting duck for a niche marketer who could offer a product with features designed for a specific subsegment. Fragmentation of mass markets was a common occurrence as products matured and customers migrated out of old segments and into new ones.

The development of cable television and the advent of literally thousands of new special interest magazines aimed at smaller target audiences created a media fragmentation that decimated the large audiences once served by the three leading television networks and the mass, general interest magazines. By the late 1980s, it became abundantly clear that the mass production and mass consumption view of business was obsolete for many marketers. Many traditional mass markets were disintegrating and the costs associated with serving them—both production and marketing costs—were too high. Mass production and mass marketing systems lacked the flexibility required by the global marketplace.

The objective of the old mass-production/mass-marketing paradigm was products in sufficient quality at low cost so that most people could afford them. The new, mass-customization paradigm is based on the goal of developing, producing, and delivering affordable goods and services with enough variety and customization that nearly everyone finds exactly what he or she wants.[12] Lowest possible cost remains a necessary condition for profitability as well as for delivering true customer value. As discussed, the movement toward mass customization as a response to the competitive demands of the global marketplace began with the new focus on continuous improvement and led to the concept of reengineering. This first step introduced new flexibility and responsiveness into the organization and its processes. (See Figure 8.2 for a model of the evolution from mass production to mass customization.) With the commitment to continuous improvement that came out of the total quality movement and rising customer expectations, firms learned to live with a concept of dynamic process change instead of the old stable processes of a mass-production world.

The next and final step is to make the form of the product as dynamic as the process that produces it. In services marketing, process improvement is often synonymous with product improvement. We noted earlier that continuous improvement often concentrated on the service bundle surrounding the product, especially order entry and delivery systems, rather than the product itself. Mass customization as a concept is easier to understand in the cases of services, where there is no factory that must be tuned for flexibility. (In services marketing, however, there is a "backroom" operation involving communications and data processing that is very similar to a "factory" defined by machines, workstations, and workers.)

In services marketing, the product is often produced at the point of contact with the customer, or even as it is being consumed, as a customized response to that particular customer's needs. Even in the production of services, however, there is usually some technology in the background, such as a computer and a database, that can be accessed in modular form, allowing the service provider to quickly assemble components into a service package that appears to be completely tailored to the customer's needs and wishes.[13]

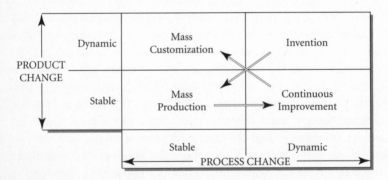

**FIGURE 8.2**   From mass production to mass customization. *Source:* Adapted from A. C. Boynton, B. Victor, and B. J. Pine II, "New Competitive Strategies: Challenges to Organizations and Information Technology," *IBM Systems Journal* 32, 1 (1993), 40–64, at p. 60. Reproduced with permission.

When a traveler contacts an online airline reservation system, a travel agent, or an airline sales representative, for example, he or she selects destination, date of travel, time of day, class of travel, preferred routing, seat location, a special meal, payment terms, and other variables that represent a unique product for that traveler. His or her product is "assembled" in the computerized reservations system where it is "held in inventory" until it is delivered at the time of travel. But it is truly a unique product. It literally has the traveler's name on it and the traveler is identified in the customer information file by a large amount of data that describes a unique individual to whom communications can be addressed and whose needs and preferences have been duly noted. If this is a frequent traveler, his or her traveling history, a series of transactions, is clearly noted and the probable future value of the relationship with that customer can be rather precisely determined.

While the concept of mass customization may appear to be more applicable to services, it is increasingly relevant for the production of physical products as well. Even in the case of products as tangible as automobiles, the number of options available to the consumer in styles, accessories, colors, and so on, makes it possible to produce a unique car for each of the millions of people who purchase a car each year. Every car moving down the assembly line has a customer identified with it, either the buyer or the dealer, and is being built to that customer's specifications. Toyota has been designing an information and production system that will make it possible for an individual consumer to specify a car that will be delivered to his or her home within a few days of ordering. A Japanese bicycle company already offers a similar service, tailoring the dimensions of each bike precisely to the physical characteristics of the rider, although delivery takes a few weeks. Personal computers can be assembled with hardware and software, chosen from hundreds of options, installed to meet the unique needs of the customer and delivered to the customer's home or business within a few weeks.

With mass customization, the product truly becomes a variable, as called for by the new marketing concept. Mass customization means working with existing product technology, in modular form, to create specific product bundles for that particular customer. From time to time, the whole process is invigorated with the introduction of new technology, created through the ongoing process of invention. It all starts with customer targeting and relationship management leading to a unique solution to the customer's problem that fits with the company's strategy and distinctive competence. That is the ultimate fulfillment of the marketing concept!

In the world of mass customization, the task of the marketing function is to understand the needs and preferences of customers as individuals, not as part of a "mass" market. It makes sense for the firm to think of itself not as a producer of goods or services for the customer, but as engaging in a process of co-development and co-production with the customer. This concept of co-production is more easily understood in the context of business-to-business marketing, as when a producer of raw materials plays an integrated role with the customer in the design and management of the customer's manufacturing process. Increasingly, however, the concept also makes sense for marketers of consumer products, from home-office personal computers to banking services to insurance to kitchen appliances and frozen foods. In every instance, the marketer must understand the individual customer and the use-system into which the product or service will be applied.

In the new marketing concept, this knowledge, understanding, and commitment is not the special province of the marketing department. Rather it is shared throughout the organization. In the words of B. Joseph Pine formerly at IBM and now head of his own consulting business, mass customization represents "the death of the marketing function . . . the triumph of the marketing discipline."[14] Marketing becomes part of the organization culture and the knowledge systems that guide decision making at all levels.

# CUSTOMER ORIENTATION AS ORGANIZATIONAL CULTURE

Implementing the new marketing concept requires that organizational culture be actively managed, along with strategy and organization structure. We have defined organizational culture as the basic set of values and beliefs that are shared throughout the organization, help members understand its functioning, and provide norms for their behavior. We reviewed research with managers in five countries showing that the most effective organizational cultures in terms of growth and profitability are those that maintain an external focus and have flexible processes for responding to a changing environment.

## Loyal Customers and Loyal Employees

A customer-oriented organizational culture is one in which customers interests come first, always. The firm stays focused on the customer in everything that it does and management constantly asks how it can do things better on behalf of the customer. People in the customer-oriented firm put the customer's interests ahead of all other stakeholders including owners, management, suppliers, and employees. Everyone's job is defined in terms of how that job helps to create and deliver value for the customer and internal processes are designed and managed to insure responsiveness to customer needs and maximum efficiency in value delivery.

The customer-oriented firm is almost certainly committed to relationship marketing and employees have a team spirit reflecting that commitment, working together to solve customer problems. Employee morale is a critical success factor in the customer-oriented company, especially for those employees who deliver some aspect of the service bundle that is part of the product offering. In the customer-oriented company, there will be a clear statement of the value proposition, which becomes the focal point for the organization. Employees will repeat the value proposition as a rallying cry. It becomes part of the symbols and rituals of the organizational culture.

Hierarchy and authority become relatively unimportant in a customer-oriented company culture. Over time, it is likely that a value-delivery definition of strategy will result in a flattening of the organization and elimination of layers of middle management as the firm attempts to improve its responsiveness by designing an organization structure that is most appropriate for its strategy, and gets management closer to the marketplace and its customers. Conceptually, and as part of the organizational culture, people may talk about the customer being at the top of the organization structure. Next in the hierarchy come the people who have direct contact with the customer and are the front-line of the value-delivery process. Then come those internal job functions that support them with products, services, and information. The role of higher level managers is to help everyone involved in the value-delivery process by giving them the resources they need, including procedures and policies as well as tangible and financial resources, to do their jobs most effectively and efficiently. The customer comes first and every person and every job is committed to creating a satisfied customer.

Relationship marketing builds an organizational culture in which the customer comes first. Customers become known by name and may even develop enduring personal relationships with members of the organization. Loyal customers are seen as a key strategic asset and resource, one that must be preserved and defended.

Loyal employees are essential to maintaining a strong organizational culture, to improving efficiency in the value-delivery process, and to building long-term customer relationships. Customer and employee loyalty are related; each reinforces the other. Experienced employees are very likely to be able to serve the customer best and to understand customers and their needs better. This knowledge is an essential part of continuous improvement. The customer's sense of confidence and trust in the organization is enhanced by knowing the employees he or she deals with as individuals, forming a bond with the organization. Likewise, this ongoing relationship helps to bond the employee to the customer and builds the commitment to customer satisfaction.[15]

Research has consistently confirmed the strong connection between customer and employee satisfaction; each reinforces the other and contributes to profitability. Each can be both cause and effect of the other, in a "virtuous cycle."[16]

## Wal-Mart's Culture Is Dedicated to Customers and Employees

Wal-Mart is often used as an example of a customer-oriented company with a strong organizational culture.[17] Until his death in 1992, Sam Walton, the founder of the company, was clearly the fountainhead of the corporate culture of Wal-Mart, its chief spokesman and cheerleader. Of the Ten Principles he articulated to guide employees, who are called "associates," nine of them concern customer service. Today, top management carries on the tradition vigorously. Among the most important and more tangible aspects of the culture are a commitment to the customer and value based on low prices; a strong dedication to associates' welfare and to their families; "greeters" who welcome customers at the store door; the famous Saturday morning management staff meeting; and a number of company cheers regularly repeated in employee meetings. Every associate pledges to greet any customer who is within 10 feet of him, "so help me, Sam!" "Be an agent for the customer" is one of the specific values articulated as part of the Wal-Mart culture.

Top management personnel, buyers, and regional managers, using a fleet of company airplanes, leave company headquarters in Bentonville, Arkansas, every Monday morning to visit stores around the country. They meet with associates in each of the stores visited, averaging two or three stores per day. At any store, they can analyze that store's performance using a data terminal to compare it with any other store, for any time period, on any item. They return on Wednesday or Thursday with up-to-the-minute information from the field about conditions in the stores, competition, customer needs and opinions, inventory problems, and personnel. This information is shared in the Saturday morning meetings, which include many other company members. The meetings have been described as a combination of business and entertainment. Weekly results are also reviewed based on information provided overnight by a state-of-the-art management information system. Every new store opening that week is reviewed in detail.

When problems are spotted at a particular location, management often takes the blame by identifying things they should have done to prevent or solve the problem. They examine the underlying processes of personnel selection, order fulfillment, delivery, or whatever, that need to be addressed to correct the problem. The discussion at the Saturday meetings usually identifies specific actions that need to be taken immediately with someone volunteering or being appointed to take responsibility to be sure that it happens and that the underlying problem is addressed as well. These meetings, and the culture that they represent, is very action oriented. Management spends a lot of time worrying about the details. Especially when it comes to fashion merchandise or out-of-stock conditions, speed is of the essence.

To perpetuate the Wal-Mart culture, each new store is headed up by a manager with at least seven years of Wal-Mart experience. Assistant Managers, on the other hand, are moved about every two years to give them additional experience and exposure to the Wal-Mart culture. Most employee/associates own stock in the company. Everyone is focused on serving the customer and beating the competition. It is the essence of a market-driven company, focused on delivering customer value through motivated employees with a sense of ownership. Customer orientation is a core value in the corporate culture.

## CUSTOMER ORIENTATION AS MARKET INTELLIGENCE

Customer orientation is more than a set of beliefs, however. It must be supported by information about the customer, information that is up-to-date and accurate. That information must focus on the needs, wants, preferences, and buying habits of customers as individuals, obtained through direct contact with them. The central question that should guide all information gathering is "How does the customer define value and how well are we providing it?" Each of the major subjects discussed in this book including customer orientation, the broader concept of market orientation, market segmentation, targeting, positioning, developing the value proposition, relationship management, corporate culture, and so on all come back to the central idea that market intelligence is the essence of marketing management.

While there is a still an important role for traditional survey research methods in specific instances, such as routine measurement of customer satisfaction with a large, valid sample of recent customers, other techniques are likely to be more valuable for management problem solving. In-depth personal or telephone interviews or small focus groups with actual or potential customers may be particularly helpful in developing new product offerings and service features, for example. For business marketers, carefully planned visits to customer sites can be invaluable in providing information to guide R&D, manufacturing planning, and salesforce development. In any company, top management's understanding of market conditions must be obtained first hand by frequent field visits and one-on-one conversations with customers. Large-scale survey research methodology is necessary primarily when the objective is to estimate key population parameters or to measure the relationship between marketing expenditures and marketplace results such as changes in sales volume, margins, and market share.

The new marketing concept calls for defining the business "from the outside in," being informed and "expert" about the customer and letting the customer define value by matching up the customer's needs and preferences with the firm's capabilities. As the founder of EDS and two-time presidential candidate, Ross Perot, so often said, "It's just that simple!" Defining the business from the customer's point of view is a simple idea but its implementation is not simple at all.

Management of the marketing information function requires professional expertise and senior management support. In most companies, it also requires up-to-date knowledge about information technology, commercially available databases, management science methods for model building and analyzing data, and the communication aspects of management information systems. As noted many times before, the over-riding responsibility of the marketing function in a customer-oriented, market-driven company is to provide decision makers throughout the organization with up-to-date information about customers and competitors, helping everyone to understand the customer's constantly shifting definition of value. In a truly customer-focused, market-driven organization, however, the market intelligence capability is not limited to marketing management. In the best companies, market intelligence gathering and analytical capability pervades the organization and becomes a core competence.[18]

## CREATING A LEARNING ORGANIZATION

An important new idea relevant for the implementation of the new marketing concept is that of the learning organization, an organization that is dedicated to continuous improvement and to reinventing itself as market conditions demand. In order to change productively, any organization must first be able to see the changes that are occurring in its markets and it must also be able to capture ideas and learn from experience that is occurring "on its periphery."[19]

John Seely Brown, director of the Palo Alto Research Center of Xerox Corporation, believes that every organization has many kinds of improvisations and experiments occurring within it at any time. In the traditional, hierarchical bureaucratic structure of a multidivision, functional organization, these learning experiences are likely to be ignored, if not actively suppressed, by normal routines, policies, and procedures. Such improvisations occur as people try in an ad hoc manner to find solutions to problems that arise in the normal course of events but that do not respond to old methods for dealing with them. In Brown's view, real learning happens as the result of improvisations and is passed on in the organization by means of informal story telling, not through formal training programs. He believes that the development of important core competences and improved practices depends on group processes within the organization. In the learning organization, these processes are nurtured and made explicit so that the results of experimentation can be shared throughout the organization.[20]

Slater and Narver have articulated a model of the learning organization that is centered on market intelligence. They draw a distinction between the most common form of organizational learning, *adaptive learning,* the process of acquiring knowledge within the constraints and assumptions of the organization, and *generative learning,* the process by which the organization actively questions established beliefs about customers, mission, capabilities, and strategy. Only generative learning can create new views of the world. Knowledge development involves three processes:

1. Information acquisition.

2. Information dissemination.

3. Shared interpretation.

The last two processes distinguish organizational learning from individual learning. The organization can learn from its own direct experiences, from the experience of others, and from organizational learning as defined earlier. Learning from the experience of others includes many techniques we have mentioned including benchmarking, reengineering, customer visit programs, marketing alliances, strategic partnering with vendors and resellers, and forming networks. The knowledge developed as the result of organizational learning leads to behavior change resulting in improved customer satisfaction, sales growth, new product development success rates, and profitability if it is combined with an entrepreneurial culture, effective leadership, and a flexible organization structure. Slater and Narver conclude with the observation that their studies, and those of others, of the relationship between corporate culture, innovativeness, market orientation, and corporate climate, as reviewed in Chapter 7, provide evidence of the impact of organizational learning on business performance.[21]

We have seen at many points how the concept of organizational learning applies to the implementation of the marketing concept. First, the market intelligence function must be committed to understanding customer needs, defining specific areas that need improvement, and identifying "best practice" wherever it is occurring throughout the organization and in other companies. Organizational learning occurs in the creation and management of strategic alliances with customers and other partners. It is inherent in the definition of an Adhocracy culture as one that is externally focused and capable of quick and flexible response to a changing market. Organizational learning is seen in the progression from mass production to mass customization. The learning organization is part of Jack Welch's concept of General Electric as a boundaryless organization in which barriers between the company and its customer environment become permeable and the walls that separate functional areas of the business break down. It continues in the General Electric process called "Workout" in which traditional ways of doing things are actively challenged as a first step in finding ways to improve. Reengineering is an attempt to make organizational learning occur in a planned way.

The concept of the learning organization becomes increasingly important in network organizations, as partners have more opportunities to learn from one another. In fact, the motivation for many strategic alliances is simply to create a learning organization, introducing change into the existing structure in order to develop and improve distinctive competence and to learn from the new partner in areas critical to developing and delivering customer value.

## STRATEGIC ALLIANCES AND NETWORK ORGANIZATIONS

In the firm committed to a value-delivery concept of strategy, management will have defined those distinctive competences that it must own and develop and those that it needs to acquire through partnership with others in the value chain. These ideas were developed in detail in Chapter 6. We saw that the role of marketing in the network organization is to keep all of the partners focused on the customer's definition of value. This is a new responsibility for marketing under the new marketing concept and it requires close cooperation with multiple business processes including purchasing, R&D, engineering, manufacturing, and distribution.

There are many kinds of marketing partners in the network organization. These include procurement, where marketing and purchasing managers must work together to be sure that suppliers of raw materials, components, subassemblies, or complete products with the company's name on them understand the nuances of the company's value proposition and customer needs and preferences. In some companies, managers have been transferred between the marketing and purchasing functions, based on the common value of negotiation skills in both areas and on the recognition that each can benefit from a better understanding of the other. This is a particularly valuable practice for bringing customer focus into the procurement process and in integrating vendors into customer-value delivery.

Technology partnerships, increasingly necessary where distinct and rapidly developing technologies converge on a particular product category, require close cooperation under the guidance of both qualitative and quantitative market research. Market orientation is often better when it is proactive, based on deep understanding of customers and their problems, than when it is reactive to the customer's articulated needs and wants. In really new areas, where customers may not be able to express their preferences for products that do not yet exist, experienced marketing managers must work with their technical colleagues to make the subtle judgments required based on an intimate understanding of customers. Their relationship with the customer must be strong enough that they can lead the customer into the new product future. Managers with experience in both marketing and R&D/engineering may be best able to make the necessary judgments on behalf of the customer.

Partnerships with resellers are perhaps the best-known marketing alliances. In fact, the academic study of strategic marketing alliances has been centered in the area of marketing channels and distribution, where there is a useful body of knowledge dealing with power, trust, cooperation and conflict, and other aspects of interorganizational relationships. In network organizations, however, the viewpoint shifts away from the traditional concern for interorganizational conflict between manufacturers and resellers and toward a new emphasis on cooperation in serving the customer. Instead of asking "Whose customer is it?" and fighting over control of the customer relationship, the participants focus their energies on the shared tasks of understanding and delivering customer value.

Simply defining *the customer* for any company as the party that pays the bill can be very helpful in developing concepts of cooperation in a marketing channel. Consumer goods manufactures have come to realize that their customer is really the reseller, not the consumer, as large retailers such as Wal-Mart, Target, Safeway, Circuit City, Staples, and Home Depot have become increasingly powerful and important to them. The end consumer is the retailer's customer in this view and the manufacturer offers the brand and its service capabilities as business assets to the retail trade. If I manufacture a branded product and sell it through distributors to retailers who in turn sell it to the household consumer, who is my customer? Under this definition, it is the distributor if the distributor takes legal title to the merchandise, pays me for it based on an invoice I send to him, and then resells it to the retailer by means of the distributor's own salesforce. If I send the invoice to the retailer, with the distributor physically stocking and delivering the product but not actually taking title, then my customer is the retailer. In this case, my salesforce will probably work directly with the retailer as well as with the distributor. (Because I would receive an invoice from the distributor under these circumstances, I am the distributor's customer!) The consumer who comes into the store to buy my branded product is the retailer's customer, not mine.

## Defining the Customer: How Samuel Cabot Succeeds

Different companies work out this question of customer definition in the network organization in different ways. One company that has successfully wrestled with the issues here is Samuel Cabot, Inc., a manufacturer of high-quality stains and paints for the exterior and interior surfaces of houses and other buildings. Cabot states their mission as follows:

> Our mission is to be the benchmark in product innovation, quality, and inspired customer support, consistent with our heritage since 1877 as the category leader in wood care. Our mission is fueled by a passion for conducting business with those who share our ideals including respect for people, integrity, and exceeding customer expectations.
>
> Although the ultimate end-user/purchaser and controller of our brand strategy is the consumer, purchase decisions are greatly influenced by retailers, contractors, builders, and architects. Due to our limited resources, and the competitive environment, the independent dealer is the focus of our selling efforts.[22]

Cabot's strategy is very selective. They focus on the high-quality, high-price end of the market with products that have a higher cost of materials and manufacturing. Traditionally specialists in oil-based stains for exterior surfaces, they have aggressively innovated new product formulas to incorporate water-based products, cleaning solutions, interior stains, and paints as these offered meaningful additions to the range of products they could offer to stocking retailers and consumers.

Cabot made a conscious strategic choice not to go to market through mass merchants such as Wal-Mart and Home Depot, even though this is the faster growing marketing channel, because this would not be in the best interests of their independent retailer partners and because they do not have the resources to work with the mass merchants as a supplier. They use distributors selectively in some parts of the country, based on their market strength and the availability of strong distributors who meet their strategic needs, but they have been moving toward direct retailer coverage with their own salesforce in order to strengthen their relationship with the retailer. However, their main commitment is to the independent retailer as a strategic partner, supported where necessary by a distributor. They have also partnered with many large cooperative buying groups that serve independent retailers, such as Ace Hardware and Tru-Serve, as more retailers have affiliated with such groups as a strategy for survival against the "big box" stores.

Cabot realized that the key to its success, given its limited resources, is the support they receive from independent retailers in stocking and promoting Cabot Stains and other Cabot products. It has spent heavily on advertising and high-quality promotional materials such as color cards and specification sheets to develop awareness and preference for the Cabot brand among homeowners, architects, painting contractors, builders, and the retail trade. In the Cabot strategy, the focus is on delivering superior value to the retailer in the form of a full product line, a tinting system, a broad spectrum of colors, advertising and sales promotion support, and so on, so that the dealer can obtain superior value from stocking and selling Cabot Stains. Both Cabot and its retailer are committed to a partnership with the objective of delivering superior value to the end-user/customer.

Developing and maintaining a strong consumer brand franchise is an important part of the process of delivering superior value to the retailer. The key to Cabot's strategy has been to define the independent retailer as their customer and to avoid competing with them by expanding into the mass merchant outlets. As a result, Cabot has enjoyed significant increases in sales volume, market share, and profitability.

## What Does It Mean to Be "Market-Driven"?

What it does *not* mean is "marketing driven," in the old sense that a central marketing department must review and approve all activities involving the company's product offering and relationships with customers. A large marketing department may be the antithesis of a market-driven company, especially if it is part of a hierarchical, bureaucratic structure dominated by rules, policies, and procedures. If the marketing department is one link in a chain as ideas get passed along from research to design to engineering to development to manufacturing and so on, it is simply one more step in slowing down the process of responding to customers and competitors. Marketing's job is to provide information to decision makers throughout the organization and to develop total marketing programs including products, prices, distribution, and communications that respond to changing customer needs and preferences.

To be "market-driven" is more than simply "customer-driven" and it requires more than customer orientation. While customer orientation remains as the prime idea within the marketing concept, to be market-driven also means being fully aware of competitors' product offerings and capabilities as they are viewed by customers. It means understanding the intersection of customer needs and company capabilities in the context of competitors' product offerings as these three things come together in the customer's definition of value. To be market-driven requires that all decision making is informed by customer information, competitive intelligence, and a clear concept of the company's value proposition.

## SUMMARY

The new marketing concept is built around a value-delivery concept of strategy. It recognizes that the individual and business customers of today have an almost unlimited set of purchase options combined with almost unlimited information about them in the global marketplace. Marketers throughout the world must develop the strategies, skills, and organizational resources required to be competitive on a global basis as their home countries strive to achieve and maintain sustainable levels of economic growth, employment, and standard of living.

Companies everywhere are driven by the fundamental need to create value propositions built on their distinctive world-class competences, supported by coalitions with multiple strategic partners in network organizations that transcend the boundaries of company, industry, and country. The old marketing concept was built around a concept of mass production for mass markets using the techniques of mass communication. The new marketing concept calls for "mass customization" of products and services for individual customers using tailored communications and super-efficient distribution systems.

The critical skills required are those of sensing and responding to the customer's ever-changing definition of value and competitors' ever-changing product offerings. Every organization must develop processes for continuous innovation, customer relationship management, and value-chain management, constantly learning from its own experiences and those of its network partners. Marketers must assume responsibility not just for responding to customers' changing needs, preferences, and buying patterns, but also for leading customers into the future with new and better solutions to their problems.

In the final chapter, we summarize the new marketing concept as a set of guidelines for creating a customer-focused, market-driven organization as required by the markets of the twenty-first century.

# 9

# Implementing the Value-Delivery Concept of Marketing Strategy

*Marketing is too important to be left to the marketing people.*

David Packard

Hewlett-Packard Company

Implementing the value-delivery concept of marketing strategy is a responsibility for management throughout the company, beginning at the top. It cannot be a one-time event. It must be done vigorously and with commitment, paying attention to details while continually assessing the total environment of the company internally and externally.

There is now a substantial body of research evidence showing that marketing competence is a major factor in company performance in terms of financial results. The research reviewed in previous chapters shows the value of implementing a customer-focused, market-driven approach to business strategy. Among the many dimensions of marketing management identified as leading to greater profitability are market orientation, innovativeness, organizational responsiveness, customer relationship management, product and service quality, customer-linking capabilities, market intelligence, brand equity, and customer loyalty.

The guidelines that follow are intended to offer specific steps that must be taken to achieve the benefits of the new value-delivery concept of marketing and business strategy. They are interlinked and they are not easy to accomplish, but they are becoming increasingly necessary for business survival.

# GUIDELINES FOR IMPLEMENTING THE NEW MARKETING CONCEPT

We can summarize the key ideas in the value-delivery marketing concept with a set of guidelines for its implementation. These are sixteen interrelated ideas that weave the fabric of the new marketing concept. While they are not listed in strict priority, some are precursors to others. All are essential to a full commitment to the new marketing concept. These are things that every business must do if it hopes to be competitive in today's global, networked marketplace:

1. Focus on the customer and build customer commitment throughout the organization.
2. Invest in market intelligence.
3. Define and nurture distinctive competence.
4. Select customers carefully.
5. Develop and communicate the value proposition.
6. Manage for profitability, not sales volume.
7. Put value capture into the business model.
8. Position the firm carefully in the value chain.
9. Develop customer relationships and manage customer loyalty.
10. Build and manage brand equity.
11. Develop strategic partnerships with vendors and resellers, focus the network on customers, and control customer relationships.
12. Innovate and improve continuously.
13. Define the business as a service business.
14. Create customized solutions for customers.
15. Don't confuse marketing with selling.
16. Destroy marketing bureaucracy.

## 1. Focus on the Customer and Build Customer Commitment throughout the Organization

Everything must begin with the customer. As in the case of the original marketing concept, the central idea of the value-delivery concept of business strategy is customer orientation—putting the customer first, *always*. From top management on, throughout the entire organization, people must commit to a single overriding purpose for the business: to create a satisfied and loyal customer by delivering superior value. The customer must be put on a pedestal, standing above all of the others in the organization including the owners and the managers.

The focus on the customer must pervade the organization and achieving that focus is a major mission for top management, aided by a strong marketing management team. The CEO must be the chief advocate for the customer, frequently stating the primacy of customer satisfaction and loyalty as the key goal of the business and making the tough decisions when necessary to show the organization that the customer always comes first. If the CEO doesn't put the customer first, he or she puts another group's interest first—probably the shareholders. The rest of the organization will sense this and behave accordingly. Only by putting the customer first are the other constituencies served best in the long run. Profit is the reward for satisfying a customer. Customers must be integrated into the organization in every way possible.

Organizational culture must be managed actively, along with strategy and tactics. The company needs customer-oriented values and beliefs that are symbolized and made visible in multiple ways. A strong mission statement is often a powerful tool for building customer orientation, provided that it is focused on the customer. The mission statement should identify those customers and how the company proposes to deliver superior value to them.

Outstanding customer service should be publicized and those responsible rewarded. Customers should be made visible to the organization through visits and publicity about them. The CEO and the top management team need to constantly remind everyone about the importance of putting the customer first, through actions as well as words. It is easy to trivialize the commitment if people in the organization hear only words that are not matched by action and the commitment of resources to value delivery and rewards for superior customer service.

Marketing initiatives represent investments in the future. Because of the difficulty of measuring immediate results for most marketing activities (unless they involve price-cutting, which is selling, not marketing!), marketing budgets are often the target of attempts to find quick improvements in short-term bottom-line results. Not only can this shortsightedness damage future earnings potential, it can have an immediate impact as a signal to the organization that the customer is not as important as investors and financial analysts. The damage done to customer orientation will be hard to repair.

Customer orientation includes a commitment to customer-defined quality, innovation, and the value-driven concept of strategy. The customer-oriented company is constantly seeking improved efficiency and lower costs, in order to deliver superior value to customers. Price is always part of the customer's value calculation, so continuous improvement in pursuit of lower costs is part of being customer oriented.

## 2. Invest in Market Intelligence

Marketing is a customer-back activity bringing the customer into the organization. It is how the customer gets to influence the company. (Selling is how the company influences the customer.) Marketing is customer-centric, not product- or company-centric. Customer orientation has to be more than wishful thinking.

There are three broad classes of market intelligence:

1. Secondary information about markets.
2. Customer databases.
3. Studies of customer behavior.

*Secondary information about markets* describes general economic conditions, industry-specific data and trends, broad customer buying patterns, competitive activities, and so on. These data are usually available from public and industry sources and are not specific to the company. They play a key role in knowledge development by the organization and contribute to adaptive learning about the environment in which the company competes.

*Databases* are large-scale collections of data about customers and their interactions with the company. Advances in information technology have put this resource within reach of virtually any company, regardless of size, although the more sophisticated marketing databases and analytics require substantial investment. The customer database is a resource for analyzing customers, tracking customer relationships, and guiding all of the activities of the customer-oriented company. Databases have value only when access to them is widely dispersed throughout the organization. Among the heaviest users will be people in customer service, the salesforce, marketing communications, new product development, logistics, manufacturing, and purchasing. They are a critical resource for customer relationship management, which is impossible today without a customer database.

*Studies of customer behavior* can include surveys, visits by customers to the company and by company personnel to the customer's location, focus groups, large gatherings of users, and many other direct interactions with present and potential customers. In a truly customer-oriented company, everyone is studying the customer all the time.

To be customer oriented requires listening to the customer. Lip service to customer orientation doesn't count; it is the customer's voice that must be heard, not the company's. The act of listening is only possible one voice at a time; you can't listen to a faceless crowd. The customer-oriented company listens to its customers as individuals and understands their perceptions, expectations, needs, and wants. The ability to listen to the customer is not a natural ability; it must be developed and the instinct to be selective and defensive must be overcome. Opportunities to listen must be sought out and captured whenever they occur, not limited to programmed occasions for soliciting customer feedback.

Customer complaints offer one of the most valuable opportunities for learning about the customer as well as about our own business. When customers complain, they are telling us how they define value and why we are not delivering it, in their judgment. They are telling us how they define the problem for which they are seeking a solution when they buy our product or service. They may help us to identify a process or a product feature that needs improvement opportunities for product and service innovation. They may be telling us something we didn't know about our competitors. They are also telling us that they care about our products and our company and that they want us to do a better job.

Other opportunities for listening to the customer occur on every sales call and service call, every time the customer calls in an order, every time there is an inquiry about an order or a delivery or an invoice. Listening to criticism is not something most people do well. Many companies tend to respond to customer complaints and suggestions by "blaming the customer" for not understanding the product and its use well enough, or for expecting too much, or for misusing the product in some way. Instead of the defensive reaction, people must be taught to listen, not just to respond. When we ask customers what they like and do not like, we must be prepared to hear what they say, to put the information into a form useful to the organization, and to follow up to see that correct action is taken.

To maximize opportunities for listening to the customer, steps must be taken to be sure that virtually everyone in the company has some contact with customers on a regular basis. Managers must get into the field, make sales calls with the sales representatives, or stand behind the counter in the store.

Production people can travel with the product to the customer's location to see how it is handled and used. Engineering personnel can make site visits to customer facilities. Everyone in the company can benefit from actually watching customers use the product. Plant workers can call customers on the telephone, in the evening, to ask them how they like their new purchase, to see if they have any questions, and to learn how the product could be improved. I have heard literally hundreds of different examples of ways in which company people are put into contact with real customers. In every instance, the report has been positive. Never has someone said it was a waste of time.

Market intelligence is absolutely essential to a learning organization, the source of knowledge that can be used to improve, grow, and adjust to the changing market environment. For the market-driven company, customer knowledge is a distinctive competence and one of its most important strategic assets. Knowledge about customers is perhaps the critical variable in defining the firm as a distinct entity, not simply as part of a network of partnerships with other organizations. It may also be the hardest of all distinctive competences for competitors to duplicate.

## 3. Define and Nurture Distinctive Competence

The by-word of the value-delivery concept of marketing is *focus*. Given limited resources, every company must focus on specific market targets, customers, product offerings, marketing channels, geographic territories, and so on. The roots of this focus must be the capabilities and resources of the company, the things that it can do well—so well that it can achieve market dominance if it can successfully link them with under-served market needs and wants.

The old marketing concept lacked strategic impact because it did not consider the difficult task of matching up customer needs with the firm's capabilities. It never really addressed the question of which customers, and which customer needs, the company should focus on except those that were relatively unsatisfied. The concept of customer value was not part of the definition of customer orientation. What the concept of value brings to the equation is the notion that there is a dynamic interaction in the customer's assessment of needs and preferences between the company's product offering and those of its competitors. What is it that the firm can offer that is better than its competitors' offering? What are the skills, resources, and knowledge required to deliver superior value to customers?

The notion of distinctive competence requires customer orientation for its definition. A distinctive competence must be something perceived as having value by the customer. Otherwise, it is not a competence that has any strategic value. A distinctive competence should also apply across product categories and multiple market segments; that is, it should offer strategic flexibility and opportunity for development and growth. It will almost certainly be knowledge-based, which means that it resides in the minds and skills of individuals, a notion that includes but is not limited to technology-based competences. A distinctive competence properly nurtured, developed, and deployed is a source of unique, sustainable competitive advantage. Customer needs and perceptions are one part of the definition of value; the other part is the set of distinctive competences that the firm brings to the competitive marketplace.

Distinctive competence and excellence are two different things. Only distinctive competence can be a true source of competitive advantage. The firm may be excellent in many things, all of them relevant to delivering superior value, but they may not be distinctive if they are merely a condition of doing business in the competitive market. Every company must strive for excellence in such areas as order entry and billing, delivery, inventory management, technical service and support, Internet access, product quality, and media buying. These are usually necessary for survival but never sufficient to achieve competitive supremacy.

The definition of distinctive competences is the starting point for strategy formulation in the market-driven company. Where in the global market is there an opportunity for us, given our skills and resources, to be the best in the world in delivering customer value? It also leads to the identification of areas where the company does not have the competences that it needs to have a complete value proposition. This awareness identifies the need for strategic partnering and for positioning the company carefully in the value chain.

The first three guidelines have concerned developing the organizational capabilities necessary to be an effective competitor: customer focus, market intelligence, and distinctive competence. We now discuss strategy formulation and the development of a business model with the goal of maximizing long-term business performance.

## 4. Select Customers Carefully

The essence of strategy is matching opportunities and capabilities. A mismatch wastes both. Opportunities and capabilities are both destroyed when they are inappropriate for one another. Customer selection is *the* critical strategic choice. Customers who cannot be served well by the company and are unwilling to pay the company for its capabilities can severely damage a business. Pursuing opportunities that the company cannot handle with its resources will destroy the opportunity for the company and leave the company weaker because it has used resources without earning a return. Once again, the key concept is that of *focus* and selectivity.

Being market-driven is to know which customers are ours and which belong to our competitors. If a strategy is not selective, it is not a strategy because it is not focused on opportunities. This concept of strategic selectivity is often the most difficult for management (as well as salespeople) to accept. It means turning away potential customers and revenue to concentrate on building relationships with customers who have the best probability of being satisfied, loyal, and profitable.

Market segmentation, targeting, and positioning remain as the critical strategic choices under the new marketing concept, as they were under the old. Positioning now takes on the added meaning of the value proposition, as opposed to the old, narrower definition of positioning as a communication exercise to position the product in the mind of the consumer relative to competition. Market segmentation is an analytical exercise that depends on solid market intelligence about customers and about competitors' product offerings. It also requires creativity to define the dimensions on which markets will be segmented. Targeting is the strategic decision making involved in matching up customer characteristics and company capabilities, selecting the customers we are best able to serve.

We must select customers carefully because we are going to make a commitment to them and agree to be judged by them. We are entering into a relationship and we are going to try to build customer loyalty. The process of relationship building and loyalty management begins with the market targeting decision.

## 5. Develop and Communicate the Value Proposition

Market segmentation, targeting, and positioning are integral parts of the development of business strategy. Positioning defines the company's relationship with its target customers. Positioning, the act of developing the value proposition, is the process of putting together the value statement that will be communicated to the customer and throughout the organization and has three parts: Who? What? Why?

- *Who* is our target customer?
- *What* are we selling; what is the frame of reference we want the customer to use?

- *Why* should the customer do business with us; what are the benefits we offer?

A strong value proposition is essential to achieving customer focus within the organization.

Customer value is defined in the marketplace, not in the factory. The market intelligence function is necessary to make sure that everyone in the company understands how the customer has defined value and how that definition continues to evolve over time. Customer orientation and market intelligence combine to create a functioning organizational commitment to delivering superior value. The development of business unit strategy and the definition of "how to compete" should be built around a clear concept of customer value. Delivering superior value to customers should be part of the basic culture of the organization, the shared values and beliefs.

The company's mission statement should incorporate the overall definition of customer value, and specify how the firm proposes to deliver that value, the commitments to excellence that are required to be successful in achieving that mission. That vision should be communicated and discussed at every opportunity, helping everyone in the company to maintain that commitment to delivering customer value and thereby maintaining the firm's competitiveness.

Individual business units (unique combinations of markets to be served and the products offered to those markets) require their own value propositions. These should be further refined by market segment. For example, market segmentation and targeting may result in three types of customers:

1. Well-informed, knowledgeable customers who value the company's basic capabilities for high quality products but perceive them as commodities to be purchased at a favorable price. The value proposition for these customers may be built around easy ordering, consistent quality, and quick delivery at low prices. These are transactions customers who value reliability, efficiency, and low price. A commercial real-estate company, for example, would handle these customers through a brokerage business that finds office space at low cost by offering superior knowledge of local market conditions and an efficient office operation.

2. Those who need help in specifying and using the products offered by the company and are not well informed about the types of products and services available. The value proposition for these customers

would include a bundle of services to assist the customer in buying and using the product. These are relationship customers who value personalized service and specific product features. The real-estate company might serve this market through a building management subsidiary with a value proposition built on efficient, professional operations using the best available technology providing a low-cost solution to the customer's office space needs.

3. Those who want a total solution to a problem that will free them from further concerns and allow them to concentrate on their core business. The value proposition for these customers would be that of a strategic partner who is able to provide an effective, low-cost, worry-free solution that can be standardized across many buying locations. These are strategic partners for whom the marketer company becomes part of their operation. The commercial real-estate company might buy, outfit, lease back, and manage these properties for its clients in cities throughout the United States.

In each case, the specific value proposition would identify the unique capabilities of the company in offering these products to these defined customers to provide a strong answer to the question, "Why should we do business with you rather than your competitors?"

## 6. Manage for Profitability, Not Sales Volume

The strategic importance of market targeting is based on the assumption that the firm should be managed for profitability, not sales volume. At several points in this book, we have made this argument. Profit is a measure of the value that the firm has created for the customer. It indicates the ability of the firm to identify unsatisfied customer needs and to define, develop, and deliver value. Value is the ratio of customer benefits to the costs of the product offering, including both its price and the costs associated with its use.

Profit indicates the efficiency of the firm in delivering value as well as its ability to understand customer value. Profit measures the difference between the value that has been produced in the marketplace and the costs of acquiring the resources, including human and organizational resources, used to create and deliver the product.

Over the long run, creating value for the customer leads to value creation for the shareholder. This article of faith lacked empirical support until recently. In Chapter 2, studies were described that discredited the direct link between market share (i.e., sales volume) and profitability. It was seen that quality and market targeting were the driving forces behind both sales volume and above average pricing, resulting in superior profit margins and better return on investment. In Chapter 7, we reviewed new research that showed the best performing businesses, in terms of return on investment and rate of growth, were those that scored high on measures of market-oriented culture and innovativeness.

Using low price to build sales volume has proven to be a serious strategic error in many cases. First, it obviously reduces profit margins that must be made up with even more volume. Second, it tends to attract customers who have a low probability of being satisfied and loyal customers who value a relationship with the company. Dissatisfied customers in turn generate negative word-of-mouth messages to other potential customers.

Managing for profitability, not sales volume, means that the company is seeking customers who value those things the firm does well, who need its distinctive competence. Relationships with those customers will help the firm continue to develop its distinctive competence. Those customers will put pressure on the firm to do things that are in its own best interests, making the necessary investments in resources and skills to maintain its competitive advantage. Customer selection is at the heart of a strategy for value capture.

## 7. Put Value Capture into the Business Model

Value capture is partly a pricing problem but more basically it is a problem of maintaining control. The ultimate objective of value creation for customers is to make the best possible use of the resources that have been committed to the business and to earn a return for the owners of those assets. It would be easy to give all of the value created to the customers, especially if they are big, powerful customers with buying power that allows them to determine the conditions under which they will do business. However, the size of the customer is by no means the determining factor.

When industries mature and the market lifecycle enters the maturity, saturation, and decline stages, product offerings become commoditized, product differentiation disappears, and price levels and profit margins erode. As managers conclude that their only competitive weapon is price and give up any attempt to achieve meaningful product differentiation, they contribute to the downward drift. When companies try to compete in these market conditions by lowering prices, reducing costs, and eliminating expenses for product development and differentiation, whole industries can enter a death spiral in which no competitor is able to earn a return greater than its cost of capital. At this stage, market conditions are probably beyond the control of any single competitor, although market re-segmentation and new strategies for differentiation are still possibilities for a well-managed, strategically adept company. Among the most visible examples of mature markets with very low or negative profit margins in today's economy are airlines, forest products, basic chemicals, telephone voice service, and electronic components. Surprisingly, these industries may attract new investment as firms think that adding new capacity may help them lower costs and compete more effectively. They may even attract entirely new competitors who think they have a different business model, typically based on lower costs, which can be profitable in these mature market conditions.

Even in growth markets, there are many companies with business models that are inadequate in their value capture. The best example is what happened in the famous Internet boom and bust of the 1990s where the vaunted "get-big-fast" strategy cost investors many billions of dollars. It is common for a focus on top-line revenue growth to dominate management attention in the belief that only the largest firms will survive an anticipated industry shakeout period. As one company told its mid-level business managers, "You just get the volume. We'll figure out how to make it profitable." Unfortunately, many companies simply don't take time to figure out how to do that, relying instead on the simplistic assumption that eventually demand will catch up with supply and higher prices will be possible. Very often, the longed-for day never comes when the marketplace settles down to a few well-mannered competitors who maintain high prices allowing everyone to earn a fair return. One reason is that few if any competitors have a sound business model that will permit a fair capture of value for the owners. If there are no competitors in the market with a sound business model, there is no one to lead the industry to profitability.

The basic question is: "How do you plan to make a profit?" High price and low cost is not a very good answer, because it is incomplete, although it captures the essence of what must be done. The correct question is: "How can we capture a fair portion of the value that has been created for the customers we have elected to serve?" The answer requires: (1) a sound profit model relating prices with costs to provide products and services to these customers; and (2) mechanisms to maintain control over the relationship with the customer. Among the tools available to marketing managers for maintaining control over the relationship with the customer are market segmentation and targeting, focusing on a relatively easy to defend market niche, branding, professional salespeople, service bundling, reseller partnerships, pricing schedules that reward desired customer behavior, product development and differentiation, value chain management, and programs for supporting the retail and wholesale trade. Each of these tools has been an important part of the discussions in earlier chapters.

These tools for profit capture must be used in a manner that ties into the customer's own profit model, for business customers, or more generally the customer's definition of utility and value. Industrial marketers may find it important to offer a service bundle when they understand their customers' overall business design and strategy for profitability. Manufacturers of consumer luxury goods often know that *high* price is one of the attractive features of their products for customers who value those products because they are, due in part to their well-known prices, a visible expression of achievement, good taste, and lifestyle. Price paid (as opposed to the asked-for price, which may be different) is fundamentally a measure of the value perceived by the customer.

To achieve value capture, the company must maintain a degree of control over its relationship with its customer. Marketing segmentation, targeting, positioning, relationship management, partnering with others in the value chain, product innovation and product differentiation, and so on all require direct customer relationship. Otherwise, the company is merely an interchangeable part in a system controlled by another marketer and must learn to compete on the basis of low cost and commodity pricing.

## 8. Position the Firm Carefully in the Value Chain

Positioning the firm in the value chain has become a key responsibility for marketing management. It has three parts:

1. Focus on distinctive competence and defining the basis for delivering superior customer value.
2. Deciding how to build and maintain customer relationships that permit value capture.
3. Selecting business partners, suppliers, and resellers, who will complete the value offering of product features and services to the customer.

Positioning in the value chain defines the scope of the firm, specifying what it will do and what it will not do. Relationships with all of the partners in the value chain must be guided by customer focus and market intelligence, which is why marketing management must take the leadership in defining that positioning. We complete the discussion of the problem of maintaining focus in the next section, but first we must emphasize the importance of developing and managing customer relationships that are the target of the entire enterprise.

Positioning the firm in the value chain is the first step in defining the relationship with the customer.

## 9. Develop Customer Relationships and Manage Customer Loyalty

As a corollary of customer orientation, market targeting, and managing for profitability, a market-oriented firm concentrates its resources and energy on developing and maintaining customer relationships and building customer loyalty. The objective of the marketing effort is to attract customers, not to make the next sale. It is another hallmark of the new value-delivery concept of marketing that management sees customers as the single most important business asset. Maintaining the base of loyal customers in an ongoing, two-way relationship is critical to the firm's survival. Customers, not products, are the lifeblood of the business.

Customer relationships must be developed over time. Not all customers will be interested in a long-term relationship, and this presents the company with a clear choice. It can either avoid customers who do not want a relationship and the commitments that it involves or it can develop separate, distinct product offerings (including prices and services), and value propositions for relationship- and transaction-oriented customers. In the latter case, it has the further choice of simply maintaining the base of transactions customers over time, or of trying to convert them to relationships. In most cases, the latter is likely to be a very difficult sell.

Most companies find it difficult to be in both types of business relationships at the same time—transactions with some customers and partnerships with others, unless through distinct strategic business units. They require different resource commitments, different management and operational skills, and different product offerings. Furthermore, customers may not understand what they see. The relationship customers may want the lower prices they know are available to the transactions customers while the transactions customers insist on the service bundle provided to the relationship customers.

Existing customers usually offer the potential for greater profitability than new customers. We examined this proposition at a number of points in earlier chapters. Existing customers are likely to perceive greater value and to be willing to pay a bit more for the additional value offered by your total product offering, including the service bundle. They provide a stream of revenue from multiple transactions over time. They may be served at lower total cost because of the operational efficiencies provided by a long-term relationship. They offer an opportunity to sell additional products and services. And they generate favorable word-of-mouth.

It costs more, in terms of communications and related marketing efforts such as developing specific product offerings, to attract new customers. If price has been part of the inducement, as it often is, the new customers, at least initially, provide reduced profit margins. To the extent that they are attracted primarily by lower prices, they offer less opportunity for profitable growth in volume, and they have a much higher probability of switching to a competitor.

In the worst of all possible worlds, the company spends a lot of money to attract transaction-oriented customers, wastes resources trying to convert them to relationship customers, and then spends even more trying to prevent them from leaving. Such is often the fate of the company that is trying to maximize sales volume rather than profitability. One study of the use of sales promotions in 25 grocery product categories over a seven-year period, for example, found that while they often increased manufacturer sales volume, especially for low-share brands, they actually reduced category revenue for the retailers. However, in 90 percent of the cases examined, the increased manufacturers' revenues were not large enough to repay their retailer customers for their lost revenues. Thus, over the long run, sales promotions appear likely to damage the relationship of leading brand manufacturers with their retailer partners.[1] Likewise, many earlier studies have questioned the ability of short-term price inducements to attract customers who will remain loyal.

## 10. Build and Manage Brand Equity

Building and managing brand equity is a key part of building customer relationships and managing customer loyalty. The brand can be defined as a relationship with the customer, and as the meaning that surrounds the product offering. Brands are found in virtually every business category, both industrial and consumer, often in the form of the name of the company. Brands have value because they connote trust in the relationship between producer and consumer. Brand equity is a major business asset. Many leading brands including Coca-Cola, Microsoft, IBM, General Electric, Nokia, Intel, Disney, Ford, McDonald's, and AT&T have values estimated in the tens of billions of dollars.[2] Another way of looking at brand equity is to translate it into the value of sustained customer relationships, although these are different concepts.

As reviewed in Chapter 4, building and managing brand equity depends on a total marketing program that begins with creating brand identity and brand meaning and ends with defining desired customer responses to and relationships with the brand. The marketing program creates customer awareness, preference, and buying actions that lead to superior market results in terms of sales volume, market share, profit margins, customer loyalty, and repeat business. Brand equity provides leverage for all marketing expenditures including advertising, product development, and trade relations. Ultimately, enhanced market performance creates cash flow, stronger earnings per share, high stock prices, and increased shareholder value. Without a brand, the company can never hope to earn superior returns. It remains a commodity business lucky to earn a return on its investment that covers its cost of capital.

## 11. Develop Strategic Partnerships with Vendors and Resellers, Focus the Network on Customers, and Control Customer Relationships

After the firm has been clearly positioned in the value chain and has defined its desired relationship with customers, the work of building the value chain continues with developing strategic partnerships with vendors and resellers. Depending on the industry and the firm's business model and strategy for value capture, the reseller partners may actually be its customers, even if there is a strong brand relationship with end-users. For example, Intel is one of the world's most powerful and valuable brands and it enjoys high levels of consumer brand awareness and preference. But Intel's customers are original equipment manufacturers, value-added resellers, and other electronics distributors who incorporate Intel components into products that are sold to other resellers and to end-users. Many of Intel's customers are other manufacturers who continue the product value-adding process.

The network organizations that result from value-adding partnerships represent a significant shift away from traditional bureaucratic, hierarchical, divisionalized, functional organizations. Marketing as a competence must be developed and maintained in these networks under the leadership of the firm that controls the relationship with the end-user customer. The competitive battles of the future will be among rival networks for customer loyalty and profitability based on efficiency and superior value delivery.

Building customer relationships and developing brand equity must take place in the context of the multiple partnerships that define the value chain. These multiple partnerships in the value chain often include firms that are simultaneously competitors, customers, and suppliers of one another. For example, General Motors has partnered with Toyota, Isuzu, and others to design new cars and to create new, efficient, manufacturing capacity. Delta Air Lines simultaneously competes with Alitalia for traffic across the Atlantic even as both are partners in the SkyTeam Alliance.

Marketing has a major role to play in keeping the entire network focused on the customer. At the hub of the network, or at the "top" of the flattened organization, marketing managers must be involved in defining the position of the firm in the value chain and in defining its core set of target customers. It must work with top management to develop a customer-focused culture and the symbolic communications that will spread it throughout the organization. In this fundamental sense, marketing management has a major role to play in defining the shape and scope of the network organization.

The firm at the center of the network must involve itself in its partners' relationships with its customer to ensure that all activities are guided by the shared sense of mission and the value proposition. In brand development, customer relationship management, customer loyalty programs, and so on, the activities of the partners must be guided by the core firm's strategy. Reseller partners must be managed as part of a team, not left on their own without guidance and support, even though they are independent businesses.

## 12. Innovate and Improve Continuously

Knowing that customers' definition of value keeps changing and being committed to delivering superior customer value, the company must commit also to continuous improvement and innovation. Global competition offers no other choice. Become complacent and you're dead. There is now strong evidence that innovativeness is a major determinant of long-term profitability, reflecting the demands of customers on the one hand and their willingness to pay profitable prices for solutions to their problems on the other hand.

Continuous improvement is part of being customer-oriented and should lead to lower costs and to a more responsive organization. When the benefits of lower costs are shared with the customer in terms of lower prices, the value of the long-term relationship is underscored for the customer. For the business customer, this support from its vendors is likely to be critical to its survival in the global marketplace. This is seen in the common practice of target pricing, where the vendor agrees to take business at prices that offer little or no profit initially, on the assumption that the customer will work with the supplier to reduce the supplier's costs so that the relationship becomes mutually profitable over time.

To maximize the value of customer relationships and to build customer loyalty, the company must be able to create new products and services that will enhance the value of the relationship for both itself and its customers. As customers' needs evolve, so must the marketer's product offering. Increased sales to present customers are a much better path to enhanced profitability than trying to find new customers for existing products. Of course, new products will also bring the opportunity to attract new customers and to build the base of loyal customers.

## 13. Define the Business as a Service Business

Customers are buying value in the form of benefits provided by the product offering. The product per se may be relatively incidental to the total value provided. Customer expectations are very often focused on the service bundle that accompanies the product offering, not the physical product itself. The service aspects of the product offering are usually the dominant dissatisfiers. The automobile customer is unhappy with the car because of lousy service from the dealer. Insurance customers have problems with agents, not policies.

Defining the product as a service leads to defining the business as a service business. It is usually the service bundle that is dominant in differentiating the product offering from those of competition. It is the processes of value delivery that set the firm apart from its competitors, and that need continuous monitoring, improvement, and reengineering.

## 14. Create Customized Solutions for Customers

In many industries, the once dominant paradigm of the standard product that best serves the needs of a majority of customers has been replaced by the idea of "mass customization," product offerings tailored to the needs of each individual. Very often, this does not refer to the physical product itself but to the bundle of product features and services uniquely tailored to the needs and wants of a particular customer. For example, when a consumer has a prescription filled by the local pharmacy for a standard product meeting a very tightly defined specification, the dosage and quantity will be packaged for that particular patient. But the total product offering will be tailored to that individual when the pharmacist goes to a database containing that patient's history, checks for possible problems of drug interaction with other prescriptions that have been written for that patient, pulls together relevant information pages and brochures about possible side effects, and updates the database. Subsequently, that patient may receive reminders about refills, instructions to ensure that the complete course of medication is completed, literature about other products that might be helpful for the medical condition indicated, and so on.

Marketers of technology-based products are increasingly relied upon by their customers to produce integrated systems of products and services to meet the unique application requirements of that customer. Good examples include management information systems, telecommunications systems, process control systems in manufacturing facilities, and jet aircraft. Transportation companies no longer offer movement from point A to point B; instead the service includes total logistics from order entry, load assembly, and transportation to inventory management, delivery to multiple locations, shipment tracking, and even recovery of used products and shipping containers. In most of these systems solutions, an information component becomes at least as important as the physical products involved.

## 15. Don't Confuse Marketing with Selling

Marketing has come a long way from the days when it was equated with selling. We began this book with a discussion of the distinction between these two activities. Selling is something you do to the customer; marketing is what the customer does to the company. Selling is focused on the company's needs and its products. Marketing is focused on the customers' needs, preferences, and buying habits. Selling is short term and tactical; marketing is long term and strategic.

This distinction is not meant to diminish the importance of selling. On the contrary: Selling is critical to the process of implementing marketing strategy. The problem is that the two points of view often get confused and when the two responsibilities are combined in the same management personnel, short-term attention to sales goals overrides long-term attention to marketing priorities. We have cited any number of instances and examples from virtually every marketing decision area to make this point: Failure to invest in long-term product development in order to protect short-term sales volume for existing products; pricing to move product in the short-term that steals revenue and profit margin from future periods; taking money from brand development budgets to maximize short-term incentives, and so on.

While this is a controversial point of view, there is a very strong argument that marketing and selling should be distinct management responsibilities, perhaps in the form of separate departments in a functional organization. The argument against this is based on the necessity to ensure that salesforce activity is guided and controlled by marketing strategy. The counter-argument is that with proper goal setting and compensation plans, selling effort can be tied directly to marketing objectives. Those objectives and rewards should emphasize long-term profitability, customer relationship management and loyalty, and other strategic objectives. For long-term survival, growth, and success, marketing objectives must take precedence over short-term volume goals wherever possible, and sales goals should be guided by marketing objectives.

## 16. Destroy Marketing Bureaucracy

Traditional marketing departments, with managers of advertising, products, brands, sales promotion, market research distribution, pricing, customer service, and so on, as the place where all marketing gets done, should be a thing of the past. While organizations must still develop professional competence in the many specific areas of marketing management, and while clear responsibility for achieving results must still be assigned, gone are the days when marketing was the responsibility of the marketing department while the rest of the organization concentrated on other things. Today, customer-value delivery and satisfaction must be *everyone's* shared responsibility.

Especially in traditional product-manager and market-manager organizations, there was a tendency to centralize all decision making authority and to move with all the slowness and caution associated with bureaucracy. Such organizations cannot survive in today's hypercompetitive global marketplace. In terms of types of organizational cultures, as defined in Chapter 7, hierarchies and clans need to be replaced with adhocracies, flexible and externally focused. Dinosaurs must develop wings!

Marketing is no longer a separate management function but the market-focused leadership of three processes for creating superior customer value and profitability: customer relationship management, innovation management, and value chain management.

The marketing professionals who remain distinct in an organization must be experts on the customer, responsible for such areas as product strategy, marketing communications, pricing, and distribution that have traditionally been the responsibility of marketing management, but also responsible for providing market information to the rest of the organization, working with people in all areas to help them deliver superior value to customers.

## SUMMARY

Superior marketing, defined by the 16 guidelines offered in this chapter, as customer-focused problem solving and the delivery of superior value, is a more sustainable source of unique competitive advantage than superior product technology in the global markets of the future.

The new marketing concept is much broader than the old. It is also more pervasive throughout the organization. The old marketing concept encompassed customer-orientation, innovation, and profit as a reward for creating a satisfied customer. It looked at the business from the customer's point of view. It was a management philosophy.

The new marketing concept is more than a philosophy; it is a way of doing business. It includes customer orientation, market intelligence, the focus on distinctive competences, value delivery, market targeting and the value proposition, relationship management, brand equity, profitability rather than sales volume, continuous improvement, and a customer-focused organizational culture. It requires hands-on involvement by management at all levels and in all functions, throughout the complex networks of strategic partnerships, to develop and deliver superior value to customers. It requires that everyone put the customer first.

To survive in the global marketplace, every business must develop world-class competence in those areas that give it some unique competitive advantage. It is the customer who will decide whether the company has created value. The competitiveness of each business, and of the nation it represents, depends on its commitment to the new marketing concept.

# NOTES

## Chapter 1   Putting the Customer First—Always!

1. Peter F. Drucker, *The Practice of Management* (New York: Harper & Row, Inc., 1954).

2. Frederick E. Webster, Jr., "The Rediscovery of the Marketing Concept," *Business Horizons,* Vol. 31 (May–June 1988), pp. 29–39.

3. Frederick E. Webster, Jr., "The Changing Role of Marketing in the Corporation," *Journal of Marketing,* Vol. 56 (October 1992), pp. 1–17.

4. See note 1, pp. 37–41.

5. See note 1, pp. 38–39.

6. *Business Week* (June 24, 1950), pp. 30–36.

7. General Electric Company, *1952 Annual Report,* p. 21.

8. Robert J. Keith, "The Marketing Revolution," *Journal of Marketing,* Vol. 24 (January 1960), pp. 35–38, at p. 38.

9. Carlton P. McNamara, "The Present Status of the Marketing Concept," *Journal of Marketing,* Vol. 36 (January 1972), pp. 50–57.

10. J. B. McKitterick, "What is the Marketing Management Concept?" in Frank M. Bass (Ed.), *The Frontiers of Marketing Thought and Science* (Chicago: American Marketing Association, 1957), pp. 71–82.

11. Ibid., p. 77.

12. Theodore Levitt, "Marketing Success through Differentiation—of Anything," *Harvard Business Review,* Vol. 58 (January–February 1980), pp. 83–91.

13. Richard T. Hise, "Have Manufacturing Firms Adopted the Marketing Concept," *Journal of Marketing,* Vol. 29 (July 1965), pp. 9–12.

14. See note 9.

15. Theodore Levitt, "Marketing Myopia," *Harvard Business Review,* Vol. 38 (May–June 1960), pp. 45–56.

16. Andrew G. Kaldor, "Imbricative Marketing," *Journal of Marketing,* Vol. 35 (April 1971), pp. 19–25.

17. See note 9, p. 25.

18. Frederick E. Webster, Jr., *Top Management Views of the Marketing Function*, Report No. 80-108 (Cambridge, MA: Marketing Science Institute, October 1980), p. 5.

19. John G. Myers, Stephen A. Greyser, and William F. Massy, "The Effectiveness of Marketing's 'R&D' for Marketing Management: An Assessment," *Journal of Marketing*, Vol. 43 (January 1979), pp. 17–29.

20. See note 18, p. 18.

21. See note 18, p. 22.

### *Chapter 2   Strategic Planning and Marketing*

1. Alfred D. Chandler, Jr., *Strategy and Structure* (Cambridge, MA: MIT Press, 1962).

2. H. Igor Ansoff, *Corporate Strategy: An Analytical Approach to Business Policy for Growth and Expansion* (New York: McGraw-Hill, 1965).

3. Ibid., p. 5.

4. Ibid., pp. 8, 40–41.

5. Ibid., p. 93.

6. Ibid., p. 41.

7. G. P. E. Clarkson, *Portfolio Selection: A Simulation of Trust Investment* (Englewood Cliffs, NJ: Prentice-Hall, Inc., 1963). Winner of the 1961 Ford Foundation Doctoral Dissertation Award.

8. H. Markowitz, *Portfolio Selection: Efficient Diversification of Investments* (New York: John Wiley & Sons, 1959).

9. See note 2, p. 50.

10. Peter F. Drucker, *The Practice of Management* (New York: Harper & Row, Inc., 1954).

11. Theodore Levitt, "Marketing Myopia," *Harvard Business Review*, Vol. 38 (July–August 1960), pp. 45–56.

12. See note 2, pp. 104–109.

13. Walter Kiechel III, "Corporate Strategists Under Fire," *Fortune*, December 27, 1982, pp. 34–39.

14. Richard G. Hammermesh, "Strategic Management," in Eliza G. C. Collins and Mary Anne Devanna, Eds., *The Portable MBA* (New York: John Wiley & Sons, 1990), pp. 292–331, at p. 296.

15. George S. Day and David B. Montgomery, "Diagnosing the Experience Curve," *Journal of Marketing*, Vol. 47 (spring 1983), pp. 44–58, at p. 45.

16. Frederick E. Webster, Jr., *Industrial Marketing Strategy*, 3rd ed. (New York: John Wiley & Sons, 1992), pp. 333–39; see also note 14, pp. 297–304.

17. See note 14, pp. 295–96.

18. Robert D. Buzzell and Bradley T. Gale, *The PIMS Principles: Linking Strategy to Performance* (New York: Free Press, 1987).

19. Sidney Schoeffler, Robert D. Buzzell, and Donald F. Heany, "Impact of Strategic Planning on Profit Performance," *Harvard Business Review,* Vol. 52 (March–April 1974), pp. 137–45; and Robert D. Buzzell, Bradley T. Gale, and Ralph G. M. Sultan, "Market Share—Key to Profitability," *Harvard Business Review,* Vol. 53 (January–February 1975), pp. 97–106.

20. Paul W. Farris, Mark E. Parry, and Frederick E. Webster, Jr., *Accounting for the Market Share—ROI Relationship,* MSI Technical Working Paper, Report No. 89-118 (Cambridge, MA: Marketing Science Institute, November 1989).

21. Thomas Peters and Nancy Austin, *A Passion for Excellence* (New York: Random House, 1985), p. 82.

22. Cathy Anterasian and Lynn W. Phillips, *Discontinuities, Value Delivery, and the Share—Returns Association: A Re-examination of the "Share-Causes-Profits" Controversy,* Research Program Monograph, Report No. 88-109 (Cambridge, MA: The Marketing Science Institute, October 1988), pp. 1–3.

23. Michael E. Porter, *Competitive Strategy* (New York: The Free Press, 1980), pp. 42–43.

24. Lynn W. Phillips, Dae R. Chang, and Robert D. Buzzell, "Product Quality, Cost Position, and Business Performance: A Test of Some Key Hypotheses," *Journal of Marketing,* Vol. 47 (spring 1983), pp. 26–43.

25. See note 18, pp. 79–82.

26. See note 18, p. 7.

27. Walter Kiechel III, "The Decline of the Experience Curve," *Fortune,* October 5, 1981.

28. See note 20.

29. George S. Day and Robin Wensley, "Assessing Advantage: A Framework for Diagnosing Competitive Superiority," *Journal of Marketing,* Vol. 52 (April 1988), pp. 1–20.

30. *Business Week,* "King Customer," March 12, 1990, pp. 88–92.

31. Adrian J. Slywotzky and David J. Morrison, *The Profit Zone: How Strategic Business Design Will Lead You to Tomorrow's Profits* (New York: Times Business, 1998).

*Chapter 3   Marketing as Process: Quality, Service, and Customer Satisfaction*

1. Stephan H. Haeckel, *Adaptive Enterprise: Creating and Leading Sense-and-Respond Organizations* (Boston, MA: Harvard Business School Press, 1999).

2. George S. Day, "The Capabilities of Market-Driven Organizations," *Journal of Marketing,* Vol. 58 (October 1994), pp. 37–52.

3. Frederick E. Webster, Jr., "The Future Role of Marketing in the Organization," in *Reflections on the Futures of Marketing,* Donald R. Lehmann and Katherine E. Jocz, Eds. (Cambridge, MA: Marketing Science Institute, 1997), pp. 39–66.

4. Rajendra K. Srivastava, Tasadduq A. Shervani, and Liam Fahey, "Marketing, Business Processes, and Shareholder Value: An Organizationally Embedded View of Marketing Activities and the Discipline of Marketing," *Journal of Marketing,* Vol. 63 (Special Issue 1999), pp. 168–79.

5. Theodore Levitt, "Marketing Success through Differentiation—of Anything," *Harvard Business Review,* Vol. 58 (January–February 1980), pp. 83–91 or Chapter 4 in *The Marketing Imagination* (New York: The Free Press, 1983), pp. 72–93.

6. David A. Garvin, "Competing on the Eight Dimensions of Quality," *Harvard Business Review,* Vol. 65 (November–December 1987), pp. 101–9.

7. "The Cracks in Quality," *The Economist,* April 18–24, 1992, pp. 67–68, at p. 68.

8. Ibid., p. 67.

9. See, for example, A. Parasuraman, Valarie A. Zeithaml, and Leonard L. Berry, "A Conceptual Model of Service Quality and Its Implications for Future Research," *Journal of Marketing,* Vol. 49 (fall 1985), pp. 41–50; Valarie A. Zeithaml, Leonard L. Berry, and A. Parasuraman, *Communication and Control Processes in the Delivery of Service Quality,* Report No. 87-100 (Cambridge, MA: Marketing Science Institute, 1987); and A. Parasuraman, Valarie A. Zeithamel, and Leonard L. Berry, *SERVQUAL: A Multiple-Item Scale for Measuring Customer Perceptions of Service Quality,* Report No. 86-108 (Cambridge, MA: Marketing Science Institute, 1986).

10. Edward F. McQuarrie, "The Customer Visit: Qualitative Research for Business-to-Business Marketers," *Marketing Research* (March 1991), pp. 15–28.

11. Katherine Tobin, "Hewlett-Packard's Customer Visit Program: Getting Closer to Customers," a presentation to the Marketing Science Institute Conference on Communicating with Industrial Customers, held on March 8–10, 1989, in Melbourne, FL.

12. John R. Hauser and Don Clausing, "The House of Quality," *Harvard Business Review,* Vol. 66 (May–June 1988), pp. 63–73.

13. "Special Report: Quality," *Business Week,* November 30, 1992, pp. 66–75, at pp. 74–75.

14. C. K. Prahalad and Gary Hamel, "The Core Competence of the Corporation," *Harvard Business Review,* Vol. 68 (May–June 1990), pp. 79–91.

15. Richard C. Whiteley, *The Customer-Driven Company* (Reading, MA: Addison-Wesley Publishing Company, Inc., 1991), p. 151.

16. Claes Fornell and Birger Wernerfelt, "Defensive Marketing Strategy by Customer Complaint Management: A Theoretical Analysis," *Journal of Marketing Research,* Vol. XXIV (November 1987), pp. 337–46.

## Chapter 4 Market Targeting and the Value Proposition

1. Saul Hansell, "A Surprise from Amazon: Its First Profit," *New York Times,* January 23, 2002, p. C4.

2. Frederick E. Webster, Jr., "Republic Airlines (A) & (B)," case studies developed for classroom use at the Amos Tuck School of Business Administration, Dartmouth College, 1985.

3. Wendell R. Smith, "Product Differentiation and Market Segmentation as Alternative Marketing Strategies," *Journal of Marketing,* Vol. 20 (July 1956), pp. 3–8.

4. Al Ries and Jack Trout, *Positioning: The Battle for Your Mind,* 1st ed. rev. (New York: Warner Books, 1986), p. 2.

5. "Ford Motor Company (B)," in Kenneth R. Davis, *Marketing Management,* 2nd ed. (New York: Ronald Press, 1966), pp. 659–73.

6. Kevin Lane Keller, *Strategic Brand Management* (Upper Saddle River, NJ: Prentice-Hall, 1998).

7. "Conceptualizing, Measuring, and Managing Customer-Based Brand Equity," *Journal of Marketing,* Vol. 57 (January 1993), pp. 1–22. See also David A. Aaker, *Managing Brand Equity* (New York: The Free Press, 1991).

8. Stuart Elliott, "P&G discovers that a new look to an old product can be seen as betraying customers' brand loyalty," *New York Times,* January 28, 1993, p. D20.

9. Kevin Lane Keller, "Building Customer-Based Brand Equity: A Blueprint for Creating Strong Brands," *Marketing Management,* Vol. 10 (July–August 2001), pp. 15–19; see also Kevin Lane Keller and Donald R. Lehmann, "The Brand Value Chain: Linking Strategic and Financial Brand Performance," *Sloan Management Review,* currently under review.

10. "Gould, Inc.—Graphics Division," in E. Raymond Corey, *Industrial Marketing: Cases and Concepts,* 2nd ed. (Englewood Cliffs, NJ: Prentice-Hall, 1976), pp. 119–39.

11. "Amicon Corporation (A)," in E. Raymond Corey, *Industrial Marketing: Cases and Concepts,* 4th ed. (Englewood Cliffs, NJ: Prentice-Hall, 1991), pp. 217–39.

12. Roland Rust and Richard L. Oliver, "Should We Delight the Customer?" *Journal of the Academy of Marketing Science,* Vol. 28 (winter 2000), pp. 86–94.

13. Lynn W. Wilson, Allen M. Weiss, and George John, "Unbundling of Industrial Systems," *Journal of Marketing Research,* Vol. XXVII (May 1990), pp. 123–28.

14. Rashi Glazer, "Marketing in an Information-Intensive Environment: Strategic Implications of Knowledge as an Asset," *Journal of Marketing,* Vol. 55 (October 1991), pp. 1–19.

15. Stephan H. Haeckel, *Business Strategies in an Information Economy,* Report No. 90-119 (Cambridge, MA: Marketing Science Institute, December 1990).

16. William Boulding, Eunkyu Lee, and Richard Staelin, *The Long-Term Differentiation Value of Marketing Communication Actions,* Report No. 92-133 (Cambridge, MA: Marketing Science Institute, December 1992).

## Chapter 5   *Customer Relationship Management*

1. Frederick E. Webster, Jr., *It's 1990: Do You Know Where Your Marketing Is?* MSI White Paper (Cambridge, MA: The Marketing Science Institute, 1989).

2. Attributed to Professor Jagdish Sheth by Richard C. Whiteley, in *The Customer-Driven Company* (Reading, MA: Addison-Wesley Publishing Co., Inc., 1991), p. 41.

3. Robert C. Blattberg, "The Marketing Information Revolution," a presentation to the Marketing Science Institute Board of Trustees, April 25, 1991, at their meeting in Tucson, Arizona.

4. Robert C. Blattberg and John Deighton, "Interactive Marketing: Exploiting the Age of Addressability," *Sloan Management Review,* Vol. XX (fall 1991), pp. 5–14. See also John Deighton, "The Future of Interactive Marketing," *Harvard Business Review,* Vol. 74 (November–December 1996), pp. 4–16.

5. Gordon A. Wyner, "Customer Profitability," *Marketing Management,* Vol. 8 (winter 1999), pp. 8–9, at p. 9.

6. Eugene W. Anderson, Claes Fornell, and Donald R. Lehmann, "Customer Satisfaction, Market Share, and Profitability: Findings from Sweden," *Journal of Marketing,* Vol. 58 (July 1994), pp. 53–66.

7. Ruth N. Bolton, P. K. Kannan, and Matthew D. Bramlett, "Implications of Loyalty Program Membership and Service Experiences for Customer Retention and Value," *Journal of the Academy of Marketing Sciences,* Vol. 28 (winter 2000), pp. 95–108.

8. Susan Fournier, Susan Dobscha, and David Glen Mick, "Preventing the Premature Death of Relationship Marketing," *Harvard Business Review,* Vol. 76 (January–February 1998), pp. 42–51.

9. Lawrence A. Crosby and Sheree L. Johnson, "What to Do Before Going 1-to-1," *Marketing Management,* Vol. 9 (winter 2000), pp. 15–21.

10. Dan Flack and Pam Evans, "Marketing on Customer Terms," *Marketing Management,* Vol. 10 (November–December 2001), pp. 19–23.

## Chapter 6   *Strategic Partnering and Network Organizations*

1. Russell Johnston and Paul R. Lawrence, "Beyond Vertical Integration—the Rise of the Value-Adding Partnership," *Harvard Business Review,* Vol. 66 (July–August 1988), pp. 94–104.

2. James P. Womack, Daniel T. Jones, and Daniel Roos, *The Machine That Changed the World: The Story of Lean Production* (New York: HarperPerennial, 1991).

3. Ibid., pp. 48–58.

4. Walmart.stores.com.

5. Gary L. Frazier, Robert E. Spekman, and Charles R. O'Neal, "Just-In-Time Exchange Relationships in Industrial Markets," *Journal of Marketing*, Vol. 52 (October 1988), pp. 52–67.

6. Robert E. Spekman, "Strategic Supplier Selection: Understanding Long-Term Buyer Relationships," *Business Horizons*, Vol. 31 (July–August 1988), pp. 75–81.

7. Jan B. Heide and George John, "Alliances in Industrial Purchasing: The Determinants of Joint Action in Buyer-Seller Relationships," *Journal of Marketing Research*, Vol. XXVII (February 1990), pp. 24–36, at p. 34.

8. Ibid.

9. Robert E. Spekman and Deborah Salmond, *A Working Consensus to Collaborate: A Field Study of Manufacturer-Supplier Dyads*, MSI Working Paper, Report No. 92-134 (Cambridge, MA: Marketing Science Institute, December 1992).

10. James C. Anderson and James A. Narus, "Partnering as a Focused Market Strategy," *California Management Review*, Vol. 33 (spring 1991), pp. 95–113.

11. Robert Krapfel, Deborah Salmond, and Robert Spekman, "Strategic Relationship Management: A Conceptual Framework," *European Journal of Marketing*, Vol. 29, No. 9 (1991), pp. 22–37.

12. Rowland T. Moriarty, Gordon S. Swartz, and Charles A. Khuen, *Managing Hybrid Marketing Channels with Automation*, MSI Work Paper, Report No. 88-113 (Cambridge, MA: Marketing Science Institute, December 1988).

13. Neil Rackham and John R. DeVincentis, *Rethinking the Sales Force: Redefining Selling to Create and Capture Customer Value* (New York: McGraw-Hill, 1999).

14. David B. Montgomery and George S. Yip, "The Challenge of Global Account Management," *Marketing Management*, Vol. 9 (winter 2000), pp. 22–29.

15. Kenichi Ohmae, "The Global Logic of Strategic Alliances," *Harvard Business Review*, Vol. 67 (March–April 1989), pp. 143–54.

16. Stratford Sherman, "Are Strategic Alliances Working?" *Fortune* (September 21, 1992), pp. 77–78.

17. See, for example, Jordan D. Lewis, *Partnerships for Profit* (New York: The Free Press, 1990); Kathryn R. Harrigan, *Strategies for Joint Ventures* (Lexington, MA: Lexington Books, 1985); and Joel Bleeke and David Ernst, "The Way to Win in Cross-Border Alliances," *Harvard Business Review*, Vol. 69 (November–December 1991), pp. 127–35.

18. C. K. Prahalad and Gary Hamel, "The Core Competence of the Corporation," *Harvard Business Review*, Vol. 68 (May–June 1990), pp. 79–91.

19. Ibid., p. 84.

20. Ibid., p. 89.

21. Louis P. Bucklin and Sanjit Sengupta, *Balancing Co-Marketing Alliances for Effectiveness,* Report No. 92-120 (Cambridge, MA: Marketing Science Institute, 1992).

22. Han Thorelli, "Networks: Between Markets and Hierarchies," *Strategic Management Journal,* Vol. 7 (1986), pp. 37–51.

23. James R. Houghton, "The Age of the Hierarchy is Over," *New York Times,* September 24, 1989, Sec. 3, p. 3.

24. General Electric Company, *Annual Report,* 1990.

25. Noel M. Tichy and Stratford Sherman, *Control Your Destiny or Someone Else Will* (New York: Doubleday, 1993). Excerpts from this book were reported in "Jack Welch's Lessons for Success," *Fortune* (January 25, 1993), pp. 86–92.

26. An earlier version of these ideas appeared in Frederick E. Webster, Jr., "The Changing Role of Marketing in the Corporation," *Journal of Marketing,* Vol. 56 (October 1992), pp. 1–17.

27. Regis McKenna, "Marketing Is Everything," *Harvard Business Review,* Vol. 69 (January–February 1991), pp. 65–79.

## *Chapter 7    Organizational Culture and Customer Orientation*

1. Peter F. Drucker, *The Practice of Management* (New York: Harper & Row, Inc., 1954), p. 41.

2. Stanley M. Davis, *Managing Corporate Culture* (Cambridge, MA: Ballinger Publishing Co., 1984).

3. William G. Ouchi, "Markets, Bureaucracies, and Clans," *Administrative Science Quarterly,* Vol. 25 (March 1980), pp. 129–41; Alan Wilkins and William G. Ouchi, "Efficient Cultures: Exploring the Relationship between Culture and Organizational Performance," *Administrative Science Quarterly,* Vol. 28 (September 1983), pp. 468–81.

4. Joanne Martin, *Cultures in Organizations: Three Perspectives* (New York: Oxford University Press, 1992).

5. Ibid., especially pages 8–13.

6. This section is based on Rohit Deshpandé and Frederick E. Webster, Jr., "Organizational Culture and Marketing: Defining the Research Agenda," *Journal of Marketing,* Vol. 53 (January 1989), pp. 3–15.

7. Linda Smircich, "Concepts of Culture and Organizational Analysis," *Administrative Science Quarterly,* Vol. 28 (September 1983), pp. 339–58.

8. See, for example, James R. Lincoln and Arne L. Kalleberg, *Culture, Control and Commitment: A Study of Work Organization and Work Attitudes in the U. S. and Japan* (Cambridge, England: Cambridge University Press, 1990); Akio Morita, *Made in Japan* (New York: E. P. Dutton, 1986); Robert T. Pascale and Anthony Athos, *The Art of Japanese Management* (New York: Simon &

Schuster, 1981); John W. Slocum, "A Comparative Study of American and Mexican Operatives," *Academy of Management Journal*, Vol. 14, No. 1 (1971), pp. 89–97; and Michael Y. Yoshino, *Japan's Managerial System: Tradition and Innovation* (Cambridge, MA: MIT Press, 1968).

9. David B. Montgomery, "Understanding the Japanese as Customers, Competitors, and Collaborators," *Japan and the World Economy*, Vol. 3, No. 1 (1991), pp. 61–91.

10. Rohit Deshpandé, John U. Farley, and Frederick E. Webster, Jr., "Triad Lessons: Generalizing Results on High Performance Firms in Five Business-to-Business Markets," *International Journal of Research in Marketing*, Vol. 17 (2000), pp. 353–62.

11. Geert Hofstede, *Culture's Consequences: International Differences in Work-Related Values* (Beverly Hills, CA: Sage Publications, 1980), and *Cultures and Organizations: Software of the Mind* (London: McGraw-Hill, 1991).

12. Thomas Peters and Robert Waterman, *In Search of Excellence* (New York: Harper & Row, Inc., 1982).

13. Terence E. Deal and Allen A. Kennedy, *Corporate Culture* (Reading, MA: Addison-Wesley Publishing Co., 1982).

14. Bro Uttal, "The Corporate Culture Vultures," *Fortune* (October 17, 1983) (unpaged reprint).

15. "I'm going to let the problems come to me," *Business Week* (April 12, 1993), pp. 32–33.

16. "IBM's New Boss," *Business Week* (February 11, 2002), pp. 66–72. The quotation is found on page 72.

17. Joseph A. Litterer and Stanley Young, "The Development of Managerial Reflective Skills," paper presented at Northeast American Institute of Decision Sciences meetings, April 1981.

18. Deborah Dougherty, "The Problem of New Products in Old Organizations: The Myth of the Better Mousetrap in Search of the Beaten Path," unpublished Ph.D. dissertation, Sloan School of Management, Massachusetts Institute of Technology, 1987.

19. Michael W. Miller, "At Many Firms, Employees Speak a Language That's All Their Own," *Wall Street Journal* (December 29, 1987), Sec. 2, p. 1.

20. Claude Lévi-Strauss, *Structural Anthropology* (New York: Basic Books, Inc., 1963) and Stephen P. Turner, "Studying Organization through Lévi-Strauss' Structuralism," in *Beyond Method: Social Research Strategies*, Gaeth Morgan, ed., (Beverly Hills, CA: Sage Publications, Inc., 1983).

21. Ajay K. Kohli and Bernard J. Jaworski, "Market Orientation: The Construct, Research Propositions, and Managerial Implications," *Journal of Marketing*, Vol. 54 (April 1990), pp. 1–18.

22. Ibid., p. 6.
23. Bernard Jaworski and Ajay K. Kohli, "Market Orientation: Antecedents and Consequences," *Journal of Marketing,* Vol. 57 (July 1993), pp. 53–70.
24. John C. Narver and Stanley F. Slater, "The Effect of a Market Orientation on Business Profitability," *Journal of Marketing,* Vol. 54 (October 1990), pp. 20–35.
25. Michael E. Porter, *Competitive Strategy* (New York: The Free Press, 1980), esp. pp. 42–43.
26. Rohit Deshpandé and John U. Farley, "Measuring Market Orientation: Generalizations and Synthesis," *Journal of Market-Focused Management,* Vol. 2 (September 1998), pp. 213–32.
27. Noel Capon, John U. Farley, and James Hulbert, *Corporate Strategic Planning* (New York: Columbia University Press, 1988).
28. Kim S. Cameron and Sarah J. Freeman, "Cultural Congruence, Strength and Type: Relationships to Effectiveness," in *Research in Organizational Change and Development,* Vol. 5, R. W. Woodman and W. A. Passmore, eds. (Greenwich, CN: JAI Press, Inc., 1991).
29. Robert E. Quinn, *Beyond Rational Management* (San Francisco: Jossey-Bass, 1988).
30. Benjamin Schneider and Joan Rentsch, "Managing Climates and Cultures: A Futures Perspective," in *Futures of Organizations,* Jerald Hage, ed. (Lexington, MA: Lexington Books, 1988).
31. See note 27.

*Chapter 8    Developing a Customer-Oriented, Market-Driven Company*

1. Rajendra K. Srivastava, Tasadduq A. Shervani, and Liam Fahey, "Marketing, Business Processes, and Shareholder Value: An Organizationally Embedded View of Marketing Activities and the Discipline of Marketing," *Journal of Marketing,* Vol. 63 (Special Issue 1999), pp. 168–79, at p. 178.
2. John Deighton, "The Future of Interactive Marketing," *Harvard Business Review,* Vol. 74 (November–December 1996), pp. 4–16, at p. 4
3. Peter F. Drucker, *The Age of Discontinuity* (New York: Harper & Row, 1968).
4. John Kenneth Galbraith, *The Affluent Society* (Boston: Houghton Mifflin Company, 1958).
5. James Brian Quinn, *Intelligent Enterprise* (New York: The Free Press, 1993), p. 6.
6. Frederick R. Reichheld, "Loyalty-Based Management," *Harvard Business Review,* Vol. 71 (March–April 1993), pp. 64–73.

7. Iain Gately, *Tobacco: A Cultural History of How an Exotic Plant Seduced Civilization* (New York: Grove Press, 2000), reviewed by John Carey, *Business Week,* February 18, 2002, p. 22.

8. Michael Hammer and James Champey, *Reengineering the Corporation: A Manifesto for Business Revolution* (HarperCollins Publishers Inc., 1993). See also Michael Hammer, *The Agenda* (New York: Crown Business, 2001) and James Champey, *X-Engineering the Corporation* (New York: Warner Books, 2002).

9. "Reengineering in real time," *The Economist,* February 2, 2002, a survey of the real-time economy, p. 12.

10. Andrew C. Boynton, Bart Victor, and B. Joseph Pine II, "New Competitive Strategies: Challenges to Organizations and Information Technology," *IBM Systems Journal,* Vol. 32, No. 1 (1993), pp. 40–64; B. Joseph Pine II, *Mass Customization: The New Frontier in Business Competition* (Boston: Harvard Business School Press, 1993).

11. Stanley Davis, *Future Perfect* (Reading, MA: Addison Wesley Publishing Co., 1987).

12. B. Joseph Pine II, "Mass Customisation of Goods and Services: The New Competitive Reality," 3rd Global Conference on Marketing, Management Centre Europe, London, June 3, 1993.

13. See note 5, pp. 349–50.

14. See note 12.

15. See note 6, p. 68.

16. Leonard L. Berry, *Discovering the Soul of Service* (New York: The Free Press, 1999), esp. Ch. 8, "Investment in Employee Success," pp. 156–81.

17. Bill Saporito, "A Week Aboard the Wal-Mart Express," *Fortune,* Vol. 126 (August 24, 1992), pp. 77–84; Sam Walton, *Made in America* (New York: Doubleday, 1992).

18. Stanley F. Slater and John C. Narver, "Intelligence Generation and Superior Customer Value," *Journal of Marketing,* Vol. 63 (Special Issue 1999), pp. 120–27.

19. Marjorie Adams, *Seeing Differently: Improving the Ability of Organizations to Anticipate and Respond to Constantly Changing Needs of Customers and Markets,* Conference Summary, Report No. 93-103 (Cambridge, MA: Marketing Science Institute, May 1993).

20. John Seely Brown, "Keynote Address: Seeing Differently," pp. 1–5.

21. Stanley F. Slater and John C. Narver, "Market Orientation and the Learning Organization," *Journal of Marketing,* Vol. 59 (July 1995), pp. 63–74.

22. Courtesy of Gregg Riskin, Vice President–Marketing, Samuel Cabot, Inc.

*Chapter 9    Implementing the Value-Delivery Concept of Marketing Strategy*

1. Shuba Srinivasan, Koen Pauwels. Dominique M. Hanssens, and Marnik G. Dekimpe, "Do Promotions Benefit Manufacturers, Retailers, or Both?" MSI Report No. 01-120 (Cambridge, MA: Marketing Science Institute, 2001).

2. "The Best Global Brands," *Business Week* (August 6, 2001), pp. 50–64.

# INDEX